INSIGHT GUIDES

MALTA

Discovery CHANNEL

APA PUBLICATIONS
Part of the Langenscheidt Publishing Group

INSIGHT GUIDE
MALTA

ABOUT THIS BOOK

Editorial
Project Editor
Paul Murphy
Managing Editor
Cameron Duffy
Editorial Director
Brian Bell

Distribution

UK & Ireland
GeoCenter International Ltd
The Viables Centre, Harrow Way
Basingstoke, Hants RG22 4BJ
Fax: (44) 1256 817988

United States
Langenscheidt Publishers, Inc.
36–36 33rd Street 4th Floor
Long Island City, NY 11106
Fax: 1 (718) 784 0640

Canada
Thomas Allen & Son Ltd
390 Steelcase Road East
Markham, Ontario L3R 1G2
Fax: (1) 905 475 6747

Australia
Universal Publishers
1 Waterloo Road
Macquarie Park, NSW 2113
Fax: (61) 2 9888 9074

New Zealand
Hema Maps New Zealand Ltd (HNZ)
Unit D, 24 Ra ORA Drive
East Tamaki, Auckland
Fax: (64) 9 273 6479

Worldwide
Apa Publications GmbH & Co.
Verlag KG (Singapore branch)
38 Joo Koon Road, Singapore 628990
Tel: (65) 6865 1600. Fax: (65) 6861 6438

Printing

Insight Print Services (Pte) Ltd
38 Joo Koon Road, Singapore 628990
Tel: (65) 6865 1600. Fax: (65) 6861 6438

CONTACTING THE EDITORS
We would appreciate it if readers
would alert us to errors or out-
dated information by writing to:
**Insight Guides, P.O. Box 7910,
London SE1 1WE, England.
insight@apaguide.co.uk**

www.insightguides.com

This guidebook combines the interests and enthusiasms of two of the world's best known information providers: Insight Guides, whose titles have set the standard for visual travel guides since 1970, and Discovery Channel, the world's premier source of non-fiction television programming.

The editors of Insight Guides provide both practical advice and general understanding about a destination's history, culture, institutions and people. Discovery Channel and its website, www.discovery.com, help millions of viewers explore their world from the comfort of their own home and also encourage them to explore it first-hand.

In this fully revised edition, we take you around the island of Malta – from the Knights' auberges in Valletta to the rural villages and their over-sized churches – and then cross the water to Gozo, with its un-spoiled character and landscapes, and finally to the barren idyll of Comino.

reference for information on travel, accommodation, restaurants and other practical aspects of the country. Information may be located quickly using the index printed on the back cover flap, which also serves as a handy bookmark.

The contributors

This new edition, which builds on the earlier edition edited by **Geoffrey Aquilina Ross**, was edited by **Paul Murphy**. Murphy has written two other guide books about the Maltese islands. He updated and restructured a large part of the current guide as well as supplying new words and pictures.

The principal contributor to this edition, Geoffrey Aquilina Ross, is a Maltese journalist currently editing the Malta International Airport Magazine, *High Flyer*. His native insights frequently lay bare aspects of the Maltese psyche which are not readily apparent to most holidaymakers.

Literally at home in Gozo is **Ann Monsarrat**, who contributed and updated the Gozo section. An experienced journalist, she is also the author of several books.

Brian Richards, a Malta aficionado, contributed the Sports pages. **Albert Fenech** updated the entire book for the 2004 printing. Other writers whose text has been adapted from earlier editions are **Rowlinson Carter**, **Maud Ruston, Daphne Caruana Galizia, Anthony Montanaro, Michael Ellul, Louis Mahoney**, and **Eric Gerada-Azzopardi**.

The proofreader was **Sylvia Suddes** and the indexer **Liz Cook**.

How to use this book

The book is carefully structured to convey an understanding of Malta and its culture and to guide readers through its sights and attractions:

◆ The **Features** section, with a yellow bar, covers Malta's history and culture in lively, authoritative essays written by specialists.

◆ The **Places** section, with a blue bar, provides full details of all the sights and areas worth seeing. The chief places of interest are coordinated by number with specially drawn maps.

◆ The **Travel Tips** listings section offers a convenient point of

Map Legend

▬ ▬ ▬	International Boundary
▬ ▬ ▬	National Park/Reserve
▬ ▬ ▬ ▬	Ferry Route
✈ ✈	Airport: International/Regional
🚌	Bus Station
P	Parking
❶	Tourist Information
✉	Post Office
❚ † ⸸	Church/Ruins
†	Monastery
☾	Mosque
✡	Synagogue
❚ ❚	Casdtle/Ruins
∴	Archaeological Site
∩	Cave
❚	Statue/Monument
★	Place of Interest

The main places of interest in the Places section are coordinated by number with a full-colour map (e.g. ❶), and a symbol at the top of every right-hand page tells you where to find the map.

INSIGHT GUIDE
MALTA

CONTENTS

Maps

Maltese Islands **140**

Valletta **146**

Three Cities **178**

Mdina and Rabat **186**

Sliema and St Julian's **206**

The North and
the Centre **210**

The South **222**

Victoria **248**

Gozo **256**

A map of the Maltese islands
is inside the front flap

A map of Malta bus routes
is inside the back flap

Introduction

Sun, Sea and History **15**

History

Decisive Dates **18**

In the Beginning **21**

The Knights of St John............ **31**

The Great Siege **37**

After the Siege **45**

Enter the British **57**

World War II **65**

Looking to the Future **77**

Features

The Maltese People **89**

A Taste of Malta **97**

Venerable Vehicles **105**

Maltese Architecture........... **111**

Superstition and Lore **119**

Sport **127**

Mosta Dome has a fine interior and can be seen from almost any vantage point in Malta

Insight on ...

The Knights of Malta Today **52**
The Festa **122**
The British Influence **156**
Secrets of the Temples **236**

Information panel

Dom Mintoff: Hero and Ogre .. **78**

Places

Valletta **145**
Grand Master's Palace **161**
St John's Co-Cathedral **169**
Three Cities **177**
Mdina and Rabat **185**
Mdina Cathedral **192**
Central Malta **198**
Sliema and St Julian's **205**

The North **215**
The South **227**
Gozo **243**
Victoria **247**
Around Gozo **255**
Comino **269**
Going to Sea **275**
A Trip to Sicily **278**

Travel Tips

Getting Acquainted **284**

Planning the Trip **285**

Practical Tips **287**

Getting Around **290**

Where to Stay **292**

Where to Eat **295**

Sport **300**

Shopping **301**

Children **301**

Language **302**

Further Reading **302**

◆ **Full Travel Tips index is on page 283**

SUN, SEA AND HISTORY

For centuries Malta lay at the heart of the Mediterranean's power struggles. Today the invaders are tourists

In the middle of a remarkably clear and unpolluted expanse of blue Mediterranean Sea, some 90 km (60 miles) due south of Sicily, the Maltese archipelago consists of three inhabited islands – Malta, Gozo and Comino – and a number of minuscule uninhabited rocks. Malta is the largest of these (but still not much bigger than England's Isle of Wight), Gozo is only half its size and Comino is smaller again. The population is around 400,000, most of whom speak English, as well as the native Malti.

The islands are relatively low lying and flat and from a distance are not easy to identify. Malta is shaped like a wedge, sloping from the southwest to the east, with most of the resort developments on the eastern shore which is indented with harbours and bays, rock beaches and sheltered coves.

Like all islands subject to the vagaries of modern tourism, Malta throws up sharp contrasts, which are made all the more striking because of the island's tiny size. Ancient temples – some of the oldest structures on earth – and the massive fortifications and *palazzi* of the Knights of St John rub shoulders with the increasing sprawl of modern Malta and its tourist infrastructure. Considerable wealth mingles with a simple hardworking rural lifestyle. The unspoiled countryside is threatened and the Maltese themselves are moving to Gozo to get back to the pleasures of a simpler, greener way of life. Nowadays, however, Gozo is under pressure too as it gears itself up, albeit on a small scale, to offering visitors the type of facilities that they have come to expect from other Mediterranean resorts.

But if this is a familiar scenario for any small nation determined to succeed in today's competitive world it should not diminish the attractions of the islands. As yacht marinas grow and welcome larger and more expensive yachts and as 5-star hotels claim the coastline and prime spots overlooking the harbour, so the overall quality of accommodation and restaurants improve. Beaches and watersports have been developed to offer a wider variety of activities, and facilities have improved for the locals as much as for the visitors.

Life is as hectic or as leisurely, as sophisticated or as rustic as you want it to be. The recent trend for staying in Gozo's renovated and highly desirable farmhouses is a case in point. Visitors come for the simple life – but with air conditioning and a large outdoor pool.

Tourism has been a vital source of income but the islands are doing well economically in other spheres too. With membership of the European Union due in 2004 most Maltese are in a buoyant and optimistic mood. ❑

PRECEDING PAGES: Manoel Island, Marsamxett Harbour and Sliema; Ta' Pinu Basilica on Gozo; casting a giant shadow at Ggantija, Gozo; rural island life.
LEFT: the glowing golden stones of Birzebbuga in late afternoon.

Decisive Dates

PREHISTORY

Before 5000 BC: First settlers arrive in Malta, either by sea from Sicily or from across the landmass that once joined Europe to the North African coast. The earliest temples are built from 4800 BC, and a religious cult of the dead is introduced.

circa **3200 BC:** The megalithic temples of Hagar Qim, Ggantija and Mnajdra are built. They survive today as the oldest free-standing edifices in the world.

circa **2000 BC:** The Bronze Age. The end of Malta's temple-building phase. Fortified villages with defensive

walls are built, for example Borg in-Nadur, near present-day Blrzebbuga.

circa **700 BC:** Hellenic influence begins.

circa **800–480 BC:** The Phoenicians, merchants from the eastern Mediterranean, settle the islands and use its safe harbours as a trading post. Inscriptions, coins and tombs are left behind.

circa **480–218 BC:** Carthage, originally a Phoenician colony, conquers Malta and controls the sea routes in the western Mediterranean.

THE ROMAN PERIOD

218 BC: During the Second Punic War between Rome and Carthage a Roman expedition captures Malta and incorporates the islands into the Republic of Rome.

AD 60: St Paul is shipwrecked in the area now known as St Paul's Bay. He converts the islanders to Christianity, including Publius, Chief Man of the island, whose house was where Mdina Cathedral now stands.

AD 117–138: During Hadrian's reign Malta is declared a Roman Municipality.

DARK AGES TO ARAB ARRIVAL

AD 395–535: Division of the Roman Empire and collapse of the western half (including Malta). Goths and Vandals descend on the islands.

AD 535: Justinian, head of the eastern Roman Empire conquers Malta and Sicily in the name of Byzantium.

AD 870: The Aghlabite Arabs arrive, bringing with them cotton, citrus fruits, figs and a language that is incorporated into *Malti*. The Islamic religion is also adopted by the islanders.

EUROPEANS TAKE POWER

1090: The Normans invade under Count Roger, who annexes Malta to the Kingdom of Sicily. Arabic remains the national language but the islanders revert to Christianity.

1194–1266: After the Norman kings die out the island passes to the Swabian (German) kings.

1266–1283: The French House of Anjou drives out the Germans.

1283–1530: The Aragonese rule Malta and Sicily.

1479–1516: Affiliation of the Houses of Castile and Aragon means that Malta becomes part of the new Spanish Empire.

THE KNIGHTS OF ST JOHN

1530: The 4,000-strong army of the Order of St John arrives to take formal possession of the islands as a gift from Emperor, Charles V of Spain. They select Birgu, where Vittoriosa is now established, as their base.

1551: Corsairs from the Barbary Coast, in the pay of the Ottoman Empire, attack Gozo and enslave almost the entire population.

1561: The Inquisition is established in Malta.

1565: The Great Siege of Malta. For three months Suleiman the Magnificent's fleet lays siege to the Knights. Eventually help arrives from Sicily and the Ottoman forces are defeated.

1566: Urgent construction begins on Valletta, in anticipation of the return of the Turks. It becomes the finest fortified city in Europe.

1683: With the defeat of the Turks outside Vienna, a century-long phase of consolidation and construction begins on Malta and Gozo, resulting in many fine baroque structures. However, with no enemies to fight, the Order of the Knights declines into decadence.

1789: The French Revolution means that property belonging to the Order of the Knights is confiscated, further weakening the faltering Order.

NAPOLEONIC PERIOD

1798: Napoleon takes Malta without a fight. The Order of the Knights of St John is despatched and the Inquisition is also abolished.

1800: The Maltese rise against French domination. Britain and Naples intercede, offering the islands its protection in the name of the King of Naples. French force capitulates.

THE BRITISH INFLUENCE

1802: Peace of Amiens decides that Malta should be returned to the Order of St John, but the Maltese people object and vote to come under the protection of the British. At the 1814 Treaty of Paris Malta formally becomes a British Crown Colony.

1850 onwards: Malta experiences an economic upswing as a trading harbour and an important British naval base.

1914–18: World War I. Malta provides care for the wounded and becomes known as the "Nurse of the Mediterranean".

1919: The *Sette Giugno* riots. As the war ends the Maltese economy fails, resulting in considerable poverty and unemployment. An angry crowd riots in Valletta causing troops to be called in. Four Maltese in the crowd are shot.

1921: Self-government is granted. The first Malta Parliament is opened; domestic affairs are finally in Maltese hands.

1930: The Constitution is suspended by the British after the Church tells people to vote Nationalist.

1932: The Constitution is restored.

1933: The Constitution is withdrawn. Malta reverts to the Crown Colony status it held before 1814.

1936: The Constitution is again restored: members of Executive Council are nominated.

WORLD WAR II

1940–43: Malta receives the most severe aerial bombardment in history while undergoing its second Great Siege. Thousands of houses are destroyed, about 1,500 Maltese civilians are killed, with many more injured, and for months supply lines are cut off, causing famine. In 1942, in recognition of their heroism under fire, Britain awards the islands the George Cross.

PRECEDING PAGES: Hagar Qim's mighty facade.
LEFT: armour of the Knights of St John.
RIGHT: Malta convoy, World War II.

POST-WAR PERIOD

1947: Self-government restored. Governor assumes administration.

1964: Malta becomes an independent state within the British Commonwealth.

1970: Malta becomes an Associate Member of the European Economic Community.

1971: The first Maltese Governor-General is appointed.

1972: An agreement is signed with Britain and NATO to use the islands as a military base.

1974: Malta becomes a Republic, with a President, but remains within the British Commonwealth.

1979: The last British forces leave the island.

1987: Malta becomes a neutral and non-aligned state.

1989: The Malta Summit. US President George Bush Snr and Soviet leader Mikhail Gorbachev use the island as a meeting-place to mark the end of the Cold War.

1990: Malta seeks full membership of the European Community.

1996: The Labour party blocks the European Union membership application.

1998: Nationalists return to power and re-open application for EU membership.

2001: Pope John Paul II makes a second visit to Malta to beatify Dun Gorg Preca as the first-ever Maltese national on the road to sainthood.

2003: Following a General Election and Referendum, Malta signs the full EU Accession Treaty in Athens for full EU membership in 2004. ❏

IN THE BEGINNING

The first inhabitants of the Maltese islands built giant temples to pagan gods, long before the pyramids were constructed

It is widely believed that the Maltese islands once formed part of a causeway which joined Europe to Africa, and so became a thoroughfare for animals escaping from the encroaching ice of Northern Europe. Many died en route or were perhaps trapped by the rising sea which turned the causeway into a necklace of island stepping stones. The best evidence we have for such movements comes from the cave of Ghar Dalam (near Birzebbuga), which contains the bones of several prehistoric and extinct animals, including dwarf elephants and hippo, from around 100,000 BC.

Of the people who were stranded or otherwise chose to live on the Maltese islands, very little is known. Among the animal bones found at Ghar Dalam were a couple of Neanderthal human teeth from about 40,000 BC, and it seems that there was a fairly sizeable human population that lived in caves along the coastal cliffs. Eventually they emerged from their troglodyte dwellings to live in settlements of tiny huts.

Temple builders

In about the 4th millennium BC, some thousand years before Minoan civilisation began at Knossos on the island of Crete, the Maltese were engaged in the construction of great megalithic temples. The Ggantija temples on Gozo were probably the first, but they were soon joined by the temples of Mnajdra and Hagar Qim on the main island of Malta.

The temples were an assembly of massive slabs of rock, similar to Stonehenge in Britain, with alcoves for altars and statues associated with ancient religious rituals. The temple at Hagar Qim incorporates a stone which is 6 metres (20 ft) long – a testament to the considerable engineering skills of those who manoeuvred it into position. These great temples were mostly erected outdoors, yet Malta's most

LEFT: the first known free-standing statue of a deity.
RIGHT: the massive stones of Ggantija, the world's oldest free-standing monument.

remarkable Neolithic remains were revealed only last century by a builder who was digging to lay foundations for a house.

The Hypogeum of Hal Saflieni (the last part of the name refers not to some ancient deity but to the area where the builder was proposing to put up the house) is a vast, three-storeyed

underground chamber carved by human hands out of solid rock. It is supposed that the chambers once housed an oracle and were used for "initiation into the mysteries of priestcraft". Later they became burial chambers, and the Hypogeum is so huge that it is estimated to have held up to 7,000 bodies. Yet, apart from the fact that they lived about 5,000 years ago, practically nothing is known about the people who built this temple.

Shortly after the Hypogeum discovery, close by at Tarxien three more temples were found, embellished with carvings which are remarkably sophisticated for their time. One of the courts of Tarxien produced the quintessential

Stone Age art of Malta: a statue of a woman whose arms and feet are normal but with all the bits in between swollen to elephantine proportions. The style is known, commendably, with no beating about the bush, as "Fat".

A Mediterranean staging post

Malta edges into recorded history on the fringes of the momentous three-cornered power struggle for the then known world between Phoenicians, Greeks and Persians. The Phoenicians set the ball rolling by sailing the breadth of the Mediterranean from the cities of Tyre and Sidon (in what is now Lebanon), to semi-secret copper and tin deposits in Spain. The Phoenicians were intrepid sailors, but they preferred to remain within sight of land and furthermore to break the journey into comfortable stages. Staging-posts were therefore needed at regular intervals along the route, which, because of hostile Greek expansion along the European shores of the Mediterranean, increasingly followed the North African coast.

Phoenicians and Carthaginians

The most famous of the new Phoenician colonies was Carthage, founded in modern-day Tunisia. Soon this was almost as prosperous

MYSTERY OF THE CART TRACKS

The strange formations found on both Malta and Gozo pose one of the islands' most taxing enigmas. Known as cart tracks, these are parallel ruts – V shaped and generally between 15 to 50 cm (6 to 20 inches) wide – which run through the hard rock. Were they first cut with tools or were they simply worn this size by constant use? What is surely beyond coincidence is that they uniformly measure around 135 cm (54 inches) apart – which corresponds exactly with the width of the axle still used on the modern Maltese country cart.

The obvious question is: to what use were these tracks put? Some lead apparently pointlessly up hills or plunge over the edge of cliffs. Maltese archaeologist, Sir Themistocles Zammit surmises that "the material handled must have been abundant, cheap, and of the greatest value to those who carted it". In Malta that could well have meant soil, as everywhere on the islands the bare rock is topped by only the thinnest layer of earth. "When the increasing population required as much land as possible under cultivation on which to grow foodstuffs, they could only do this by carrying earth from the valleys up on the sides and tops of hills where terraces were built and the soil spread". Later experts believe the tracks are evidence of an elaborate transport and communication system.

and powerful as the Phoenician homeland, but the connection between the two was severed after a bungled attempt by Phoenicians and Persians acting in concert to crush the Greeks. The Greeks beat both enemies in surprise victories that are reputed to have taken place on the same day in 470 BC and the Mediterranean was effectively cut in half: with Greeks supreme in the east and Phoenicians (now more properly called "Carthaginians") in the west. Planted in the middle of the dividing line was little Malta.

The Carthaginians used Malta as a training base for their galley crews. They also began to cultivate olives and carobs and used the excel-

would have been of no great interest, but astoundingly, next to the cursive Phoenician script (the progenitor of the European alphabet) was a Greek translation. These *cippi* – one in Malta's Museum of Archaeology, the other in the Louvre in Paris– thus became the key to deciphering Phoenician in exactly the same way as the Rosetta Stone unlocked the secrets of ancient Egypt's hieroglyphics.

The Malti language

By modern analysis, *Malti*, the language of the Maltese, appears to be a living legacy of spoken Phoenician (subject of course to 2,000 years of

lent quality local clay for pottery. These innovations must have improved the islands' economy, but the terrible price paid by the local inhabitants was to see many of their number carried off as slaves to Carthage.

Today, aside from some cave tombs, there is little to tell us that the Carthaginians were ever here, but there is one priceless exception. In 1697 a pair of marble *cippi* (columns) were discovered, inscribed with a dedication by two brothers to the god Melqarth. Normally this

LEFT: the deep furrows of Malta's enigmatic cart tracks, near Dingli.
ABOVE: chamber entrance at Mnajdra temples.

natural evolution and later additions), which helps to explain its often outlandish appearance to European eyes.

In its earliest form the language was only spoken, never written. It was the language of a simple people, and, possibly because of this, had a basic vocabulary, short of the flowery pretensions that mark the language of a sophisticated society.

When the Arabs arrived in the 9th century they brought their own language and, because of similar Semitic language roots, many of their words were incorporated by the Maltese. Similarly, in later centuries the European nations began imposing their influence on Malta, and borrowed words from the Romance languages were also assimilated into *Malti*.

The Punic Wars and Roman rule

The three Punic (Phoenician) Wars raged between Rome and Carthage between 264 and 146 BC and culminated in the destruction of the Carthaginian empire.

Malta was tossed about in this struggle to the death between the two superpowers although there are few specific references to its fate in Roman accounts of the war. We know, however, that Great Harbour, as it was then called, served as a Carthaginian naval base and must

have been subject to attack, as Rome realised that the Carthaginian threat would have to be met at sea as well as on land.

After the first Punic War, records also tell us that Malta was ceded to Rome as part of Carthage's indemnity.

According to Livy, Hamilcar (Hannibal's father) was in Malta when he surrendered with 2,000 men. But the Carthaginians must somehow have regained Malta because it was ceded again after the second war. In any event, the islands were firmly in Rome's orbit for a good millennium after the Punic Wars.

Although Malta had a certain degree of autonomy under Roman rule, it was generally lumped together with Sicily for administrative purposes and prospered under unobtrusive Roman rule.

Diodorus of Sicily, one of the very few Latin historians who so much as mentions Malta, describes the inhabitants as "Phoenicians". In fact the Maltese coins of the period bore Phoenician symbols with Latin or Greek inscriptions and the tradition of cremation and burial in pit tombs was maintained. In general, therefore, it would seem that the Roman presence was confined to a garrison which had no impact either on the local culture or on the language.

St Paul

The greatest single upheaval in Maltese culture occurred in AD 60, when a ship bound for Rome with 275 passengers, including a famous prisoner, was caught in a dreadful storm off the northeastern coast. "They knew not the land but they discovered a certain creek with a shore, into which they were minded, if it were possible, to thrust in the ship...The forepart stuck fast, and remained unmoveable, but the hinder part was broken with the violence of the waves... And when they were escaped, then they knew that the island was called Mel-i-ta. And the barbarous people shewed us no little kindness: for they kindled a fire, and received us every one, because of the present rain, and because of the cold."

The author of the quotation was St Luke (Acts of the Apostles: XXVIII) and the prisoner was St Paul. The shipwreck victims clambered ashore at what is known today as St Paul's Bay and remained on the island for three months. During this period St Paul is said to

---

THE CORRUPT GOVERNOR

During its period under Rome rule, Malta had the misfortune to have been governed, from Sicily, by Verres, one of the most corrupt officials of Roman republican history. He was impeached in 70 BC and at the beginning of proceedings was mocked by Cicero. "I don't need to be told where you obtained 400 jars of Maltese honey and a huge quantity of Maltese cloth, or for that matter 50 sofa cushions and 50 candelabra, but I am curious as to what you proposed to do with so much stuff, unless of course you merely intended to make presents of it to the wives of all your friends." Cicero was still warming to the task when Verres fled the country.

have lived for most of the time in a grotto at Rabat but also, for three days, as the guest of Publius, "the chief man of the island", whose father he also cured "of a fever and of a bloody flux."

According to tradition, St Paul not only converted Publius to Christianity but also made him bishop, with his house being nominated as Malta's first church. The present-day cathedral is reputed to stand on the very site.

If, as is surmised, the Maltese were still speaking a fairly pristine form of Phoenician

ISLANDS OF HONEY

It was the Greeks who first called the islands Melita, meaning honey, after the rich sweet variety produced by the local bees.

best examples of these can be seen at St Agatha's and St Paul's Catacombs, in Rabat.

After the Romans

Malta seems to have escaped the attentions of the Vandals and the Goths, who between them first destroyed the Roman provinces in North Africa and then Rome itself, and life continued in what must have been blessed obscurity. However, history records that in 535 Belisarius, the Byzantine conqueror of the northern scourges was despatched to win Malta

with its Canaanite origins, St Paul's preaching would have been greatly facilitated by the fact that he, as a native of Tarsus, also spoke a Canaanite dialect. In any case, Malta was one of the first Roman colonies to become Christian, which is reflected in the existence of catacombs from the 2nd century onwards.

One of the characteristics of these are the *agape* tables cut into the rock walls of the vestibule, on which mourners reclined for a ceremonial feast in honour of the deceased. The

Left: St Paul's Grotto, where the Apostle is said to have lived for a while, and was perhaps held captive.
Above: Roman remains found at Rabat, Malta.

on behalf of Justinian, the emperor of the Eastern Empire.

The islands seem to have been relatively unaffected, too, by the Islamic tide which swept westwards across North Africa in the 7th century. Malta was not in fact occupied by Arabs until 870 and even then probably only as an adjunct to their wider ambitions in Sicily and on the European mainland.

No doubt influenced by the same strategic military considerations, the Arabs took over the old Roman fortifications, including what was later to become Fort St Angelo, and the city which they renamed Mdina. The latter became their island capital and stronghold and parts of the walls they added are still in evidence today. A number of Arab graves have been found, but the greatest legacy of their 200-year rule undoubtedly lies in the Arabic words and phrases added to Malti, a language which they would have readily understood.

The return of Christianity

The Muslim hold on Malta was ended in 1090 by the Norman count Roger I of Sicily, who fooled the Arab garrison with a mock attack on St Paul's Bay, while other troops scaled the perilous western cliffs.

Roger was probably less interested in taking over the island than in making sure that the Arabs living there were not in a position to trouble him in Sicily. This was no religious inspired invasion. In fact Arabic remained the island's national language for some time and Islam was only gradually replaced as the principal religion with Christianity.

Malta was thus for centuries in the shadow of the higher priorities of whoever ruled Sicily, a good enough reason for concise histories of Malta (including this one) to skip lightly over the Normans with names like William the Bad and his offspring, William the Good, and a whole succession of Angevins, Aragonese and Castilian dynasties.

The islands passed from hand to hand, by marriage, inheritance or war, the Maltese themselves having little say in the matter – although a rebellion in 1428 managed to exact certain rights under a Royal Charter. Eventually the islands reached the hands of Spain's redoubtable Catholic Monarchs, Ferdinand of Aragon and Isabella of Castile.

Seeds of conflict

Ferdinand and Isabella's determination to rid Europe, particularly Spain, of the "Moors" (a catch-all term for the Arabs and North African Berbers who had crossed the Mediterranean under the protection of Islam), was to have unforeseen consequences for Malta. The implications would be fully realised when, in 1530, their grandson, the Emperor Charles V, made a gift of the islands to the homeless Knights of the Order of St John of Jerusalem. ❑

RIGHT: the Catacombs of St Paul in Rabat, dating from the 4th and 5th centuries – evidence of early Christianity on the islands.

THE KNIGHTS OF ST JOHN

From peaceful monastic beginnings the Knights of St John evolved to become the armed champions of Christendom

Whatever the tawdry truths that lie behind the romantic image, once upon a time the Knights of the Order of St John of Jerusalem were the most fabulous figures in Christendom. They were, quite literally, gallant white Knights on chargers, heroes who at heart deplored violence, but, as a last resort in the face of unspeakable evil, were more than capable of climbing into suits of armour and proving their worth on the battlefield.

Humble beginnings

The Order was originally formed in about 1085 as the Knights Hospitallers, a community of monks set up to nurse Christians who fell ill while on pilgrimage in the Holy Land. As pilgrims came increasingly under attack from the Infidel however, they needed physical protection rather than cures for minor ailments, and young Knights were recruited specifically to provide that protection.

These fighting Knights were drawn from aristocratic families in France, Italy, Spain, Portugal and England. Nobility was an essential qualification for knighthood, and even the lesser ranks and servants had to prove that their family background was "respectable". This was not considered to be ordinary mercenary work. "To volunteer in a Crusade against the Infidels in possession of the Holy Land", relates E.W. Schermerhorn in her masterful history of the Order, *Malta of the Knights*, "aside from the great service rendered to Christianity, and the safe and sure place it promised in the world to come, was the sport *par excellence* of the Middle Ages."

The Knights of Rhodes

As powerful as the Knights had become, the rising tide of Islam eventually drove them out of the Holy Land. They regrouped on the island of Rhodes, turned it into a stronghold and from

there sailed in their fleet of resplendent galleys to harry the Infidel. However as leadership of the Islamic world had now passed to the Ottoman Turks, Rhodes, just off the Turkish coast, was an intolerable provocation. "That abode of the Sons of Satan" was one of numerous unflattering terms of Turkish reference for

PRECEDING PAGES: war helmet of the Knights.
LEFT: armour sentinels in the Grand Master's Palace.
RIGHT: Grand Master Manoel de Vilhena (1722–36).

Rhodes. Ottoman forces seized Constantinople in 1453 and Belgrade in 1520. The whole of Europe knew Rhodes would be next, but when the assault came "no Christian King lifted a finger; all were too busy killing each other."

The opposing commanders in the battle for Rhodes, which raged for six months, were Suleiman the Magnificent, greatest of all the sultans, and, for the Knights, Philippe Villiers de L'Isle-Adam, now in his seventies but still "tall, lithe, graceful, alert, with delicately sensitive face, high cheek-bones, an aristocratic aquiline nose, soft, flowing white beard and hair... the embodiment of the soldier and gen-

tleman." But Rhodes fell. "It is not without some degree of pain", the victorious Sultan sighed, "that I force this Christian, at his time of life, to leave his dwelling."

In contrast to their brutal stereotyped image the Turks were gracious in victory and allowed the Knights to make a dignified departure with all their possessions, not least the cherished relic of the hand of St John the Baptist. The Greek inhabitants had misgivings about remaining on Rhodes under Turkish rule, so 100 families were given places in the Christian galleys. As Suleiman the Magnificent suspected, however, the Knights had no idea where they were going.

Between a rock and a hard place

The prospect of these illustrious veterans adrift in the Mediterranean was more than could be countenanced by the King of Spain, Charles V, who was also Holy Roman Emperor and therefore the symbol of almost everything the Knights stood for. Nor could he bear the thought of having to accept the disbandment of Christendom's most prestigious fighting force in such ignominious circumstances. A new home had to be found for them. He had, as it were, a couple of surplus properties in his inheritance. One was Tripoli, capital of what is now Libya, the other consisted of the islands of Malta.

The Knights were familiar with Tripoli as a beleagured Christian outpost among notoriously hostile natives and the worst kind of Barbary Coast pirate. Needing more information about the comparatively unknown Malta, the Knights sent commissioners to look into what was on offer.

Malta, they reported disdainfully, was "merely a rock of a soft sandstone...scarcely covered with more than three or four feet of earth... no running water, nor even wells... wood was so scarce as to be sold by the pound... about 12,000 inhabitants, of both sexes; the greatest part of whom were poor and miserable." In short, "a residence in Malta appeared extremely disagreeable – indeed, almost insupportable – particularly in summer."

Tripoli however, was an even worse option. Malta it would be. But the arrangements were not finalised for seven years, by which time the shiploads of Knights, with their servants and their Greek passengers, were understandably "battling with pestilence, poverty and discouragement."

An island of mongrels

The arrival of the Knights and hapless Greeks put Malta under the spotlight of Europe for the first time. The 12,000 poor inhabitants of the islands were regarded, in so far as they were given any consideration at all, as the human detritus of a vaguely perceived concoction of Phoenicians, Arabs, Norman princes and diverse vagabonds.

One of the results, according to the Knights' commissioners, was that the inhabitants had been left speaking "a sort of Moorish". The true nature of the language was later to provoke intense academic speculation. Until that happened, a typical assessment of the language was that it made the islanders sound "more rough than they really are, it being much akin to Turkish." The Italian knight who passed this opinion was no scholar: he believed, for example, that Arabs and Turks were the same. Like most Knights, he made no effort to learn the language.

The barefooted fishermen and peasants of Malta welcomed the influx of Knights as prospective employers and customers and as protectors against Barbary Coast corsairs who routinely raided the islands for slave labour.

But in spite of the sullen reservations of the indigenous ruling class, the face of Malta was soon transformed. Before, it had been little more than a small fishing village, the Borgo, an old fort called St Angelo and an "old deserted town" in the interior (meaning Mdina), a description which did not please the local worthies who lived there.

Accommodation had to be found or built immediately for several thousand newcomers, and great urgency was given to the construction of defences which had to be capable of withstanding the attack by the Ottoman troops that was only a matter of time in coming. ❑

Verdala essendo Governatore dell'Artiglieria accresce e risarcisce gli strumenti di guerra, e si diporta in que sta carica con universale soddisfazione l'anno 1561.

Verdala amministrando in convento molte e principali cariche, con somma diligenza e intiera fedeltà, viene eletto ricevitore e procuratore, del comun tesoro per Tolosa

An island transformed

Although the Maltese peasants welcomed the protection of the Knights, the local nobility were not at all keen on being displaced by a superior force enjoying a special relationship with the Pope and Holy Roman Emperor. Moreover, they had managed to secure a guarantee from one of Charles's predecessors that Malta would not be passed around the Crowns and Dukedoms like a parcel. This promise was clearly now being ignored.

LEFT: Grand Master Philippe Villiers de L'Isle Adam.
ABOVE: fresco scene of daily life at the Grand Master's Palace.

A NEW HOME

A document in the National Library records the gift of Malta to the Knights "that they may perform in peace the duties of their Religion for the benefit of the Christian community, and employ their forces and arms against the perfidious enemies of the Holy Faith, we have determined on granting them a fixed home out of the particular affection we bear the Order, that they may no longer be compelled to wander about the world. All who may now be dwelling in said island shall receive and consider the Grand Master as their true and feudal lord and shall perform and obey his behests as good and faithful vassals should always obey their lord".

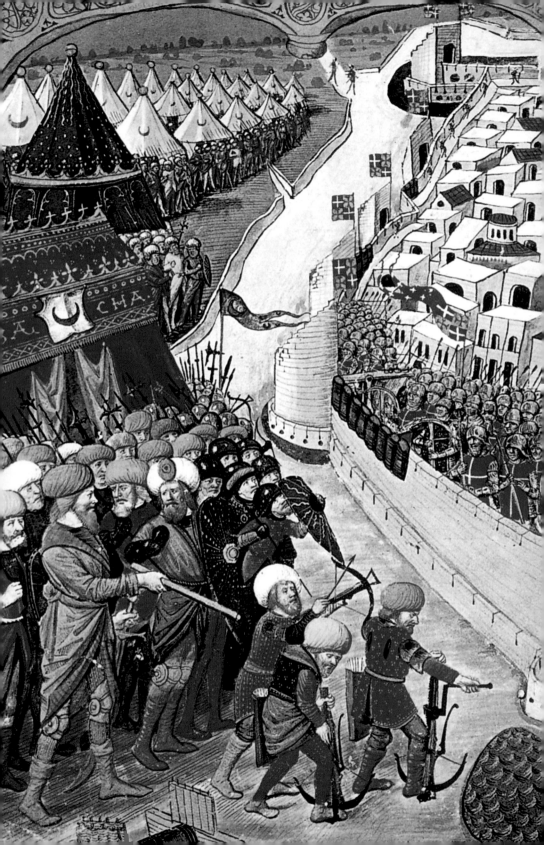

THE GREAT SIEGE

The battle for Malta was much more than a fight between Knights and Turks. It was East versus West, Islam versus Christianity – the key to world domination

There can never have been more natural enemies. Well before the arrival of the Knights, the Barbary Corsairs, as the pirates of North Africa were generally known, had been frequent raiders in this part of the Mediterranean. Malta was often hard hit but was not alone in its suffering. It is said that one particularly lucrative Corsair expedition to Italy netted no fewer than 11,000 captives. Prisoners were either enslaved or put up for ransom, the latter arrangement being run like a well-regulated business with recognised prices being placed on the heads of various ranks and nationalities.

The Barbarossa band

The profits from piracy enabled the Ottoman *deys* and *beys* in control of the Barbary ports to employ the finest fighting commanders and crews available. The best (or worst, if you were a Christian) at the beginning of the 16th century, were the brothers Barbarossa from the Greek island of Lesbos. Their protégé Dragut was equally infamous.

Born on the Caramanian coast opposite Rhodes, Dragut joined the Turkish navy as a boy and was recognised as "a good pilot and a most excellent gunner". He joined the Barbarossa band based at Algiers and quickly rose to the rank of lieutenant with the command of 12 galleys.

"From thenceforward this redoubtable Corsair passed not one summer without ravaging the coasts of Naples and Sicily: nor durst any Christian vessels attempt to pass between Spain and Italy; for if they offered it, he infallibly snapped them up: and when he missed any of his prey at sea, he made himself amends by making descents along the coasts, plundering villages and towns, and dragging away multitudes of inhabitants into captivity." "Imprisonment" (in the galley of Admiral Doria)

had sharpened his appetite for Christians, and he harried the Italian coasts with more than his ancient zeal." According to a contemporary Turkish chronicler, he had become "the drawn sword of Islam."

The Duke of Bourbon, the Viceroy of Naples and the Pope all financed unsuccessful expedi-

PRECEDING PAGES: the Turkish invasion of Malta, 1565.
LEFT: the Christian garrison besieged.
RIGHT: Grand Master Jean Parisot de la Valette.

A CHANCE MEETING

There is a legend that some 25 years before the Great Siege two of the principal protagonists met face to face. In 1540, Dragut was captured and put to work as a galley slave in a Christian ship. One of the ship's officers had once been captured by the Turks, and had been a galley slave under Dragut. He spotted him straining at the oars and cried: "Señor Dragut, usanza de guerra!" ('tis the custom of war!). To which the prisoner, recognising the officer, replied *"Y mudanza de fortuna!"* ("a change of luck!"). The Christian officer was Jean Parisot de la Vallette, the future Grand Master. Dragut was ransomed soon afterwards by the Barbarossas for 3.000 crowns.

tions to eliminate Dragut. At last Doria believed he had his former galley slave cornered in an inlet at Jerba, the Tunisian island, "and sent joyous messages to Europe, announcing his triumph." He spoke too soon. During the night Dragut had a canal dug and escaped to open water. "Never did Doria curse the nimble Corsair with greater vehemence or better cause."

Tiring of solitary roving, Dragut decided to join the Ottoman navy, and in 1551 he sailed out of the Dardanelles as second in command (under Sinan Pasha) of a fleet of nearly 150 galleys and 10,000 soldiers – "witherbound no Christian could tell."

corsair was in fact the brother of Dragut and now he had come for revenge. The Turks devastated the island and carried off almost the entire population of 5,000 into slavery.

Preparing for the worst

La Valette, approaching 70 years of age, did not expect to wait long before his old adversary Dragut came looking for him. He had been in action at Rhodes 43 years earlier, a tall, handsome man, devoutly religious and an inspirational leader. He had learned Turkish during his spell as a galley slave, and his sufferings "had increased his hatred of the Infidel".

The sack of Gozo

The Ottoman fleet was in fact heading straight for Malta. By then the Knights had been on the island for 20 years, steadily improving the defences. When the Turks landed on the tongue of the promontory, between the two great harbours, they were intimidated by the mighty sight of Fort St Angelo, even though it was not yet complete. Instead of attacking Malta they redirected their assault and plundered the relatively defenceless island of Gozo.

Five years earlier the Gozitans had captured a corsair, and the people, who were infuriated by years of terror and plunder, had burned his body on the bastions of their citadel. The

To face the impending invasion, the fortification of Malta was augmented in the great harbour to include the fortress of St Michael, which protected the approach to the Senglea peninsula. Fort St Angelo was further strengthened and Fort St Elmo, facing the sea on the point of Mount Scebberas (where Valletta would one day stand), was also fortified.

The entrances to the harbour and the sheltered creeks of the Borgo were guarded by a ferocious chain of stakes and metal. La Valette ordered the granaries filled and the cisterns kept topped up with water. A chain of warning beacons was erected around the coast. He asked the Viceroy of Sicily to be ready to help and appealed to all absent Knights to return to Malta at once. In the meantime, 700 Knights and 3,000 Maltese troops, supplemented by about 5,000 mercenaries, waited.

The siege begins

On 18 May 1565 the huge Ottoman fleet hove into view. It consisted of 180 ships carrying more than 30,000 of the best troops the Sultan could muster: Janissaries, reared from infancy for fighting, Thracian horsemen, Anatolians and volunteers from all parts of the dominions. But Dragut himself was delayed and word was received that it would be two weeks before he

works ready for an attack on the relatively small garrison of St Elmo before moving on to the main targets, Birgu and St Michael. Arriving at last, Dragut disagreed with these tactics but the preparations were too far advanced to be abandoned. Mustafa professed himself confident that St Elmo would fall within five days.

The sheer weight of the attack when it was launched put the Turks in possession of the ravine in front of the gate within just three hours. The defenders, no more than 60 Knights and a few hundred men, doubted that they could withstand a second assault and sent a message to the Grand Master. La Valette replied

could assume overall command of the operation. Mustafa Pasha, the senior army officer, and the fleet admiral, Piali, had little choice but to begin without him.

The beacons along the coast flared warnings. Peasants rushed into the fortresses with the last of the food and their livestock. Mdina, the cavalry headquarters, closed its gates and poison was dropped into the wells at Marsa, where the enemy were expected to make their camp.

The Turks took their time, building earth-

LEFT AND ABOVE: the fresco scenes from the Grand Master's Palace are the most accurate known depiction of the Great Siege of 1565.

AN EYE FOR AN EYE

The Great Siege was a brutal and bloody fight to the finish. During the battle for St Elmo the ravine beneath Dragut's bridge overflowed with putrefying corpses, while the flowing white robes of the Christian defenders on the wall were set alight by fire hoops and plunged into the ravine like comets. After the battle was over, the Turks – trying to demoralise the knights further – sent five wooden crosses floating across the harbour towards St Angelo, each bearing the headless body of a knight who had all died so bravely. La Valette's riposte was to execute all his Turkish prisoners and to fire their heads back at the Turkish lines as cannon balls.

that if necessary, he would personally come to take over St Elmo's defence. Dragut threw a bridge across the ravine and ordered his men to take the fort.

The battle raged on the bridge for five hours, in the course of which the Turkish losses were heavy. Having been denied a quick victory, Dragut encircled St Elmo with his heaviest guns and poured in 7,000 rounds a day while the Janissaries repeatedly charged the walls.

The many stories of the Battle of St Elmo are the stuff of legend but one incontrovertible fact is that during the action Dragut himself was mortally wounded – according to the Maltese,

by the shrapnel of a shot fired from Mount Scebberas. Mustafa is said to have thrown his cloak over the prostrate Dragut until he could be carried to the safety of his tent.

The fall of St Elmo

The battle continued. La Valette gave up asking for the promised help from Sicily and the St Elmo defenders in turn asked no more for reinforcements. Having committed their souls to God, they "made ready to devote their bodies in the cause of His Blessed Son." On 22 June the St Elmo Knights set to their final hand-to-hand combat with the Turks and by the next day a Turkish flag was run up over the fort.

It is said that word reached the dying Dragut in his tent that St Elmo had at last fallen without a single survivor, whereupon he lay back dead. In fact there may have been a handful of Christian survivors – some say there were nine Knights, who were never heard of again, and five Maltese, who swam to safety across Grand Harbour. The Turks had lost 8,000 men. "If the child has cost us so dear", said Mustafa, contemplating what lay ahead at St Angelo and St Michael, "what will the parent cost".

Mustafa proposed terms of capitulation to La Valette. His reply was to point at the depth of the ditch around the two as yet untouched forts with the remark: "Let your Janissaries come and take that".

The final assault

Turkish guns were manoeuvred into position to bombard the forts, but the rock-hard ground provided little cover for crews who were exposed to brisk counterfire. Engineers were brought in under cover of darkness to cut trenches, but the sound of their picks gave the Christian gunners something to aim at.

Mustafa would have liked to have brought the Turkish ships to lend fire support to his infantry and gunners; La Valette's spiked barrier, however, blocked the entrance. An attempt by Turkish swimmers to cut the chain with axes led to a battle with Maltese troops who dived in with knives between their teeth to see them off.

The Turks threw 10 assaults at St Michael supported by fire from ships dragged across the lower slopes of Mount Scebberas to circumvent the defences laid at the harbour entrance. Janissaries swarmed up scaling ladders but were hurled back, "a huddled mass of mangled flesh". Knights defended by dropping huge blocks of masonry on to the heads of their assailants. "The scimitar", we are told, "was no match for the long two-handed swords of the Christians" and the water was red with Turkish blood and "mottled with standards and drums and floating robes". The Christians spared only two prisoners, although their respite was brief; they were "delivered over to the mob to be torn in pieces".

Still no help came from Don García de Toledo, the Viceroy in Sicily, although it seems that messages passed freely backwards and forwards during the long weeks. Then on 7 August Mustafa threw 20,000 men at the two bastions.

A mine brought down a long line of battlements and with a gigantic roar the Turks, sensing victory, poured through the breach into the town of Birgu itself. "At that supreme moment even the aged Grand Master... came down to the front of battle and used his sword and pike like a common soldier."

Reinforcements at last

The Turks seem to have been distracted at the very moment of their victory by the sight and sound of cavalry riding down from the Old Town, Mdina. Assuming that they were the long anticipated reinforcements from Sicily, the

7 September by reports of the arrival of 28 enemy ships and some 8,000 men. This time the rumours of reinforcements were true; the exhausted Turks marched to engage them at Naxxar. Realising that he must withdraw, Mustafa formed a rearguard with Dragut's son, Hassan, to protect a retreat which nevertheless left St Paul's Bay choked with Turkish bodies.

Victory

At nightfall on 8 September, the battered gates of Senglea and Birgu were opened and the Knights' Cross again flew over St Elmo. The survivors emerged, blinking on to the ruined

soldiers turned tail, retreating over the 2,000 dead who lay after 8 hours of fighting and ignoring their commander's entreaties that this cavalry was merely the 200 members of the Old Town garrison.

Mustafa managed to regroup but his men had lost the stomach for a fight. The Turkish offensive thereafter was left to the gunners amid growing concern about the prospect of being stranded in Malta during the approaching winter. Mustafa's concern was increased on

LEFT: the Knights in their role as hospitallers, tending the sick in the Great Ward.
ABOVE: Valletta and the Three Cities.

battlefields outside their fortifications. "The Grand Master and his few surviving Knights (the entire force was reduced to some 600 men) looked like phantoms, so pale and grisly were they, faint from their wounds, their hair and beard unkempt, their armour stained and neglected... men who had hardly slept without their weapons for more than three memorable months."

The anniversary of the ending of the siege on 8 September has, ever since, been the most important holiday on the Maltese calendar. It was thought that no moment of pain or glory could equal it – until Malta's second Great Siege in 1940 *(see page 65)*. ❏

AFTER THE SIEGE

The defeat of the Turks was the most heroic chapter in the Knights' history, but ultimately it was also to prove their downfall

Grand Master Jean Parisot de la Valette was the hero of Europe. Even Queen Elizabeth of England, whose father Henry VIII had withdrawn the English Knights from the papist Order, was moved to remark that a Turkish victory would have imperilled the rest of Christendom – as indeed it surely would have. La Valette declined a cardinal's hat but accepted a magnificent sword with a gold hilt and an enamelled and jewelled dagger from Philip II. Other monarchs vied to lavish honours and money on the Grand Master and the Order.

Rebuilding

The first task in devastated Malta was to build a city fortified against any future attack. With the Order's coffers overflowing, expense was no object. The site chosen was Mount Scebberas, the high ground from which the Christian forces had taken so much Turkish fire.

The Grand Master, after whom "The Most Humble City of Valletta" was named, did not see the city completed. He suffered a stroke, after a day's hawking, and earned the distinction of being the first person buried in Valletta. His body was placed in the crypt of the Cathedral of St John as soon as that was ready, the inscription reading: "Here lies La Valette, worthy of eternal honour. Once the scourge of Africa and Asia from whence he expelled the barbarians by his Holy Arms, he is the first to be buried in this, the beloved city which he founded."

Artists, sculptors, jewellers and craftsmen were eager to be associated with such a prestigious project. Levelling the site on Mount Scebberas proved more difficult than expected and was abandoned prematurely; this accounts for the number of streets that end in a steep dive down a flight of stairs to the sea. In general, though, Valletta was laid out as a pure example of Renaissance symmetry, a homogeneous

PRECEDING PAGES: the Great Ward, Sacra Infermeria.
LEFT: siege hero, Grand Master Jean de la Valette.
RIGHT: detail of portico, Auberge de Castile.

blend of large and small, public and private buildings. Visiting in 1830, Benjamin Disraeli remarked that it was a city which "equals in its noble architecture any capital in Europe."

The forts of St Angelo and St Michael were rebuilt and enlarged, as were the fortifications around Birgu – renamed Vittoriosa to com-

memorate the victory – and Senglea, which sensibly resisted attempts to impose on it the pompous name "Invitta" (Invincible).

Ever mindful of the possibility of another attack, engineers were worried that loose earth and stones around the new city might be used by some resourceful enemy to improvise breast-works and trenches. The Order therefore bought all fields between Valletta and the plain of the Marsa and had the soil scraped away down to bare rock.

Although the Turks made sporadic raids on Malta well into the 17th century, any real threat from that quarter evaporated with the defeat of the Turkish fleet at Lepanto in 1571, an action in which the Knights' resident fleet of galleys played an enthusiastic part.

La Sacra Infermeria

In 1574, almost as a symbol of intended reversion to its less belligerent function in the Holy Land, the Order built La Sacra Infermeria, a great hospital immediately outside Fort St Elmo. Technically, it was the most advanced in Europe. Boiling surgical instruments in water was meant to reduce the agony suffered by patients but was of course an important step in the as yet unrecognised matter of sterilisation.

The hospital could accommodate 746

sented eight major divisions on the political map of Christian Europe as it then existed: Auvergne, Provence, France, Aragon, Castile, Italy, Germany and England, although the latter was withdrawn following Henry VIII's conjugal disagreements with the papacy. The Order as a whole was often referred to as the "Religion" and its base as the "Convent."

The Knights' standards of living seems to have been high. "I never failed", wrote an enthusiastic visitor to one of the French establishments, "to admire the quantity of the viands that are served and to wonder how so dry and barren a rock can produce such refreshment and

patients, and the principal ward was, at 155 metres (508 ft), the longest room in Europe. Lunatics and galley slaves were "treated" on a lower floor. Patients were well fed – 200 chickens went daily into broth alone – off silver plate which, when melted down (in scandalous circumstances, as we shall see) weighed 1,600 kg (3,500 lb).

Langues and *auberges*

The Knights were divided into *langues* (literally "tongues") and each lived in their particular *auberge* (or inn), which was not unlike an Oxford or Cambridge college or, perhaps, an American fraternity house. The *langues* repre-

so much game. Every day the market is full of vegetables and of almost every kind of fruit; the bread is excellent; beef and mutton of a marvellous taste. Veal and poultry are eaten at all seasons, notwithstanding the fact that there is little pasture. Partridges, pigeons, rabbits, thrushes and other game are fatter than anywhere else in Europe..."

Brotherly love... and differences

"No nobler sight can be imagined", exclaimed one traveller, "than to behold the Grand Master and the Grand Crosses at their devotions." Others too observed that "Mortal enemies are dearest friends here and leave to their countries the ennui of sustaining their masters' quarrels. The French skip, the Germans strut, the Spanish stalk, but nevertheless all are so well amalgamated that, while national peculiarities are retained, like national dress, none are striking."

If the same travellers had returned at other times they may have formed a different opinion. It took four years of patient papal diplomacy to settle a state of near civil war between the respective *langues* when a Spanish knight was murdered by an Italian soldier. At this time the Spanish were in deadlock with the French for several months over who was entitled to service first in the meat market. There were terri-

and privileges by a stranger sent here solely for jurisdiction over heresy?" The objectionable stranger was the Inquisitor, a key figure in a power struggle as interminable as the Order's energy-sapping sporting activities.

The Grand Master was officially on a par with the monarchs of Christendom but, as Sir Harry Luke wrote, "he had to endure two rival authorities, the Bishop and the Inquisitor, who in their several ways sought to make his life a burden and often succeeded in their purpose."

In granting Malta to the Order, the Emperor had reserved the right to nominate the local bishop who, moreover, had to be Spanish and

ble arguments about the order of precedence in church processions, and there was even a dispute between two officers over who should open the city gates if it was reported that the Turks had landed so that the battalion within could be unleashed upon them.

Religious interference

"Who can answer for the just indignation of a high-spirited company of warriors of illustrious birth, against the usurpation of their liberties

LEFT: the City Gate entrance to Valletta, with its original drawbridge and narrow bridge over a dry moat.
ABOVE: the Auberge de Provence.

WINE, WOMEN AND SONG

The archives of Valletta contain 14 folios of procedures against members of the Order for various offences. Most were violations of the vow of celibacy, either "adulterous association with loose or public women" or, in the case of two Italian knights, dressing as women in order to infiltrate the females attending Midnight Mass. Another convicted of sneaking into a nunnery at night was banished to Gozo, where there were no nuns at all. Grand Master Lascaris, believed temptation was best frustrated by exercise. "Wine, women and song sap virility", he warned and knights were expected to neutralise their libidos by playing a kind of football.

be given a say, if not a vote, in the Order's affairs. The bishop therefore came to be regarded as a semi-secret agent reporting to the King of Spain. The Inquisitor, originally invited to Malta by the bishop to look into "pestilential heresies", stayed on to emerge as the papal agent. They thereupon schemed to maximise their influence within the Order.

The simple expedient employed by the bishop to obtain information was to "confer the tonsure" which, apart from the unusual hair-style, signified that the persons concerned (many of whom had absolutely no intention of abandoning the lay life) were "clerks" in his

issues, like the right to shoot rabbits or in daily rules of precedence and protocol.

At audiences with the Grand Master for example, it mattered greatly whether the curtain between the antechamber and the adjoining room ought to be fully drawn, as it would be for the bishop, or merely raised a few inches by the hand of a chamberlain, as in the case of the Inquisitor.

"Each dignitary conceded to the hated rival the absolute minimum of deference while observing that outward appearance of formal courtesy which was regarded as all-important in those days."

service and therefore technically beyond the jurisdiction of the Grand Master.

The Inquisitor dispensed with such subtleties, offering potential informers the unattractive alternative of being thrown into the dungeon of his palace in Vittoriosa on suspicion of heresy. When Bishop Cagliares decided to build a new palace for himself, the Pope refused to allow him to include a dungeon.

Protocols and trivia

The three-cornered struggle for power between an independent-minded Grand Master and the two church agents, bishop and Inquisitor, was most likely to show itself in petty occasional

Right of way

Unforeseen encounters in the street between any two or, heaven forbid, all three of these worthies were very tricky.

If, for example, Grand Master and Inquisitor both happened to be in their coaches, the Inquisitor was expected to stop to allow the former to pass. If the Grand Master happened to be on foot, the Inquisitor was required to descend from his coach and compliment the Grand Master, who was equally obliged to stop to receive the compliment. If the Grand Master was in his coach and the Inquisitor on foot, the latter was supposed to salute but not to advance towards the coach.

Protocol was no less stringent when the time came for the three of them to wish each other a happy Christmas. The tension built up over several days, the end result being "the least convivial series of Christmas dinners on record."

The Quaker incident

One of the oddest challenges to the Inquisitor came in the improbable shape of two middle-aged English Quaker ladies, Katherine Evans and Sarah Chevers, who proposed nothing less than to save Malta from Catholicism. They went straight into his dungeon but found a window from which they kept up an uninterrupted flow

edicts and counter-edicts flew furiously between Valletta and Rome.

As if to compensate for a decline in their real power and importance, the Grand Masters adopted ever more ostentatious uniforms, not to mention redundant suits of armour. Some pursued eccentric interests, such as Grand Master Emanuel Pinto, who employed a notorious scoundrel known as Cagliostro (involved in a scandal with Marie Antoinette) to carry out experiments "to concoct an elixir of life designed to keep a man sound in health." Whether or not Cagliostro deserves any credit, Pinto lasted until he was 92.

of theology, necessarily but unfortunately in English, which no one understood. This continued for three years and was only brought to an end by a papal order for their release.

Decline into decadence

With no enemy to fight and in this kind of climate, the religion began to lose its sense of purpose. Knights drank, brawled and duelled over honour, as well as for the favours of local women. Petitions and counter-petitions,

LEFT: the slaves' prison in caves by Grand Harbour.
ABOVE: the grand interior of the Knight's Conventual Church, St John's Co-Cathedral, in Valletta.

PIRATE KNIGHTS

The Knights could support their extravagant lifestyles only by indulging in the type of brutal piracy that they were supposed to contain. The oars of their galleys were manned by whomever came to hand: usually prisoners-of-war, or convicts, who were stripped naked, chained six to a bench, and flogged with whips – "ten, twelve, even twenty hours at a stretch, without the slightest relapse or rests, and on these occasions the officer will go round putting into the mouths of the wretched rowers pieces of bread soaked in wine to prevent them from fainting". If someone did faint, "he is flogged until he appears to be dead and is then flung overboard".

The once-dreaded fleet of the Knights similarly sacrificed efficiency for show. A traveller in the late 18th century reported: "the ships are defended by an incredible number of hands; the flagship had 800 men on board. They were superbly ornamented, gold blazed on their numerous bas-reliefs, and enormous sails, striped blue and red, carried in the centre a great cross of Malta painted red. Their gorgeous flags floated majestically. In a word, everything rendered them a magnificent spectacle.

> ### STRATEGIC IMPORTANCE
> Negotiating with the British, Napoleon said "I would put you in possession of the Faubourg Saint Antoine (an abbey just outside Paris) rather than Malta".

"Their construction, however, was little adapted either for fighting or foul weather. The Order kept them as an emblem of ancient splendour rather than for practical purposes."

The Knights were soon to be looked down on as "a corrupt, fanatical and hypocritical lot, as cruel as the Turks and as morally loose as the Popes and Cardinals they catered to."

The French Revolution

The Order was usually dominated by the French contingent, and it was to be expected that when the French Revolution came along they were firmly on the side of the monarchy, even to the extent of sending money to Louis XVI. The victorious revolutionaries exacted revenge. A large part of the Order's income was derived from property and investments in France. These were sequestered and the French *langue* was stripped of its nationality.

The Little Emperor

Napoleon felt he needed Malta to pursue his designs on British influence in the Mediterranean in general and Egypt in particular. The Grand Master, the German Ferdinand von Hompesch, could see trouble coming and opened negotiations to bring the Order under the protection of Tsar Paul of Russia. These were in progress when 300 French warships appeared off the island demanding the supply of water. Von Hompesch insisted on not more than four ships entering at a time; Napoleon demurred. Within two days the islands were in French hands.

The feeble surrender to the French cost the Knights the last vestiges of Maltese respect. "To the educated and the aristocratic Maltese, well-informed on local history", says Miss Schermerhorn, "the memory of the imperious Order that took away their parliament and free institutions, interfered with the sacred privileges of their Bishopric, snobbishly refused membership to the sons of families whose titles of nobility ante-dated the occupation of Rhodes, and after boasting that its Standard had never been lowered to any foe, surrendered the island to the French warships without a struggle, is simply not to be defended."

The island looted

On Napoleon's orders, French troops looted the various *auberges* and palaces of paintings and tapestries. Napoleon personally helped himself to the jewelled sword presented to La Valette by Philip II of Spain. The magnificent silver service in the hospital was melted down and used to pay for Napoleon's troops in Egypt. Although the majority of Grand Masters had been French, the language of the Order was traditionally Italian. French became the official language of Malta overnight.

Napoleon stayed only a week before launching himself on Egypt. He left behind a garrison of 1,000 men under General Claude Vaubois. The Royal Navy under Nelson, however, caught up with him at Alexandria and, at the ensuing Battle of the Nile, the French fleet was annihilated. One of the notable casualties was the *Orient*, which took to the bottom much of the treasure so recently looted from Malta.

The French garrison left behind was not deterred by these setbacks from plundering Maltese churches further; the crowning insult was a public auction held in Mdina of the contents of the Carmelite Church.

The local backlash

This was the final straw for the furious Maltese who slaughtered the small garrison in Mdina and set off in pursuit of Vaubois, who

The French are ousted

Although Vaubois proved remarkably resilient, initially the British commanding officer, Captain Alexander Ball, was not inclined to do more than patrol the coastline to prevent French reinforcements from slipping in. It was left to the Maltese to sustain the pressure on the ground with the help of fifth columnists within the walls. The French unmasked some of these and on one occasion executed 43 men.

However, as the 19th century dawned, Britain decided to turn the screw by sending additional forces, who raised a local regiment. The mass of volunteers who came forward

speedily locked himself in the safety of Valletta. A siege was laid by a local force, under the command of the Canon of Mdina Cathedral, aided and abetted by the British ship *Orion* who supplied 1,000 muskets, and the King of Naples and Admiral Lord Nelson who provided ships to blockade Valletta.

Vaubois was not to be intimidated, however, and he led his men out of the city against the 10,000 islanders who had now declared themselves to be subjects of the King of Naples.

LEFT: General Marmond and his French troops land to take Malta.
ABOVE: Napoleon is rowed ashore in a longboat.

thereby the Maltese Light Infantry – part of the British Army, a new departure in Maltese military history. The French hung on in Valletta for two months, eventually giving themselves up when their bread was reduced to just three days' supply. The British flag was run up over Malta on 5 September 1800, yet in spite of their substantial contribution to the outcome, the Maltese were given no say in the final negotiations and were outraged when the French were given leave to depart with their possessions, a large proportion of which the Maltese recognised as having been looted from them. The departing French took with them the ghost, if not the corpse, of the Knights. ❑

THE KNIGHTS OF MALTA TODAY

The warrior knights began as Hospitallers, caring for pilgrims to the Holy Land, and have never forgotten their healing tradition.

The Sovereign Military Hospitaller Order of St John of Jerusalem of Rhodes and Malta, to give its full name, is still a powerful force. It has 11,000 Roman Catholic members spread around the globe and co-operates with many other Christian and non-Catholic orders. Its modern mission is purely humanitarian, from the running of refugee camps, to caring for children in South American slums. It has leprosy hospitals in Africa and Asia and, quite appropriately, a maternity clinic in Bethlehem. It also runs blood banks and dispatches field hospitals to disaster areas.

The Order's headquarters in Rome's elegant shopping street, Via Condotti, is, like the Vatican (with which it is closely linked), a sovereign state. It issues is own stamps, has its own diplomatic corps and has a sovereign head with the title Prince and Grand Master. But these days only the top echelons of the Order take vows of chastity and poverty, and they require an impeccable pedigree of more than two centuries of nobility.

Depite its chic address there is a real desire to return to the site of its most famous victory, Fort St Angelo, Malta's last bastion of defence during the Great Siege. The Order has a lease on part of the fort and would like to turn it into a mini state. The Maltese government, however, is less keen on the return of the Order.

▷ **IN GUARDIA**
The changing of the guard, staged at Fort St Elmo and at the Citadel in Gozo, re-enacts an old Knights' ceremony and is a great crowd pleaser.

△ **MEN OF IRON**
These model knights in shining armour carry on a legacy of metalworking which was first introduced by the Knights.

◁ **DRESSED TO KILL**
Recruits in fine plumage – the old garb of Knights' officers and men-in-arms.

△ **THE INN PLACE**
The Auberge d'Angleterre, in the narrow streets of Vittoriosa, was the first residence of the English Knights before the Order decamped to Valletta.

ST JOHN AMBULANCE

In Britain, the Protestant Order of St John carries on the hospitaller tradition of the Knights through two separate foundations: the St John Ambulance Association, formed in 1877 to train the public in first aid, and the Ophthalmic Hospital in Jerusalem. The St John Ambulance, a worldwide charitable association, still offers first-aid courses and is most conspicuous when putting what it teaches into practice. Present at almost all public events, its members are adept at dealing with all manner of diasaster.

Since 1888, when Queen Victoria granted a Royal Charter to the British Order of St John, its Sovereign Head has been Britain's ruling monarch.

△ **TOP BRASS**
A gathering of senior Knights and clerics with the 78th Grand Master, Fra Andrew Bertie, a Scotsman descended from Mary Queen of Scots.

◁ **KNIGHT LIFE**
The Knights as tourist attraction: in Mdina *The Knights of Malta* is just one of many island-wide attractions that re-creates the days of the Order.

ENTER THE BRITISH

With the Knights and Napoleon both expelled, Malta was pleased to take the hand of Britain in a friendly marriage of convenience

The negotiation of the Peace of Amiens, between France and Britain in 1802, took an alarming turn, in Maltese eyes: there was talk of Britain handing back all previously French-owned territories, after two years of occupation. The island's bitter taste of French rule made the prospect of this as unsavoury as the resurrection of the discredited Knights. Malta stated its case unequivocally in a Declaration of Rights: Malta must come "under the protection and sovereignty of the King of the free people, His Majesty the King of the United Kingdom of Great Britain and Ireland."

Ancient experience of the islands being passed around as chattels necessitated the proviso that "his said Majesty has no right to cede these Islands to any power... if he chooses to withdraw his protection, and abandon his sovereignty, the right of electing another sovereign, or of governing these islands, belongs to us, the inhabitants and aborigines alone, and without control."

Anglicisation

Malta's political institutions and law were gradually anglicised, but it was probably in the matter of language that the nuances showed through most clearly. While spoken by all sections of the Maltese people, *Malti* had never acquired any status – it remained, as far as most foreigners were concerned, "a kind of Moorish." As the language of its nearest country in Europe, Italian was the language of the Church and the law and was generally used by society in Maltese drawing-rooms.

The commercial community in Valletta had picked up some English because of contact with English men-of-war and merchantmen which had been regular callers at Grand Harbour from the 17th century, but the language was no more widely known than that. Instructions to Sir Thomas Maitland on his appointment as the first British governor in 1813 contained the note, significant in the light of later events: "You will be pleased to issue all Proclamations in English as well as Italian, and in a few years the latter may be gradually disused." He added that, as yet, "no permanent or definite system had been laid down for their Government."

PRECEDING PAGES: symbol of the British Empire.
LEFT: statue of Queen Victoria in Republic Square.
RIGHT: a British ship in Grand Harbour.

DON'T CALL US...

The Civil Commissioner who guided Malta into the British way of doing things was Sir Alexander Ball. His first task had been to let the Order of the Knights know that it would definitely not be returning to Malta. However, oblivious to Maltese local feeling, Grand Master Tommasi was waiting in Sicily fully expecting the call to return. When it didn't come, he sent his plenipotentiary, the Bailiff Buzi, to investigate the reasons for the delay. Buzi assumed he could move into the Palace in Valletta; instead, he was politely advised that Sir Alexander was in residence and found it "absolutely necessary" to remain so. Buzi was told to wait – in vain as it transpired.

Subjects of the Crown

The final shadow of the Knights that hung over the island was removed when Russia let it be known that, having broken with Napoleon, it no longer wished to pursue the restoration of the Order of St John to Malta. Now the people of Malta and Gozo could formally be made "subjects of the British Crown and entitled to its fullest protection."

As Sir Harry Luke, a British Lieutenant-Governor of Malta (1930–38), observed, the history of Malta under British rule, at least until World War II, may have lacked "the glamour, the international ramifications, the world-wide

reign a Maltese marchioness became entitled to kiss her cheek (like an English peeress) instead of kissing only her hand. A similar footnote shows Victoria doing her bit for the Maltese lace-making industry with an order for "eight dozen pairs long and eight dozen pairs short mits, besides a scarf."

Literary visitors

One of the first of Malta's illustrious British visitors was the poet Samuel Taylor Coleridge, who arrived in Malta in 1804 for health reasons. The governor, Sir Alexander Ball, appointed him Private Secretary and, after having found

appeal of the Knights." But what it did bring to the islanders was the beginnings and development of modern Maltese politics, education, the liberation of the Maltese church from Sicilian domination and the regulation of the rights of the Maltese nobility.

In various government proclamations, for example those nominating His Majesty's judges, the switch from the earlier routine could hardly have been more simple: the words "Grand Master" were crossed out and "The King" substituted.

The history of the British period includes, in one of the smaller footnotes, the implications of having a Queen on the throne. In Victoria's

other accommodation for himself, Ball left Coleridge to live alone in the vast palace. Coleridge recorded that he felt like "a mouse in a Cathedral on a fair market day."

Grand Tourists were close in the wake of the British takeover, including another famous poet. Lord Byron, just turned 21, was offended by the paucity of the reception laid on by Ball for his arrival in 1809. He was pleased, though, with the accommodation in Old Bakery Street, Valletta, and he began to take Arabic lessons but was distracted by what was to become a notorious weakness. The woman concerned was appropriately special. Still in her mid-twenties, she was the Austrian-born daughter of the Austrian Internuncio in Constantinople and married to Charles Spencer Smith, the British representative at the same court.

Adieu from Byron

Their affair lasted a furious three weeks, during which Byron had to be restrained from fighting a duel on her behalf with an aide-de-camp. She appears in his poetry as "Florence" and they talked about running away together to Friuli in northern Italy.

Almost inevitably, Byron let her down badly and knew it. But he was probably not so diffident about the collapse of the affair because he was

More men of letters

Sir Walter Scott, paralysed and apoplectic by strokes brought on by his literary efforts to buy off creditors, spent three weeks of the last year of his life in Malta. He attended a ball given in his honour, and noted privately that it was "an odd kind of honour to bestow on a man of letters suffering from paralytic illness."

William Makepeace Thackeray's visit started inauspiciously in quarantine on Manoel Island. On being released he was enchanted by "beggars, boatmen, barrels of pickled herrings and maccaroni; the shovel-hatted priests and bearded Capuchins; the tobacco, grapes, onions

moved to write a lamenting and, it has to be said, a fairly lamentable farewell to Malta (it is regarded as among his very worst work).

> *Adieu, ye joys of La Valette!*
> *Adieu, sirocco, sun, and sweat!*
> *Adieu, thou Palace rarely entered!*
> *Adieu, ye mansions where*
> *I've ventured!*
> *Adieu, ye cursed streets of stairs!*
> *(How surely he who mounts you swears!)*
> *Adieu…*

LEFT: monument to Sir Alexander Ball in Lower Barracca Gardens, Valletta.
ABOVE: daily business in the Grand Master's Palace.

DRESSING AND DINING

In 1810, Dr Charles Meryon logged in his diary: "The upper classes of the inhabitants dress like the French; but the common people wear a dress resembling Figaro in the opera, with this difference, that they have trousers instead of tight breeches. The women are small and have beautiful hands and feet. They are fond to excess of gold ornaments which they estimate by value more than taste; their ears, necks and arms are stiff with rings, chains and bracelets. They wear shoe-buckles of gold or silver. Although very brown, they are often handsome. The repasts are plentiful; it is common to have three courses, and from five to ten different sorts of wine".

and sunshine; the signboards, bottled-porter stores, the statues of saints and little chapels which jostle the stranger's eyes…"

Dizzy's debates

Of all these visitors, the one whose impressions had the most profound influence on Britain's political and diplomatic stance towards the islands in the latter half of the 19th century was the future prime minister, young Benjamin ("Dizzy") Disraeli.

"Highly unpopular and unwanted at the regimental messes and parties", Disraeli was too clever by half for the taste of the British

Disraeli never forgot his enjoyment of Malta when it was relevant to the diplomatic tangles which ground towards World War I. Britain and France had of course patched up their differences by then and Winston Churchill, then First Lord of the Admiralty, invited his French counterpart "to use Malta as if it were Toulon". It was then that Malta became "the Nurse of the Mediterranean", providing more than 25,000 beds for the care of the wounded.

Self government

Malta's first self-governing constitution came into being in 1921. The constitution separated

officer corps. "What rendered matters worse was his great knowledge and memory, which enabled him to make short work of any bold soldier who encountered his argument." And even if Disraeli knew what people thought of him, he probably didn't care. "You should see me in the costume of a Greek pirate", he wrote home to his father.

On another occasion: "Here I am sitting in an easy chair, with a Turkish pipe six feet long, an amber mouthpiece and a porcelain bowl. What a revolution! But if I tell you that I have not only become a smoker, but the greatest smoker in Malta! The fact is I find it relieves my mind."

responsibilities pertaining to the island's role as an imperial fortress – such as defence and foreign relations – which remained with Britain, from domestic affairs, which were put into the hands of a Senate and Legislative Assembly. Political activity was fused into the Nationalist Party until, in 1927, it was defeated by the Constitutional Party under Sir Gerald (later Lord) Strickland, who had been Chief Secretary of Malta and was Maltese through his mother, the Contessa della Catena.

Ecclesiastical interference

Lord Strickland and the Church did not get along, and he was none too pleased when the bishop circulated a pre-election pastoral letter to his flock which stated: "You may not, without committing a grave sin, vote for Lord Strickland and his candidates." Moreover a post-script to priests reminded them that they were "strictly forbidden to administer the Sacraments to the obstinate who refuse to obey these our instructions."

The British government sent a protest note to the Pope over this ecclesiastical intrusion into the freedom of voters in a British colony, only to be told that Lord Strickland and his party's attitude was "undoubtedly and consistently injurious to religion, since it discredits

the situation and, having discovered that "only about 15 percent of the population can speak Italian" and that English was "far more widely used and understood" suspected that Italian fascists were at work.

Mussolini's ambitions

And so it turned out. Mussolini's propaganda was determined to persuade Italians that the Maltese were a branch of the Italian race, their speech was an Italian dialect and that they, the Italians, ought to be ready to back his plan to sieze Malta – plus other choice bits of the Roman Empire – when he gave the word. ❑

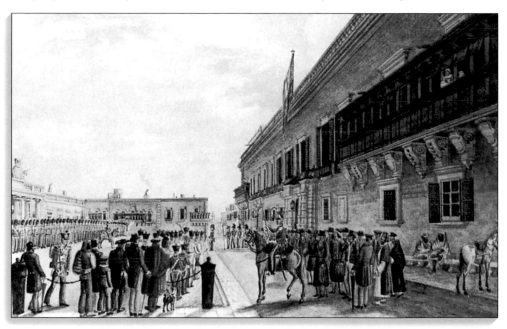

Bishops and clergy, upsets ecclesiastical discipline and tends to destroy the religious traditions of a people so deeply attached to the Church." The British government promptly suspended the General Election.

The new elections resulted in the return to office of the Nationalists, who thereupon took the curious course (for Nationalists) of reversing the previous encouragement given to the use of the Maltese language by imposing Italian. The Secretary of State for the Colonies looked into

LEFT: lithograph of Valletta, seen from Grand Harbour, by the Schranz brothers, 1840.
ABOVE: watercolour of palace and ceremonial, 1822.

A DIFFERENT LANGUAGE

In order to refute Mussolini's claim that the Maltese spoke a form of Italian (and that Malta ought, therefore, to be handed over to him), the British governor Sir Harry Luke, in his entertaining and informative book, *Malta*, pointed to a translation of the first part of Longfellow's *Psalm of Life*, ("Tell me not, in mournful numbers…")
Tghidulix li id-dinja hi holma,
Mhiex hlief frugha, u niket, u hemm;
Dak li jidher fil-wicc hu qarrieqi,
U jekk torqod ir-ruh taghna tintemm.
As Sir Harry remarked in typical British style, "It doesn't really look much like a dialect of Italian, does it?".

PRESS ONLY

WORLD WAR II

Isolated on the edge of Axis-held Europe, Malta looked doomed. But history was about to repeat itself in the island's second Great Siege

On 10 June 1940, Italy's dictator Benito Mussolini cast his lot with Adolf Hitler. Italy was at war with Britain and France. That night Malta heard *Il Duce* broadcast to jubilant crowds from his balcony overlooking Piazza Venezia in Rome. His "million bayonets", he shouted, would be on the march as from midnight. What they did not know, nor did Hitler for that matter, was that Mussolini's first action would be against Malta, the following day, 11 June.

Ernle Bradford, the renowned Maltese historian who served as a naval officer in the Malta convoys, recalls in his book *Siege: Malta 1940–1943* that Hitler "tried to persuade the Duce to withhold his entry into the war but eager to lay his hands upon the spoils, the other partner in the Axis had determined to rush in as soon as it was clear that France was falling." It was, as Winston Churchill described Mussolini's move, "the behaviour of a jackal" seeking to gorge itself on smaller meats while backs were turned.

The battle begins

At 7am the next morning, air-raid sirens wailed for the first time and minutes later, the whistle of falling bombs could be heard around Valletta and the Grand Harbour as ten high-flying bombers escorted by fighters droned overhead. A barrage of rapid fire came from the anti-aircraft guns of Malta's artillery batteries accompanied by the staccato of the 4-inch guns of *HMS Terror*, a survivor from World War I berthed in Pieta creek. It was the first of what were to be eight raids that day.

Faith, Hope and Charity

To face the enemy aircraft Malta had but three aged Gladiator biplanes, apparently left behind accidentally at the RAF base at Kalafrana when the carrier *Glorious*, to which they belonged,

set sail for the North Sea at the time of the German invasion of Norway. They had become known as *Faith*, *Hope* and *Charity* and on that first raid one was lost. Folklore has it that it was *Charity* because "Malta never lost Hope or Faith in the final victory." (Heroic *Faith* is now at the National War Museum for all to see.)

AIR RAID SHELTER
KENN
GHAL ATTAKKI MILL-AJRU

PRECEDING PAGES: Grand Harbour in 1945.
LEFT: July 1942, after the "raiders passed" signal.
RIGHT: heading for the safety of a shelter.

SECRET TALKS

What the Maltese did not know, as Mussolini spoke to the mob, was that the islands' destiny had already been secretly discussed. In a bid to keep Italy from joining Germany, Britain's War Cabinet had, some days earlier, received a proposal from the French suggesting the Allies offered Italy "belligerent status" and therefore the right to a seat at an eventual peace conference. There, her territorial claims to Malta could be discussed.

It was a close call. The two doves of the War Cabinet, Neville Chamberlain and Lord Halifax, voted for the proposal; the three hawks, Churchill, Clement Attlee and Arthur Greenwood voted against, and so rejected it.

To fight or to flee?

Even though the War Cabinet had voted against ceding any claims on Malta to Italy, whether the islands were physically defensible was quite another matter. Both the Army and the Royal Air Force had considered Malta too vulnerable to attack from enemy planes based on neighbouring Sicily and favoured evacuation. The Royal Navy had thought otherwise and its voice carried. It was to be proved right – though at high cost.

The Governor of Malta, Lieutenant General Sir William Dobbie, issued an Order of the Day: "The decision of His Majesty's Govern-

Malta strikes back

As new allied planes arrived, the island also took on an offensive role. On 11 November an airborne torpedo attack by planes from the carrier *Illustrious* hit the Italian fleet sheltering in Taranto harbour, accounting for the loss of three battleships and two cruisers. They had been located with the help of reconnaissance planes flying from Malta.

By December more than 200 Italian air raids had been logged but Malta held fast; Operation Hercules – Italy's code name for the planned invasion and occupation of the islands – was indeed proving a herculean task.

ment to fight until our enemies are defeated will be heard with the greatest satisfaction by all ranks of the Garrison of Malta... I call on all Officers and other ranks humbly to seek God's help, and in reliance on Him to do their duty unflinchingly."

The islands were soon fully embroiled in the rigours of 20th-century war. Wartime restrictions were put into force, blackout introduced and already deep shelters were dug deeper into the limestone rock. The sirens sounded their warnings and their all-clears. The 30,000 troops divided into equal numbers of British and Maltese. The civilian population stood at about 255,500.

The key to the Mediterranean

Churchill was utterly convinced of the islands' strategic importance. Malta, he insisted, must be held, whatever the cost. And the strength of Malta's strategic position was not lost on the German forces either.

As the Allies made advances in North Africa, and Italy suffered setbacks with her disastrous venture into Greece, so Hitler turned his attention to the Mediterranean arena. Rommel's Afrika Korps was attempting to advance along the North African coast to Egypt but sitting astride his key supply lines from Europe was Malta, a solid military base possessing both airfields and a dockyard. If the German forces were to succeed in North Africa then Malta would have to be disarmed.

To achieve this it was decided that the full might of the German Luftwaffe would be thrown against the islands and against the warships and the convoys of merchant ships they escorted. Cut the supply lifeline and Malta would be starved into submission.

The battle for *HMS Illustrious*

The island suffered a major blow in January 1941 when the vital aircraft carrier *Illustrious* was attacked while escorting a convoy coming from Alexandria. The flight deck was put out

the sky. In spite of a relentless onslaught, (a 500kg bomb penetrated the flight deck armour), the *Illustrious* sailed on with fires raging and her steering gear out of order.

On the night of 10 January, she limped in to harbour and berthed in Dockyard Creek. Here she was sheltered by the heights of Kordin on one side but was otherwise exposed to full view. Every hand in the area was called out. Casualties were evacuated and men from the dockyard swarmed over the carrier. Working around the clock they carried out repairs.

It was six days before the enemy returned to their attack, time enough for them to re-arm

of commission, putting the carrier's own airborne planes in the predicament of needing somewhere else to land. They decided to head for Malta, their mother ship limping towards the Grand Harbour with the remnants of the convoy that evening.

On reaching Malta, as the first two merchantmen passed safely through the defensive nets at the breakwater entrance into the comparative calm of the Grand Harbour, so waves of Stuka dive-bombers and Junker 88s filled

---

LEFT: a fighter pilot scrambles into action at Luqa.
ABOVE: fires rage deep in Grand Harbour after another raid by bombers.

themselves for the final kill. But it was six days not wasted in Malta; the Allies had planned their defence. The Gunners proposed the best their guns could offer, a "box barrage", an umbrella of exploding shells, above the carrier. In order to achieve this, every gun around the harbour – like those in the forts St Elmo, St Angelo and Tigne – as well as those within range of the harbour, would be coordinated so that they threw up a theoretically impenetrable curtain of fire around the prize target. No pilot would choose to fly through it.

On the afternoon of 16 January the attack came. Buildings shook as bombs exploded and the barrage of anti-aircraft fire opened up.

Malta had never known noise like it before. People ran to nearby air-raid shelters only to see dive bombers flying at roof-top level, screaming down to where the carrier was berthed. Shrapnel rained down from the bursting barrage above.

It was a massive raid. Ten enemy planes were destroyed; five by the few fighters Malta could deploy, five by the ground artillery. And the damage to buildings on both sides of the Grand Harbour was the heaviest recorded in any one raid. Casualties were so high it was decided to evacuate the so-called Three Cities of Senglea, Cospicua and Vittoriosa bordering

needed to escort essential convoys through the gauntlet now known as Bomb Alley.

The stakes increase

The battle for Malta, which had begun almost as a personal crusade on Mussolini's part, took on a different complexion with growing German involvement.

Rommel's Afrika Korps had joined battle in North Africa, and Malta was now pivotal in the North African theatre because its aircraft, ships and submarines were a constant threat to the German's exposed supply line between Naples and Tripoli. Massed Panzers engaged

the dockyard area. Yet only one bomb hit the *Illustrious* and even that did little damage.

Undaunted, the enemy returned on the 18th. This time their objective was to put the land-based planes out of action by making the runways unusable. They succeeded, but only briefly. As they always did, teams of willing hands soon filled in the craters again.

In a lull a few days later the *Illustrious* set sail for Alexandria en route for the United States and major repair. The Luftwaffe had lost 30 aircraft in two days and, for a while, Malta enjoyed a respite. But the Mediterranean fleet was without its carrier and Malta now lacked the combined air-sea fire power

over the expanse of the desert consumed enormous quantities of fuel, every drop of which had to be imported.

German convoys were careful to pass by only at night and never closer than about 240 km (150 miles). If Malta-based aircraft missed the supplies as they crossed the sea, they were given a second chance as the supplies trundled east along the North African coast. There was no practical port in the hundreds of miles that separated Tripoli and Tobruk, hence the determination by both Allies and Axis to win and hold the latter. Field Marshal Albert Kesselring repeatedly reminded Rommel of this vulnerability, and on one occasion was overheard to say: "You risk everything if you try to reach the Nile while the British still hold Malta."

Wing Commander Laddie Lucas, the highly decorated RAF ace, compared the island to "some wounded and enraged beast of prey", a menace not only to Rommel but a hindrance to Hitler's strategy in the Middle East and, by tying down 600 German bombers and fighters in Sicily and Southern Italy, a relief valve for the Western Front.

Malta got off more lightly in the first half of 1941 than would have been the case if Rommel had not gone against Kesselring's advice with a decision to secure Tobruk first and worry

German invasion of Russia, planes that would have been deployed in Sicily were now serving at the Russian front. The odds on getting a convoy through were steadily improving.

The Blitz of Malta

The Germans, becoming increasingly frustrated by this depleting thorn in their side, felt that they could not allow the strategic outpost of Malta to remain in Allied hands any longer. Rommel pressed Berlin for action with urgent messages. In one he wrote: "without Malta the Axis will end by losing control of North Africa." The German objective now was to

about Malta afterwards. In fact, fewer allied convoys were getting through the blockade. Many ships were sunk before they reached sight of harbour, others met their fate as soon as they anchored.

But while few convoys were getting through, Malta's submarines and bombers armed with torpedoes could, and did, still inflict heavy damage and losses on ships carrying supplies destined for the Afrika Korps. The good news for Malta was that with the

LEFT: reinforcements disembark in Valletta.
ABOVE: a survivor of the Santa Marija convoy, the damaged tanker *Ohio* just reaches harbour.

UNDER SIEGE

In spite of the hardships and danger, morale was generally high during the siege. Many of the population watched the aerial dogfights and learned to distinguish the types of planes and could gauge exactly where the bombs were falling by the reverberating sounds. However, by February 1941 there were shortages of everything; stocks of staple foods had run gravely low and food rationing was introduced. Kerosene, the fuel then used in many kitchens, was also rationed. The black market thrived. Ammunition was also becoming scarce and anti-aircraft gunners were given hours when they were to hold their fire, no matter how tempting the target.

neutralise Malta, and the islands were about to enter the second Great Siege of their history.

The first waves of bombing came in the middle of January 1942, and then continued with such brutal force that air superiority seemed to be firmly in the hands of the Axis powers. In March and April twice as many tons of bombs rained down on Malta as in a whole year at the height of London's Blitz.

To crush the population's will to fight on, there were 154 days of continuous day and night raids (London had 57), and 6,700 tons of bombs were dropped on the Grand Harbour area (by comparison, the worst night of destruction

in Coventry was achieved with 260 tons). Buildings were flattened, 40,000 homes were destroyed and casualties were high. "Victory Kitchens" were set up to feed the population who were suffering acute malnutrition. Ammunition was rationed.

The blockade was complete; nothing could reach the islands. Churchill signalled: "The eyes of Britain are watching Malta in her struggle day by day. We are sure success as well as glory will reward your efforts."

He also signalled President Roosevelt: "Air attack on Malta is very heavy." With the *Ark Royal* recently sunk, could Roosevelt allow the United States aircraft carrier *Wasp* to air-lift essential Spitfires to Malta. "*Wasp* at your disposal", came the reply. On 14 April she set course from Britain for Gibraltar. On her decks were 47 vital fighters. Perhaps Malta's luck was changing.

The next day King George VI awarded the islands the George Cross. The citation read: "To honour her brave people I award the George Cross to the island fortress of Malta to bear witness to a heroism and devotion that will long be famous in history."

Taking cover

It was a traumatic time. Remote villages of no conceivable military significance suffered like everywhere else. Although houses built of stone did not burn, the confined blast of a bomb landing in a narrow alley was lethal. A low-flying plane could drop a bomb and be gone before an unsuspecting pedestrian knew what was happening, so during the worst of the bombing offensives the villagers took shelter

SECRET WEAPONS

In July 1941, the Italians revealed a secret weapon that they had not yet called on, a special unit of fast E-boats and manned torpedoes.

According to the commander of this unit, these small, deadly craft had been designed as long ago as 1935 specifically with a Malta campaign in mind, when the claims of territorial rights by Italy first surfaced.

The job of the pilot was to drive his craft at the target, wait until the last moment, throw a lever which activated the charge, and abandon the torpedo, which would explode on impact. If the shockwaves did not incapacitate the pilot and he was lucky, he would be picked up by an attendant

E-boat. Such manned torpedoes had already been used with some success in Gibraltar and Crete, and would be used again in Alexandria.

In the event, however, the bravery of the Italian pilots was to count for nothing. They had recknoned without the island's superb radar systems and coastal defences and were spotted leaving Sicily. They were tracked and allowed to enter well into Maltese waters, then within minutes were shot to pieces by concentrated firepower. Only three pilots survived, and they were taken prisoner.

The defeat of the secret weapon provided another boost to the morale of the island defenders.

underground. Many passed the danger periods reciting their rosaries, a bucket of water always at hand to wet a handkerchief which went over the nose as a filter against choking dust mixed with the smell of cordite. And if a meal in the "Victory Kitchen" included a morsel of meat, then it was goat.

Flags and bells

As an emergency reaction to each and every air-raid warning would have prevented any work from being done, the degree of probable danger was denoted by a system of signals, a red flag when bombers were expected, a red and white

Reinforcements

For nearly two years there had been raids at the rate of about three a day, but a chink of hope interrupted this gloomy situation. The American carrier *Wasp* was on its way with 47 more Spitfires. They took off unarmed (to save weight) but with extra disposable fuel tanks which enabled them to reach Malta with barely 90 litres (20 gallons) to spare. The Germans had previously been aware of the arrival of new aircraft and had timed raids to catch them en masse on the ground during the day or so it took to make them fully serviceable. Now, however, two soldiers and two airmen were

one for fighters or mere reconnaissance flights.

The flags were run up on the Governor's Palace and on the Auberge de Castile, but as these were invisible from certain places, Boy Scouts took it upon themselves to relay the appropriate signal with miniature flags on hand-held poles. Nearly 1,000 Scouts were awarded the Bronze Cross for their efforts.

Church bells, whose peal was the concomitant of normal life in Malta, were silent, now for use only to warn of imminent invasion.

LEFT: carrier with relief planes.
ABOVE: the Royal Opera House, Republic Street, reduced to rubble.

waiting for each Spitfire, which was led to a pen as soon as it landed, refuelled, armed and loaded – all within the space of 6 minutes.

The new arrivals were already in the air and waiting when the Luftwaffe made its customary call. The German pilots were evidently caught completely off guard, their radio channels suddenly clogged with cries of "Achtung Spitfeuer" and lost 30 aircraft that first day under the new rules. The Luftwaffe returned in even greater force the following day – and lost another 63. Their Stukas were extremely vulnerable to modern fighters as they came out of their vertical dives with pilots reeling under the effect of the G-forces.

Aerial superiority

Between August 1940 and October 1942, 718 fighters were flown to Malta, 367 of them Spitfires. On 10 May, the month that logged the 2,000th air raid, it appeared as if the tide of fortune had turned. The Spitfires that day seemed to be clawing the enemy out of the sky in spectacular dogfights that were watched excitedly by Maltese leaving their shelters.

By contrast the larger picture was bleak. Malta was only two months away from the date

JOLLY BOATING

At one time the rubber dinghies of so many downed Stuka bombers were bobbing in the sea between Malta and Sicily that one of the Spitfire pilots likened it to "Henley on Regatta Day".

forces, are in urgent need of replenishments of food and military supplies. These we are taking to them…Malta looks to us for help. We shall not fail them."

Day and night, a moving target, the convoy was attacked by sea and air taking heavy losses as it sailed through a corridor of fire. Of the carriers, the *Eagle* was ripped open and sunk by torpedoes and the *Indomitable* put out of action. A merchantman was lost. Nearing Sicily the heavier warships turned back to the task force in Gibraltar;

the authorities had decided would have to be the day of surrender if supplies did not get through. Conditions had now become so dire that they would have no other choice.

But relief was on its way. Heading towards Malta was a convoy of 14 supply ships with an enormous escort of three aircraft carriers, two battleships, seven cruisers and 24 destroyers. This one had to get through.

Malta expects

"The garrison and people of Malta," read a signal from the flagship, *Nelson*, "who have been defending their island so gallantly against incessant attacks by the German and Italian air

the convoy's protection was reduced to four cruisers and 12 destroyers. Now the enemy concentrated the attack, but somehow the remnants continued to progress. Two cruisers were put out of action, five merchantmen sunk.

On 13 August word spread in Malta as the first ships were sighted. Crowds gathered. First to reach harbour were the supply ships *Port Chalmers*, *Melbourne Star* and *Rochester Castle*. Two days later, on 15 August – which was an important day on the Catholic calendar, the feast day of Santa Marija (the Assumption of the Virgin Mary) – in came the *Brisbane Star* and the battered, charred hulk of the tanker *Ohio*, which was barely above water and was being towed by two mine-sweepers and a destroyer. Lining the battlements, crowds cheered and waved and wept for joy.

In the nick of time

But for the arrival of the Santa Marija convoy the islanders would have had to surrender in two weeks. The courageous *Ohio* symbolised the islands' determination to hold out.

Commenting on this event that was so crucial to the island's survival, Churchill recorded: "Thus in the end five gallant merchant ships out of 14 got through with their precious cargoes. The loss of 350 officers and men and of so many of the finest ships in the Merchant Navy and in the escorting fleet of the Royal Navy was grievous. The reward justified the price exacted. Revictualed and replenished with ammunition and essential stores, the strength of Malta revived."

Thereafter the Afrika Korps was primarily concerned with defending its retreat to Tobruk and from there to Benghazi, Tripoli and ultimately to Tunisia. The changing tide manifested itself to the Maltese when four merchant ships bobbed into Grand Harbour having made the run from Alexandria unscathed. At Christmas it was even possible to announce that there was a special treat in the rations: about half a pound per head each of beans and sugar and a quarter of currants.

Glad tidings

There was better news to come on 23 January 1943 with the announcement that the Allies had taken Tripoli – or, as the Maltese preferred to think of it, the Italians had lost it.

General Eisenhower sent a message: "The epic of Malta is symbolic of the experience of the United Nations in this war; Malta has passed successively through the stages of woeful unpreparedness, tenacious endurance, intensive preparation and the initiation of a fierce intensive."

On 12 May the Afrika Korps capitulated, Malta having barred the way to the evacuation of 291,000 Germans and Italians who might otherwise have fought another day. The following month it was possible for King George

LEFT: anti-aircraft battery in action across the harbour from Senglea.
RIGHT: citation with George Cross, 20 June 1943.

VI to visit the island while Montgomery and Eisenhower planned the invasion of Sicily. The Maltese people got a hint of the invasion plans when the Msida Creek was filled in. It was assumed at first that this was simply part of a cleaning-up exercise, but one morning they woke to discover that it was a kind of slipway for numerous landing craft that had suddenly materialised.

The Allied springboard

Equally mysterious – though not for long – was the arrival of Scottish troops who bristled with equipment and kept themselves to themselves.

The landing craft, the Scots and all the rest of a vast invasion force were gone on 9 July.

The islands thus became the Allied springboard for the invasion of Sicily (and for the subsequent push into mainland Europe), with operations planned from the depths of the subterranean Lascaris War Rooms adjacent to Grand Harbour in Valletta.

On 8 September the Italian fleet surrendered, as Commander-in-Chief, Admiral Cunningham notified Admiralty in London: "under the guns of the fortress of Malta." By coincidence, that momentous day was a feast day of the Virgin Mary and also the anniversary of the victory over the Turks in the Great Siege of 1565. ❑

LOOKING TO THE FUTURE

Free of the domination of higher powers, Malta is no longer at the centre of world events, but with independence comes a new set of challenges

While World War II raged on, the British government announced that Malta's "outstanding gallantry" called for "special recognition" in the grant, there and then, of £10 million for the restoration of war damage, with a further £20 million in the pipeline. The government also pledged to restore "Responsible Government" as soon as possible after the end of the conflict.

Elections in 1947 gave Malta its first Labour government under Dr (later Sir) Paul Boffa. The party proposed a referendum on whether the Maltese people, in post-war circumstances, wished to "submit Malta's case to the United States of America with a view to Malta receiving economic aid and, as a quid pro quo, the USA use of Malta as a base." It later transpired that the original draft, by Dominic (Dom) Mintoff, a future premier, had left the door open for the USA or "any major power", an implicit invitation to the Soviet Union. The draft alternative was attributed to "human error" and quickly deleted.

The call for independence

Mintoff came to power in 1955 and suggested that Malta should be "integrated" into the United Kingdom and therefore be represented in the House of Commons. A referendum showed 67,607 out of 90,343 votes in favour of integration, but the British government, while generally sympathetic to the idea, was not confident that the result reflected the feelings of the non-voters.

The matter was still under discussion with Mintoff when it was announced in 1957 that Britain would be cutting back its defence expenditure, with unavoidable consequences for the Malta dockyard, the islands' greatest single employer providing work for 13,000 people. Mintoff lost his enthusiasm for integration and raised the cry for full independence.

PRECEDING PAGES: the armed forces on parade.
LEFT: political party meeting at Marsa.
RIGHT: demands for independence.

Farewell to the British

Following Mintoff's appeals a constitutional deadlock ensued, leading to Britain taking over full responsibility for the islands' government.

By 1959, Malta's dockyard had outlived its usefulness (at least to Britain), and the Colonial Administration published a five-year develop-

MINTOFF'S BARGAINING CARD

In 1957, Dom Mintoff, feeling the need for the Church's support for independence, resorted to one of the more bizarre manoeuvres in Malta's political history.

Malta's two great pictures *The Beheading of St John the Baptist* and a *St Jerome,* both painted for St John's Co-Cathedral, had recently been sent to an exhibition in Rome. When they were returned to Malta, to the astonishment of the Church authorities, they were forcibly impounded on Mintoff's orders. Then, as abruptly as they had been siezed, they were released. The following day a declaration of solidarity was issued by the Archbishop demanding independence from Britain.

Dom Mintoff: Hero and Ogre

There was a time when the name Dom Mintoff was synonymous with that of Malta. Indeed, during his time as prime minister, Malta's problems were often given an airing far in excess of their worth, especially when linked to Mintoff's apparent friendship with Libya's Colonel Gaddafy. Although he stepped down in 1984, many assumed that up to 1987 his influence still held sway over political matters.

Over a period of 17 years Mintoff was prime minister four times. He made his presence felt and his demands international news. He was inclined to come over as an ogre, both feared and disliked; but, as Britain's *Sunday Times* recorded, had Malta been a larger country with Dom Mintoff at the helm, it would have been a country to reckon with.

The British press have always been hard on him, seeing his action as anti-British in spite of his English wife of patrician stock and the marriage of both his daughters to Britons.

At home his supporters regarded him as being propelled by a love for the Maltese islands; his ruthless determination seen as a sign of strength as he strove to give the people a better life.

Born of humble stock in 1916 in the crowded confines of Cospicua, where the British naval dockyard was the major employer, he was very much a man of the people. The young Dominic Mintoff's dreams were formed by the poor world in which he lived, resenting the poverty and the scant regard the Maltese were given in their own country by an unthinking and insensitive regime – when Malta meant nothing but a colonial garrison. The Maltese, he determined, would prove they were as good as anyone else.

After training as an architect and civil engineer, he worked in Britain between 1941 and 1943 before returning home to help reorganise the Malta Labour Party ready for the first post-war elections. The elections took place in 1947 and Labour won. By 1955, Mintoff was prime minister, calling for the British to leave the island.

At home, Mintoff's actions polarised the nation. People either loved him or hated him. Mintoff could talk with charismatic oratory to crowds of thousands, holding their attention and making promises. From the back of a workers' truck, in shirt sleeves, he would inspire and harangue. When he finished he would cry "we are strong, we shall win". Violence flared, communities divided. Life became dominated by politics.

In the days when everyone was a practising Catholic, he was not. He considered the Church to be dangerously authoritarian and challenged it directly. The Church supported the Nationalists and told parishioners to do so too. Mintoff made intentionally ambiguous statements to frighten the Church, frequently saying that they should be seen to be poor, not rich. He attempted to confiscate their land and treasures and, in one final show-down before handing over power, demanded all church schools be free, and achieved a compromise.

And he did improve the standards of living for oridinary people. Wages rose, social services improved and government found land for newly marrieds as housing plots. He introduced free tertiary-level education with students being sponsored.

Mintoff's political career ended on a sad note in September 1998 when, at odds with his Labour Party, he crossed the floor of the house in a vote of confidence, condemning them to a single vote defeat. They lost the ensuing general election and Mintoff declined to stand. We look foward to reading his memoirs.   ❑

LEFT: under Dom Mintoff, Malta went from being a small dependency to being truly independent.

ment plan which concluded that "put briefly... Malta must get out into the world and earn its own living in other ways than it has done in the past." The means to do so clearly demanded full independence, and this was duly granted on 21 September 1964, albeit subject to a 10-year Mutual Defence Agreement with Britain.

The British naval base was finally closed on 31 March 1979 amid politically orchestrated celebrations that were joyous for some and sad for others.

ships that followed World War I might be repeated. There was, in addition, the need for an extended settlement from Britain that would not only repair the heavy damages caused by the severe bombing but also help the construction of improved housing and infrastructure. For years Malta and Gozo had been poor colonial relations.

Employment was looking bleak. British dockyards had employed over one in six of all Maltese workers, and British service establishments had

Shortly afterwards came independent Malta's first (and to date only) experience of a hostile foreign act when a gunboat threatened an Italian company drilling for oil on Malta's behalf. It seems rather appropriate to the history of the islands that its home port was on the Barbary Coast.

Post-war worries

The main problems after the war concerned the economy, with growing worries that the hard-

ABOVE: a familiar sight on today's landscape: construction in progress from a towering crane (here, above the island's famous dockyards).

injected considerable cash into the economy.

The most dramatic result of this was two decades of mass emigration to Australia and Canada, which eased the problems and softened the blow of the inevitable run-down of jobs. The legacy is that even today there are as many Maltese and Gozitans living abroad as on the Maltese islands.

Courting trouble

In the years leading up to the long-planned British withdrawal, the demands of Malta's controversial Prime Minister Dom Mintoff were always emphatically made, most concerning money. Malta approached other countries for aid in establishing itself in the commercial world – but only those accepting Mintoff's socialist leanings would be welcomed. The result was suitors unacceptable to the West.

In the US, where the press was equally cool, Mintoff's leftish leanings spelled Communism and although during World War II both Roosevelt and Eisenhower lauded the islanders' bravery, Mintoff's request for Marshall Aid to help rebuild the shattered islands was turned down out of hand. It left a festering wound and barbed his tongue. Later, when he asked for US courtesy, no president would receive him.

With no foreign income to bolster the econ-

tion was hardly unbiased. But his relationship with Colonel Gaddafy, although ambiguous, paid dividends. Libya provided Malta with oil at cost price as world oil prices rocketed.

Looking towards Europe

Yet even before the British departure Malta had already taken a serious step into the future by signing an Association Agreement with the European Economic Community. The first approach was made on 4 September 1967, when the Nationalist prime minister, George Borg Olivier, asked the Community for negotiations to establish "some form of relationship".

omy, Mintoff was forced to cast around. Potential friends were wary of such a volatile man. President François Mitterrand, although a socialist, took much wooing before he issued an invitation to visit France, and the former USSR set up dialogue only through satellite states. Yet Mintoff was the first leader to be given a stupendous welcome in China, preceding all other Western leaders including America's Richard Nixon.

Mintoff the mediator

It was one of Mintoff's dreams in those heady days to become a world mediator, to reconcile Jew and Arab. Because of his unconcealed support for the Palestinian cause, however, his posi-

Three years afterwards an Agreement was signed. In 15 years, it was concluded, the Maltese islands would be well on the way to economic viability if they could be assured of an export market free of tariff barriers and quota restrictions. The objectives of the Association were clear. The government emphasised that Malta and Gozo were part of Europe geographically as well as through culture, religion, sentiment and way of life.

Borg Olivier spoke of a growing awareness among the Maltese that they were living "in an age of economic groupings and trade areas which will make it difficult for those countries which do not join the group to achieve economic progress and this applies particularly to small countries."

Planning to forestall future criticism from the Socialist party about following in the steps of the former Mother Country, the prime minister pointed out that Malta's approach to Europe was made before Britain's. The fact that Britain planned to become a member of the European Community made it more evident that Malta's commercial future lay in such a relationship.

In July 1990, convinced that the Association had produced economic benefits, Malta applied for full membership. All seemed set for a future that would allow Malta to develop trade

EU membership; the MLP wanted close relations with the EU but not full membership. When Labour returned to office in 1996, after 10 years in opposition, it froze Malta's application for membership. Two years later, however, the returning Nationalists asked for the islands' application to be reinstated. It was, and a national referendum held in 2003 confirmed the majority desire for full EU membership to which Malta will evolve in 2004.

The introduction of value-added tax in 1995 had prepared the ground for Malta's eventual entry, even though the debate on Malta's neutrality had always been a burning issue.

between Europe and the countries around the Mediterranean, even if this would also mean competition from larger European neighbours.

Political divisions

The transition to full European integration in 2004 has been far from smooth. The two main political parties, the Nationalist Party (PN) and the Malta Labour Party (MLP), were always at odds on Malta's stance within the European Union. The PN were always in favour of full

LEFT: policing the roads.
ABOVE: the Kalafrana Freeport terminal at Pretty Bay, south of Valletta; no longer pretty, but very profitable.

A UNIQUE NEUTRALITY

Malta became neutral and non-aligned in 1987 when it was agreed that the islands would not participate in military alliances or permit foreign military bases on its territory, or allow foreign interference in its elections. The days when Malta and Gozo formed part of another country's protectorate were long passed.

However, the prime minister of the day, Eddie Fenech Adami, called together diplomats accredited to Malta to explain that Malta's neutrality was *sui generis*, a unique arrangement, with Italy (a NATO member) undertaking to come to Malta's defence if so requested, and after consultation with other NATO members.

Seeking unity

Neutrality doesn't mean going it alone however. As well as being a member of the Commonwealth, Malta joined the United Nations in 1964 and has played its part in the Council of Europe since 1965. Malta also endorses the principles of democracy and the rule of law as embodied in the Single European Act.

To quote the official view: "Malta seeks to continue the development of its bilateral and multilateral relations with Europe as a full member of the European Community. Its European credentials are not in doubt; its Western democratic values have deep roots that have withstood

the test of provocation; and its neutral status and unpretentious but sober efforts for peaceful dialogue are a positive contribution to a new, larger and closer, but outward-looking Europe."

When the Nationalist Party took the reins of government in 1987, areas of foreign policy previously clouded in uncertainty and ambiguity dissipated. Malta's profile improved all round and although the islands held a decisive pro-Western stance, relations with neighbouring Arab countries remained friendly and strong. Malta has healthy relations with both Israel and Palestine and supports their rights to nationhood; it is also active in confirming the rights of all Mediterranean countries to secure their borders.

Malta today

Lacking any natural mineral resources – vast volumes of commercially viable oil still a pipedream – Malta relies on tourism as one of its main sources of foreign currency. There has been considerable investment in five-star hotel accommodation, the latest addition being the Intercontinental Malta at St George's Bay.

Several ambitious tourist projects are currently under development. These include the Tigne' (incorporating Manoel Island) and Cottonera projects, localities that will vie to match the sophistication of the exclusive Portomaso and Hilton Malta private yacht marina and apartments. Also under development is the Valletta-Marsa Pinto Wharf, whose refurbishment aims to establish Malta as a central Mediterranean cruise-liner terminal, to capitalise on an increasing popularity of cruise holidays and the enchantment of the Grand Harbour.

In parallel with EU requirements and its own policies, the government has embarked on privatisation campaigns to liberalise several key sectors of the economy. A leading bank and the Malta International Airport have already been privatised. The Malta Freeport, Maltacom, Air Malta and the public state lotteries are all potential targets for privatisation too.

Education remains a high priority. Schooling is compulsory up to the age of 16. The system includes both technical and trade schools, and every town and village has a state primary school and kindergarten. Both Church-run and private schools flourish. The University of Malta is the oldest in the Commonwealth outside Britain. The presence of sophisticated technological industries on Malta is reflected in the high profile given to technology in education, with specialised apprenticeship schemes and a strong engineering faculty at the University.

As ever, Malta and Gozo are islands of contrast and change. Use of internet and mobile phone facilities rate among the highest per capita in Europe; cable and satellite companies transmit scores of international channels into homes across the islands. This new way of life coexists alongside deeply entrenched Christian traditions and village *festas*, as do all-night discos, rap and salsa bars and three casinos. ❏

LEFT: tower blocks at Sliema.
RIGHT: the island's soft-limestone quarries yield the building blocks for the construction boom.

THE MALTESE PEOPLE

Ask any visitor what appeals most to them about the islands, and there is a very good chance that they will say the people – Malta's greatest asset

It hardly seems credible that in the long and chequered history of the islands the Maltese should have remained so steadfastly themselves, a proud nation distinct from any other. But they most certainly have, and they would not want it any other way.

In spite of being conquered, subjugated and led over the centuries by the powerful nations of the times – and bearing faces that even now reflect some of that past with features recalling the Romans, Arabs and Phoenicians – the Maltese have doggedly clung to insular individuality. With roots planted firmly in a group of tiny islands, whose total area adds up to no more than 316 sq. km (122 sq. miles), there is a strong sense of identity born out of a mixture of self-preservation and stubbornness, qualities the Maltese have in abundance. And the same applies to Maltese emigrants settled abroad.

Home and away

Of a population of 400,000, a total of 389,000 are Maltese living in Malta and Gozo, with about an equal number in Australia, Canada, the United Kingdom and the United States. These are the emigrants and families of emigrants who set sail for the lands of golden promise in the expansive days of migration at the end of World War II when hope was offered to poorer communities. Many, homesick after making their fortunes in a modest manner, return to build modern villas that are named in fond memory of chances given: Villa Wallaby, Melbourne Court, Brentford House, Casa Orlando and, simply, Bondi. The islands have that kind of draw.

Turning Maltese

To their surprise, many outsiders who have married a Maltese have found that it is *they* who adapt to a Maltese way of life, wherever they live, rarely the other way round. Man or woman, they equally accommodate and find it is they who quickly become part of the extended Maltese family and adapt to its customs. Even when living abroad, they return with their new families whenever they can to their adoptive homes. Undoubtedly the subconscious spirit behind this urge is another facet of the Maltese sense of self-preservation.

PRECEDING PAGES: altar boys at Ghaxaq; daily chores.
LEFT: bakery lady, providing Malta's daily bread.
RIGHT: fishing is still vital to many Maltese.

DOING THE *PASSEGIATA*

The Maltese people are friendly and hospitable, and above all are great lovers of home and family. This is most obvious at *festa* time *(see pages 122–3)*, when on balmy summer evenings families stretch their legs for the *passegiata*, or promenade, just as they do all over Italy and Spain.

Dressed to impress, young and old alike wander along the seafront, chatting, laughing and flirting with friends, pausing to pick up an ice cream or a pizza, downing a Kinnie or a Hopleaf. In high summer the promenading crowds on The Front at Sliema or the Bugibba Promenade form an almost impenetrable mass.

Of course, this may be helped by the fact that the Maltese, almost without exception, are gregarious, friendly and welcoming to foreigners – if not always to each other. The Maltese love the opportunity to be generous, especially during the parish *festa* when the patron saint is celebrated. Even in the simplest rural community they enjoy being hospitable and sharing what they have, a whisky, a soft drink, a cup of tea, their friendship.

House proud

The Maltese are proud of their homes. These are spotlessly clean inside, with gleaming pat-

hosts if a man accepts whisky. That a guest accepts hospitality is what really matters.

Dirty streets

But if the houses are clean, often the streets are not. Although there is an efficient daily refuse collection, and special services for removing household items like old mattresses or rusting refrigerators, old habits die hard. Refuse tipping still occurs. However, the government has been trying, through television campaigns, to create pride in the environment and, thanks to better organised teams of sweepers, the streets, after years of neglect, are becoming much

terned marble-tiled floors, and everything in its prescribed place. Almost everyone, whatever their social level, maintains a formal sitting room, to be used only when guests are invited to the house. It is here that wealth and social achievement can be demonstrated. Even in the most unsophisticated villages, these rooms will have furniture made to order, sofas and armchairs and wall units to hold pieces of whimsical china figurines and framed pictures. Close by will be drinks to offer guests – most likely Johnnie Walker or Chivas Regal, Martini and Aperol, the least alcoholic of aperitifs. It is acceptable for a visitor to request a soft drink, although it gives far greater pleasure to the

cleaner. Money is also being spent on the infrastructure and Valletta is finally being returned to its former architectural glory.

But other equally important aesthetic considerations are regarded as of lesser consequence. Beauty spots and sweeping panoramas are under threat. Perhaps it is because the Maltese see new building, or rebuilding, as an object of envy, putting money to conspicuous use. Elegant turn-of-the-20th-century seafront villas are flattened to make way for faceless blocks of apartments, housing estates or factories are built on valuable arable land, and villas or holiday compounds appear where the landscape was picturesque and unspoilt. Trees lining the roads are ruthlessly pruned, stone pavements are replaced with concrete, and roads are driven through open countryside so that ribbon housing development can be built shamelessly along them. No land is sacred. Like all Latin countries, it is who you know that matters if you want to bend the rules.

When the Nationalist government decided to erect a new electricity generating station, they chose to site it at a pretty waterside section of Marsaxlokk Bay adjacent to some excellent rock beaches.

POLITICAL CHOICES

Surprisingly, despite the Maltese passion for politics, there are only two parties to choose from – Nationalist or Labour. And until recently no amount of rhetoric changed a voter's allegiances.

normally lasted a lifetime, for better or worse. Business people expected to do better when their side was in power. As the governments changed so did the people in key positions in the civil service and in government-run organisations. As bureaucratic power changed, so were new ropes oiled. The "floating voter" status hardly existed.

However, the pattern began to change dramatically from 1995 onwards when it became evident that increasing numbers of youths became more independent from

No one can claim it enhances what was once a beauty spot. And the fact that the site chosen was also outside the windows of the previous (opposition) prime minister's summer house was not thought to be merely a coincidence.

Politics

Up to the mid-1990s politics played an important part in daily life. All Maltese seemed to be politically aware and were "born" into the party supported by their parents, an allegiance that

the political influence of their parents and were definitely much less interested in politics and political issues. The zenith of cross-voting was reached in the 2003 General Election when thousands of Labour Party supporters cast their votes in favour of the pro-EU Nationalist Party, to defy the MLP's anti full EU membership policy, thus assuring Malta of full membership in the European Union.

Religion

For many years the Church played a key role in life, both secular and political, making its views known on all key issues as well as running many of the better schools. In election years

---

LEFT: reminiscing about the good old days at Xewkija on Gozo.
ABOVE: newlyweds toasting future happiness.

parish priests often exhorted congregations to vote for the Nationalist party. But, as has happened elsewhere in Europe, the sway of the Church has become less important. The parish *festa* (*see pages 122–3*) is still the most important event on the annual calendar, but church attendance, although still proportionately among the highest in Europe, is declining.

The tourist influence

Nowadays, parish priests have ceased to function as moral policemen, with the ability to prescribe and enforce standards of conduct within their territory. And the fact that foreign

visitors now easily outnumber local people has undoubtedly exercised a greater influence than most Maltese would care to admit over their attitude towards unorthodox behaviour and established authority.

Yet to every cloud there is a silver lining, and perhaps there is a good opportunity for directly confronting and dealing with modern-day issues. No longer can all the clergy be charged with being narrow-minded, and the islands have come a long way since the days when girls were whisked away by police for wearing bikinis.

Contraception and abortion are now accepted subjects for discussion and, while the clergy

may insist on decorum in dress on the streets and in churches, topless bathing is tolerated on some beaches. However, nude bathing is still against the law and those who bare all may well face prosecution.

Sadly, since the increase of tourism and the arrival of the widest variety of visitors, so the drug problem has surfaced among the young and cases of Aids have been registered.

Joie de vivre

The Maltese, although industrious, are determined to enjoy life to the full. They delight in a party or wedding and seize any opportunity to gossip and tell jokes, There is a ribald sense of humour devoted, for the most part, to *double entendre*. *Malti* may be unsophisticated but gives ample opportunity for double meanings.

On the minus side, the Maltese, in true Latin tradition, can be hard on each other, prone to jealousy and quick to take advantage or pick a quarrel. A crossed Maltese stays crossed.

Although thrifty by nature, the Maltese also enjoy gambling. The weekly government lottery succeeds because of thousands of small stakes. There are often neighbourhood raffles in the smaller towns where a few cents will buy a ticket that could win the Saturday prize of a pair of rabbits or a brace of cockerels.

Conspicuous wealth has its place, too, especially in clothes and jewellery. Wealth in the home, however, is kept concealed behind doors, away from prying eyes and the temptation of burglars. In many patrician houses there are reputed to be collections of paintings and silver that would fetch stupendous prices at any international auction. This wealth sometimes leads to problems with inheritance and provokes inter-family quarrels. Many a grand house is falling to ruin because sons cannot agree about its disposal and many a daughter tells of receiving nothing in settlement.

And then there are cars, a Maltese passion – whatever their age; expensive roadsters too fast for any country and jaloppies that belch enveloping clouds of black fumes and would fail any roadworthiness test. The only thing that they have in common is the style in which they are driven – very erratically. ❏

LEFT: lack of road sense is one of the island's less endearing traits.
RIGHT: every inch of land is worked if possible.

A TASTE OF MALTA

Maltese food has no pretensions, instead just a basic, nourishing and hearty
simplicity, both in its ingredients and in its homely preparation

First-time visitors to Malta may be surprised to discover that these tiny islands have a cuisine of their own. And anyone who passed this way before the 1970s may be surprised to learn that nowadays you can find it in places other than private houses.

Given the fact that their predecessors succeeded in remaining doggedly "Maltese" over the centuries in spite of outside interference, it is little wonder that there is a local style of cooking. If the Maltese have managed to remain their own people with their own personality and impenetrable language, why should they not keep their favourite dishes, too?

Tasty mix

Geographical position has meant that the people have been subject to many culinary influences: from the north, from Sicily and Italy, and from the south, from the length of the North African coast, Tunisia to Egypt, where many Maltese communities were comfortably established until driven out by World War II.

Some of these origins show, but Maltese cooking is governed primarily by the kind of produce found on the islands – similar to that of neighbouring Sicily. So, although the likes of asparagus, kiwi fruit and other exotic imported items can be readily found now, this availability is comparatively recent. Truly Maltese dishes are those produced by ingredients that are indigenous to the islands and local waters.

Typical dishes

Ask the Maltese and Gozitans for the names of the best local dishes and you will hear the same answers wherever you are – even if some profess not to like one or two of these particular dishes themselves. The Maltese repertoire is made up almost entirely of a half dozen or so favourite dishes, such as *fenek, timpana, minestra, kawlata, mqarrun fil-forn, bragoli* and *torta*

PRECEDING PAGES: morning catch for the market.
LEFT: *fenek* (rabbit) about to be served.
RIGHT: *ghaqaq ta'l-ghasel*, sweet treacle ring.

tal-lampuki. Two of these, *timpana* and *mqarrun fil-forn*, are baked pasta and, although a large slice of either might seem a meal in itself, here it is considered a starter. Both are made of macaroni layered with meat, eggs and cheese and, in the case of *timpana*, a casing of light flaky pastry too. They're delicious, if heavy on

COMMUNAL COOKING

Often on Sundays, after the baker's own bread has emerged from the oven, you will catch equally delicious smells as the capacious bakery oven becomes a communal village oven and is filled with family roasts.

This is a custom left over from the old days when few houses had ovens and the roast was the week's treat. The habit continues, and on Sunday mornings baking trays covered with spotless tea cloths can be seen being carried to the village bakery. Under the cloth is meat sitting on a bed of halved potatoes and onions and covered liberally with seasoning and knobs of lard. Somehow it tastes better cooked here.

the carbohydrates. A variation of this recipe is *ross fil-forn*, with rice replacing the pasta. It is baked with minced meat, eggs and lots of bright yellow saffron.

Pasta is as popular here as in Italy, although it is unlikely that the average family will have it daily at home as the Italians do. It is not unusual for the spaghetti sauce to be made using the delicious juices from another dish being prepared, such as squid, octopus or rabbit.

Soup and vegetables

A favourite first course is soup, such as *aljotta* (a thin, clear fish broth) in summer, when fish

lean piece of pork or some Maltese sausages have been simmered. The meat is usually eaten separately.

Just add a thick chunk of Maltese bread to any of these soups and you have a nourishing meal in its own right. In fact, soups are staple to every Maltese family who, with much justification, have a high regard for the basic ingredients – local vegetables. Farms may be small but their richly worked soil produces some excellent vegetables, salads and fruits. Little is done by way of spraying to extend the life of the produce, so vegetables must be eaten within a day or two of purchase.

is abundant, or *minestra* (a chunky vegetable soup) in winter. *Minestra* is Malta's answer to minestrone, although in this soup the vegetables – preferably nine or ten different ones – are cut into rough chunks; dried beans, chick-peas, lentils and small pasta shapes are then added. It is a thick, hearty and filling dish, perfect for a cold winter's day.

Other favourite winter soups include *soppa tal-armla* ("widow's soup") and *kawlata*. *Soppa tal-armla* consists of finely chopped white and green vegetables only. When the dish is served, a *gbejna* (a soft, round fresh goats' cheese) is placed in each bowl. *Kawlata* is a similar vegetable soup, in which either a

Because of this organic policy, housewives often shop daily for fresh food and can be seen in the street markets or with the vegetable sellers with their painted trucks, selecting from the piles of seasonal produce.

These include giant cauliflowers, kohlrabi, artichokes, aubergines, green peppers and *qara' bali* (a round, small marrow of the courgette family typical to these islands and served boiled or stuffed).

Main meats

One of the simpler pleasures of Maltese cooking is the good old-fashioned roast dinner, usually beef or pork. (Lamb is mostly eaten at

Easter.) The meat is placed in a large greased tray, surrounded with chunkily sliced potatoes and onions, liberally sprinkled with herbs, rock salt and pepper and oil; then the tray is topped up with stock and the whole thing placed in the oven for slow roasting. As the stock evaporates, keeping the meat moist, the potatoes and onions pick up the flavours of the juices.

Unfortunately this homely skill has not spread to many restaurants. But many are adept at another dish worth trying, *bragoli*. This is not unlike the Italian beef olive, but here the sliced topside beef is rolled, stuffed with boiled eggs and bacon, and simmered in red wine.

lower fronds from the island's palm trees which they plait into flat rafts. These are taken out to sea where they are floated and the *lampuki*, finding nice patches of shade, gather beneath them. Quickly the fishermen encircle them with nets. The trick never fails.

Depending on their size, *lampuki* are grilled, fried or made into a wonderful pastry-covered pie with cauliflower, spinach and olives, called *torta tal-lampuki*.

Of course, these waters are abundant with other excellent fish. There are tuna and swordfish and smaller fish like sea bass, grouper, amberjack, mullet and skate. Highly favoured

Fruits of the sea

Rivalling rabbit as the national speciality is *lampuka*, a much more refined dish. *Lampuki* (plural of *lampuka*) are dorado, a fish that migrates past the islands between September and November. A sleek and elegant fish, it has white flesh and a distinctive flavour of the sea. It's a curious fact that *lampuki* have been caught in the same manner by Maltese fishermen since Roman times. As the season approaches, so fishermen cut and gather the large,

LEFT: fruit sellers at Cospicua's outdoor market.
ABOVE: *mqaret*, a traditional pastry with a sweet date filling, which is deep fried and served piping hot.

RABBIT AND CHIPS

Malta's favourite food is *fenek* (rabbit): fried, casseroled or roasted. Rabbit is often the prize in village raffles and there is even a special outing, known as a *fenkata*, when a family or group of friends get together for a picnic or in a simple village restaurant to enjoy fried rabbit with chips and lots of red wine.

It has been many centuries since rabbits were freely seen wild on the islands – though hunters, who have shot them almost to extinction, say there are signs of them still on barren coastal stretches. All the rabbit eaten here is specially bred for the table and is on sale, alive and cuddly, in the markets.

are saddled bream, white bream and dentex. And then there are octopus and squid, which the Maltese are adept at cooking deliciously.

Fast food

Pizzas, burgers and Chinese takeaways are readily available in places like Bugibba and St Julian's, but the islanders also have their own fast food. It might only be a slice or two of bread, but then Maltese bread is surely one of the world's best, good enough to be almost ad-

and/or garlic. You will find it on the restaurant menu, toasted like the Italian *bruschetta.*

Then there are the gloriously inexpensive *pastizzi.* Baked on trays in special ovens, they are made of flaky pastry into which a pocket of filling is folded. The choice is cheese (*rikotta,* seasoning and a little egg), mushy yellow marrowfat peas or, more rarely, an anchovy filling. As the *rikotta* filling is undoubtedly the best, so *pastizzi* came to be popularly translated as cheesecake, but they are always

dictive. Made traditionally as a cottage loaf, the sour-dough is baked directly on the oven surface. It has a crisp firm crust, with a soft white centre punctured with random holes that are caused by the sour-dough system.

It is full of flavour and is delicious spread with butter. But the Maltese prefer it as *hobz biz-zejt* (literally, bread with oil), which is eaten at any time of the day as a snack. To make it, first slice the bread thickly and then cut in half some ripe, tasty tomatoes. Rub them on to the bread until it turns pink. Leave the tomato on the bread and add salt, pepper and capers to taste, then generously add some olive oil. Extras can include basil, onion, tomato purée

savoury, never sweet. They are remarkably inexpensive and on sale most of the morning from bakeries, cafés and bars. Two or three, always eaten warm, fresh from the oven, make a favourite mid-morning snack.

Something sweet

The Maltese have a very sweet tooth. Shops, cafés and stalls are laden with all manner of cakes and biscuits, some garishly bright and powerfully sweet, others farmhouse-simple.

One particular inexpensive favourite is quickly recognised by a delicious aroma that wafts wherever it's on sale – outside Valletta's bus terminal gate is the favourite location (and also in the evenings at *festas)*. Called *mqaret*, these are small flat diamond-shaped pastry cases filled with a soft date mixture that is flavoured with aniseed. Sold by vendors seated at small carts on which there are shallow bubbling oil friers, *mqaret* are served deep fried, cooked to order, and eaten piping hot. It's the frying and the aniseed that give the tempting aroma. Another unusual sweet treat to look for is *kannoli*, crunchy cylindrical biscuits resembling large cigars, filled with ricotta cheese and candied fruit.

With so much available, it's odd that menus carry few sweet dishes or desserts. In a restaurant the choice is usually limited to ice cream (mostly commercial rather than home-made), crème caramel, or a variety of gâteaux.

At home, although European desserts are often prepared by hand, many families will order a *torta* from a leading confectioner when a special dessert is required: something rich and sweet and preferably with extravagant use of ground almonds. In the villages once or twice a week there are deliveries of the most delightful, simple biscuits, made by local bakeries. Like the crops, many of the most popular Maltese sweets are seasonal.

Holiday specials

For the Carnival weekend that heralds Lent, there is *prinjolata* (a kind of gâteau made with pine nuts). During Lent there is *kwarezimal*, a sweet almond biscuit covered with honey and pistachio nuts that originally answered the prescribed Lenten rules because it contains no eggs or shortening. And, in the winter months, there is *qaghaq tal-ghasel*, a ring of sweet pastry filled with a mixture of dark treacle, semolina and candied peel. In fact, these are so popular that they can often be found year round.

The best, however, are *figolli*, an Easter treat. These are biscuity cakes which are shaped into figures, then decorated with brightly coloured icing, a small chocolate Easter egg and, the most important part, old-fashioned oleograph faces to give them character. In the biscuit there is a layer of sweet almond paste. On the whole the more expensive it is, the thicker and better is its almond centre.

LEFT: crusty Maltese bread is baked and delivered fresh each day.
RIGHT: pizzas are a favourite Maltese import.

As final proof of the passion for sweets, there is *qubbajt*, the local nougat sold at every *festa* from decorated stalls, each stall with a large pair of chrome scales as a centrepiece. There is a choice of hard (dark and brittle) or soft (pale and chewy).

Drinks

The local brews, Hopleaf Pale Ale, Blue Label Ale and Cisk Lager, are all very drinkable and will certainly appeal to older British drinkers. A nice cool refresher with just a drop of alcohol is Farson's Shandy, that good old-fashioned combination of beer and lemonade.

The wines of Malta and Gozo are also unpretentious and enjoyable though do remember that you get what you pay for. The two major wineries are Marsovin and Delicata. Look for their Superior quality labels and you should not be disappointed. Gozitan red wines are hearty, hefty brutes, excellent with red meat and game, and perfect before a siesta.

Perhaps the island's most distinctive drink is Kinnie, sometimes described as the Maltese answer to Coca Cola. This splendid soft beverage definitely originates from the cola stable but its bitter-orange tang makes it much more a "grown-up drink". Well chilled, it is a perfect midday refresher or an evening aperitif. ❑

VENERABLE VEHICLES

In prosperous European countries, Malta's aged fleet might be accorded Classic status. Here, they are flogged as rusting workhorses or raced as dodgem cars

There are about 150,000 cars on Malta and Gozo and about 400,000 people: that is roughly one car to every two adults. Almost every family runs one. And if there are adult offspring, they will usually have one each. New cars are not cheap – not even relatively. The most basic models free of any luxury can cost more than the average worker will earn in a year. Yet cars proliferate. Few are scrapped and such is the reverence of ownership that many achieve heirloom status.

All our yesterdays

At least 10 percent of the islands' cars are more than 20 years old and look it. Cars like those in 1950s British movies are not uncommon; they never attract so much as a passing glance. A modest proportion of the remaining 80 percent are between 10 and 20 years old too. The Maltese do not change their cars regularly; that sort of north European custom is not the national habit. This is not because of parsimonious conservation. When a Maltese does buy a newer model it is because he or she wants a bigger, more expensive car to emphasise upwardly mobile status, not because the older one is fit only for the scrapyard.

But this habit is slowly changing. Younger people are becoming aware of the trade-in syndrome and there is an upsurge of interest every time a major European or Japanese car manufacturer launches a new model with customary hyperbole.

What happens to the older vehicles they replace? Nothing much. They stay in the system, handed on, or sold against cash for not much less than when they were first bought, which creates a buoyant, secondhand market.

Make do and mend

Most drivers of the old-timers also insist that the cost of spare parts and regular trips to the mechanic/electrician/insurance man are less expensive than the amount it would take to buy something flashier. And the islands' mechanics appear to have a near-magical way of whizzing up spare parts, no matter how old the vehicle. Could this be because similar cars are constantly being stolen for spare parts? There is a

THE MALTA BUS EXPERIENCE

Some buses are older than the oldest cars. Passengers hold their breath as these dinosaurs strain up a hill then plummet down the other side. They are unbearably hot in summer because most were originally driven on British roads where heating, not air-conditioning, was important. However, on the plus side, they are a very cheap means of getting around the island, and also provide a good way to meet the locals.

There is often a sign behind the head of the driver, perhaps reading *Ave Maria*, or, more ominously, *In God We Trust*. Others have a small plastic statue of the Virgin surrounded by a dried-flower arrangement.

PRECEDING PAGES: decorative truck front.
LEFT: many trucks are painted red or green.
RIGHT: souped-up Ford Prefect, with a message.

high rate of theft of cars on the islands, and the rate of recovery is low.

Mechanics operate from private garages in quiet neighbourhoods and drive residents to distraction. So do their colleagues, the panel beaters. On Malta, car repair work is considered a steady job.

The introduction of cheaper makes like Skoda, Lada and Dacia from Eastern Europe affected the market to some extent, but not so effectively as to force the old rusting models to be scrapped. There will always be those conservative Maltese who would rather spend a sum on a car of doubtful condition from a prestige manufacturer's range than spend the same amount on a new car with "inferior" origins. Fords are the most popular – if not a Capri or Escort, then at least an Anglia or Prefect.

However, Malta's cheerfully chaotic road conditions are set to change. With new Vehicle Road Testing (VRT) standards imposed on private vehicles, Malta and Gozo's much-loved old bangers are coming to the end of the road. Vigorous campaigns have been mounted to encourage higher standards and road courtesy amongst drivers. European-style road signs and traffic lights proliferate. Traffic wardens now prowl the streets and are clamping down on traffic infringements, particularly illegal parking and obstruction; and offending vehicles are towed away.

Colours, decals and names

Many trucks and vans are museum pieces, too. At one time every truck seemed to be painted red and green but now there are all colours, including some remarkable builders' trucks dressed up in glorious pink or yellow. Traditionally, bakers' vans are cream with a red stripe on the back door; butchers have a blue stripe. Many a car carries stickers on their rear window. Some of these are advertisements – like Ferrari or Evermond (cosmetics) – or speak religious texts – like Jesus Loves Me and Think God.

Many commercial vehicles have a name on the sides of their bonnet; old-fashioned titles like Tarzan, Rio Rita, Roy Rogers and more up-to-date soubriquets such as Rambo and Terminator. There is a giant, 30-year old mobile crane called Lambada Dance and a bus called Paul's Toy. Paul's Toy? Why not? This is Malta.   ❑

RIGHT: flamboyant vehicle figurehead.

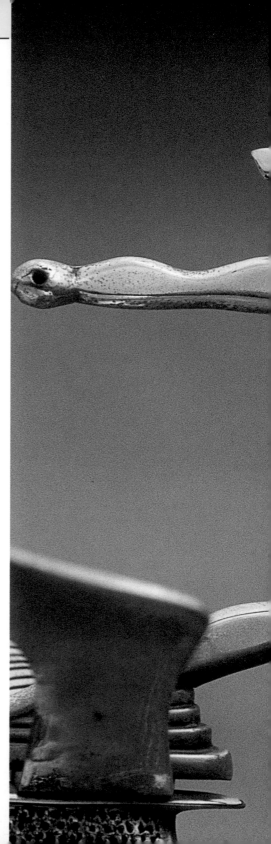

MALTESE ARCHITECTURE

Urban sprawl may disfigure much of Malta, but at the heart of even the tiniest community is usually a clutch of dignified houses and a handsome church

Malta reached its first peak of architectural achievement around 3000 BC. The archaeologist Professor Colin Renfrew describes the Maltese Neolithic temples of that time as "the earliest free-standing monuments in stone in the world" and the "memorably imposing" facade of Gozo's Ggantija temples as "perhaps the earliest architecturally conceived exterior in the world".

Later, the excellence of Maltese houses that were "very beautiful and ambitiously adorned with cornices and stucco works" caught the attention of the Sicilian-Greek historian Diodorus Sicullus (80–20 BC). At that time Malta was ruled by the Romans and, as elsewhere, they built temples, town houses, baths and villas. There was an active harbour in the Marsa basin end of the Grand Harbour, its quays built with massive masonry blocks that were perfectly cut and jointed. The capital Melita (where Mdina and Rabat now stand) was a city with handsomely built houses. But only the merest traces now remain.

Into the darkness

The Dark Ages cast a shadow over Malta as they did the rest of Europe; but, while the latter emerged triumphantly out of the torpor to beget the great monuments of the Romanesque and Gothic period, the Maltese islands slumbered on. All through the Middle Ages the islands remained desolate, sparsely inhabited and isolated. At that time Mediterranean shipping tended to hug the continental coastline, shying away from Malta to avoid shipwreck and the pirates that might be lurking in the island's coves and bays. Outside influences passed the islands by.

Indigenous Maltese architecture of the medieval period is almost non-existent and such buildings as there are were strongly influenced by Arab tradition. In Mdina, Vittoriosa and in Gozo's Citadel there are surviving late-medieval houses with windows on the first floor of a characteristically Catalan inspiration. They typically feature round-headed double lights separated by an excessively slim colonette. Mdina Cathedral dates from the 13th century but was considerably altered centuries' later and has thus lost its medieval character.

Enter the Knights

It was in 1530, at the height of the Renaissance, that Emperor, Charles V handed over the islands to the Order of St John. It was a momentous event, ushering in a long period of building activity that would produce superlative architectural monuments.

With the arrival of the Knights, Malta was linked once more to international currents and with owners who represented a concentration of wealth combined with an incredible reserve of human resources. The rich aristocratic knights, particularly the Grand Masters, would in time shower their riches on their new headquarters and endow the islands with fine buildings and

PRECEDING PAGES: Vittoriosa glowing gold at sunset.
LEFT: the imposing portals of the Auberge de Castile.
RIGHT: typical wooden balconies in Valletta.

works of art. Eminent artists, military and civil engineers, architects and artisans were lured to Malta as the Order was a good paymaster. Painters such as Preti and de Favray, and engineers and architects such as Buonamici, Mederico Blondel and Charles François de Mondion, called in at Malta expecting to stay only a few days, but remained much longer to benefit themselves and Maltese posterity.

The knights chose Birgu as their initial base because its position, straddling a promontory in the Grand Harbour, had deep creeks on either side to provide shelter for their fleet. They were fully aware that their immediate task was secu-rity; the new Malta headquarters would become an Ottoman target sooner rather than later.

In fact, their immediate position was unten-able; but with the help of some of the foremost military engineers of the day provided by Christian states, walls were built that rendered it sufficiently strong to withstand the great Turkish force sent by Suleiman the Magnifi-cent in 1565.

The building of Valletta

After the Great Siege, the Order decided to build a new fortified town on the higher promontory (Mount Scebberas) that dominates

THE REPUTATION OF GEROLAMO CASSAR

The greatest Maltese architect was Gerolamo Cassar (*circa* 1520–92), who was to Valletta what Christopher Wren was to London. He designed the Grand Master's Palace, the Conventual Church/Co-Cathedral of St John, the *auberges* of the Knights, the Hospital of the Order, the slaves' prison, the Ferreria (arsenal) and several more churches and monastic buildings; many survive today.

Before embarking on his works, Cassar was sent on a short tour of the foremost cities of Italy, and so his buildings rose in a somewhat rigid variant of Italian Mannerism. But his designs, as it transpired, also perpetuated many traditional features that appeared on early buildings in Mdina and Birgu. They set the character of all the buildings in Valletta and influenced all subsequent Maltese building.

Cassar's emphasis was strongly horizontal, with huge masses of plain masonry predominating, the whole tied in with "rusticated" corners – that is, with sunken joints and roughened surfaces. These corners became his hallmark. Cassar also believed that all his buildings should echo the fact that they were constructed in a fortified city and have, therefore, a military cast. Even his masterpiece, the (now riotously decorated) Conventual Church/Co-Cathedral of St John, was designed to be as severe internally as it is externally.

the two main ports of Marsamxett and Grand Harbour. Pope Pius IV sent Francesco Laparelli da Cortona, one of his best engineers and an assistant to Michelangelo at St Peter's, to advise and supervise the project.

The first stone was laid on 28 March 1566 and the city was named Valletta after the heroic siege victor. The massive fortifications that encircle the town were completed in less than five years with a local labour force being augmented by foreign labour from Italy.

When Laparelli left the island, in around 1569, the task of completion was put into the hands of his able assistant, Gerolamo Cassar.

with the addition of the occasional element recalling the late medieval Maltese church. Unfortunately, as parish wealth increased, many were later enlarged and, in the process, ineradicably changed.

One, however, the parish church of Attard, was almost untouched, and is the best example of this period on Malta. Another, Santa Marija, in Birkirkara, is remarkable for the richness and crispness of its carving.

Francesco Buonamici

It was Francesco Buonamici, an architect from Lucca in Italy, who designed the first impor-

Maltese baroque

Cassar went on to become the city's foremost architect *(see box opposite)*. His crowning glory was the Co-Cathedral of St John. However, the interior of this landmark building was subsequently transformed, mostly by the Calabrese painter Mattia Preti, into the magnificent baroque interior we see today.

During the first part of the 17th century, a number of parish churches were built in a style strongly reminiscent of the Italian Quattrocento

LEFT: handsome housing above the bastion walls in Valletta facing into Grand Harbour.
ABOVE: the fortifications of Valletta.

tant baroque buildings in Valletta. He was the Order's resident engineer between 1634 and 1659, and was primarily responsible for overseeing the extensions to the Order's fortifications (notably those protecting Floriana) as well as the maintenance of all other fortifications. His designs, in the then current baroque style, include the church of St Nicolas in Valletta; the plan of the church of St Paul at Rabat, with the adjoining church of St Publius; part of the facade of the church of St Philip in Zebbug; and several altar retables (the frames enclosing decorated panels behind the altars).

Buonamici's civic buildings include the Jesuit College and Hostel de Verdelin in Valletta, Wignacourt's College at Rabat and, possibly, the facade of the Inquisitor's Palace, Vittoriosa. In the first two facades Buonamici shows how it was possible to articulate a long front by means of panelling while at the same time retaining the columnless treatment of Valletta's earlier palaces.

By the mid-17th century, Mederico Blondel from France had succeeded Buonamici as resident engineer. In Valletta he designed the splendid facade of Valletta's church of St Mary of Jesus, and it is quite likely that he was also responsible for the churches of St Rocco and St Francis. In Mdina, the splendid Carmelite

church is his masterpiece. Also active during this period was the great Maltese architect Lorenzo Gafa' *(see box, below).*

The 18th century

During the next century a number of florid baroque buildings rose in Valletta and Mdina. They were designed by Romano Carapecchia who worked in Malta for 30 years from 1706, and a Frenchman, Charles François de Mondion, resident engineer from 1715 to 1733.

The major building from this period, however, is the Auberge de Castille, originally designed by Gerolamo Cassar, but remodelled by Andrea Belli in 1741. A Maltese architect who had studied in Italy and travelled through Austria and Germany, Belli designed several other outstanding buildings that give Maltese architecture its authority. His are the Bishop's Seminary (1733) in Mdina (now the Cathedral Museum), the Augustinian Priory in Rabat (1740), the Archbishop's Curia (1743) in Floriana and in Valletta's South Street, the building that houses the Museum of Fine Arts (1761).

Another architect of note during this period was the Sicilian Stefano Ittar, responsible for the neoclassical Biblioteca – the National Library (1786–96) and the Customs House.

Building a future

Malta's most important recent architectural treasures are well over a century old. In 1833 the Mosta Dome (also known as the church of Santa Marija), was designed by Grognet de Vasse. In 1841, St Paul's Anglican cathedral, designed by William Scamp, replaced the Order's Auberge d'Allemagne. Then, in 1860, the Royal Opera House was designed by Edward Middleton Barry. Sadly, along with many other buildings of architectural interest, this was destroyed in World War II, though there are plans to restore it to something of its former glory, possibly through EU funds.

During the 20th and early 21st century, Maltese architects have made their mark – some good, some indifferent, some excellent – though there is no single surviving monument or building which takes the eye. But the talent is still here and so, of course, is the soft limestone that gives the islands their architectural quality. ❑

LORENZO GAFA'

Lorenzo Gafa' (1630–1704) is Malta's greatest baroque architect. After beginning his career as a sculptor, he turned to architecture and is responsible for many of the splendid churches that have come to typify and symbolise the Maltese islands. His most important works include the church of St Lawrence in Vittoriosa, Gozo Cathedral and the Cathedral of Mdina. The latter masterpiece, set in a dramatic position on the ramparts of the old city, is an unforgettable sight. The encircling walls of the city look like part of the church building itself, and the whole is surmounted by a dome such as only a great baroque sculptor could have fashioned.

LEFT: Zabbar's splendid baroque parish church.
RIGHT: patrician building, Valletta.

SUPERSTITION AND LORE

Malta is a staunchly Catholic country, yet this is also an island of superstition where pagan symbols are omnipresent and where luck is a way of life

It is said, with some justification perhaps, that most Maltese are superstitious and a traditional wariness about things unknown is an important facet of the national character. This may not be so true today, but in days when there were fewer outside influences to distract, like television and the cinema, everyone knew what brought good luck or bad luck. This was particularly noticeable away from sophisticated town society but, even there, many a mother would never tempt fate by wearing green the day her child was to sit an important exam.

Saints preserve us

Much superstition is handed down through families and much has a religious slant to it. At an early age, for example, pupils are encouraged to write JMJ on the top left of each exam paper to bring luck, though what examiners make of this code – JMJ being Jesus, Mary and Joseph – is anyone's guess. But, don't do it and you fail. And you know why.

Later, as university students, taking the same precautions, they make their promises to St Jude, patron saint of students, and have printed in the local *Times* newspaper a few anonymous lines of thanks if they are successful.

St Rita, St Anthony and the Virgin Mary are equally popular and, in Gozo's Ta' Pinu Sanctuary, a corridor is devoted to paintings of shipwrecked sailors being saved by the Virgin Mary as well as macabre remembrances of other miraculous cures after invoking her name – like gall-stones in jam jars, discarded crutches and baby's trusses.

God and the devil

Many buses have little shrines too, close to the driver, often with the words *Verbum Dei Caro Factum Est* (the word of God was made flesh), a salutary reminder of in whose hands we really are. Older passengers, taking no chances, cross

themselves before the bus starts and do so each time the bus passes a shrine or church door. In God we trust.

To confuse the devil, who roams endlessly, churches have two clocks in their towers, one real, the other a *trompe l'oeil*. Tradition says the devil is confused by two clocks and so

cannot come to collect departing souls – though many cynics point out that few churches could have afforded more than one clock when they were built.

Warding off evil in a more overtly pagan manner, many houses in rural communities have bulls' horns tied, points outwards, on the highest corner of a roof or perhaps above the front door. Many, trying to get the best of both protections, attach horns on one corner and a saint's effigy on another.

In the 18th century, young girls in society were given simple coral necklaces to ward off evil and, until recently, many men wore tiny amulets shaped like a horn on a chain around

PRECEDING PAGES: eyes bring good luck to *luzzus.*
LEFT: holy reliquary at St Paul Shipwreck Church.
RIGHT: strange roadside memorial.

the neck. In the old Latin tradition, many still make the *qrun*, that is, point the fore and little fingers of the hand like bulls horns, to ward off the evil eye or to wish someone ill. Children can often be seen secretly making this sign when playing games in order to bring bad luck to their opponents.

Keeping an eye open

Since bad luck is not confined to humans, the *luzzu* and *dghajsa* – the beautiful brightly coloured, traditional boats, which have been used by Maltese sailors since Phoenician times, have their protection too. Each boat may be

named after a Catholic saint but each also has on either side of its prow the wide-open, ever alert eye of Osiris, one of the most important of the ancient Egyptian gods, ready to ward off the worst.

In a similar effort to ward off evil, horses puling carts or *karrozin* often have red tassels or feathers attached to their harness or bridle.

Old wives and young mothers

Many old beliefs have faded away, but old wives' tales still abound. Old wives are experts where fertility and birth are concerned; it has always been deemed that the best months for marriage are January, April and August when

bodies are at their most fertile; that women should not work in fields or pick vegetables during menstruation or the produce will be ruined; that black underwear ensures pregnancy, white the opposite; and, if a pregnant woman craves special food and does not eat it, her child will have a birth mark in that shape.

Young mothers are especially wary of the evil eye. It may be possessed by someone, invariably female, who does not know that she has it. And if she should say to the mother "what a beautiful baby you have" then the next day something awful will happen to the child – it will develop spots, a cold or a squint. The baby has been "given the eye". It is therefore common for a woman to cross the road with her child if she sees a woman approaching who she believes has the evil eye.

Life and death

An enjoyable custom, now dying out, often takes place on a child's first birthday when the family gets together for what is known as the *quecija*. They assemble a tray of small objects varying them slightly for a boy or girl. Among them might be a thimble, pen, rosary, egg, and some money. The tray is put in front of the child and the object chosen foretells the child's future – as a tailor, clerk, priest, farmer, banker, or whatever. It used to be said that if you did not carry out this ritual your child would not succeed in life; nowadays it is just an excuse for a party.

There is another home ritual that mimics the pagan celebration of rebirth and which has become incorporated into Catholic ritual too. About two weeks before the Christmas crib is assembled near the Christmas tree, the child is given saucers or shallow bowls on which to sow seeds of wheat, or canary seed. The seedlings are then kept in the dark and watered every two days. As soon as long pale shoots begin to sprout, the bowls are brought out by the child and put near the figure of the Baby Jesus.

On a sadder note, if a family member should die at home, a glass of water or a saucer of salt must be placed near the front door. The spirit must never leave the house thirsty or without salt to flavour its food. ❑

LEFT: this white bow is a wedding-day symbol.
RIGHT: the ever-watchful eye of Osiris wards off evil.

FIREWORKS, BANDS AND SAINTS

When petards explode deafeningly overhead it might sound as if war has broken out, but don't worry, it is just another of Malta's many festas

Like Christmas and Easter, the *festa* is one of the most important events on the Maltese calendar. There are many people who don't look forward to these festivals because of the noise and crowds they bring, but to most villagers it is one of the highlights of the year. *Festas* used to be celebrated all year round, but recently they have been restricted to the May–September season, when good weather is all but guaranteed. There are some 30 different *festas* celebrated each year throughout the islands.

Once upon a time, the *festa* was exclusively a religious event, but nowadays it is more simply an excuse for a village celebration, with big bands, fireworks and a procession. It has also changed from being a one-day event to a weekend of festivities.

A *festa* literally gets off to a bang with exploding petards, but the real celebrations begin in the evening, when the villagers come out wearing their Sunday finery. The local church, too, will be splendidly dressed with red damask hangings, the altar garlanded with flowers and the best silverware will be on display. Outside, the church will be brilliantly illuminated by hundreds of light bulbs. The streets are also decorated, and vendors sell all sorts of fast foods from *pastizzi* to hot dogs and chips. Accompanied by more petards and a brass band, the statue of the village patron saint is paraded through the streets. The day ends at around 11pm or later with a superb firework display – both aerial and floor-mounted in ingenious tableaux.

◁ **LOVING TOUCH**
The local patron saint's effigy is carefully re-gilded and restored ready for the grand parade through the streets.

▷ **SWEET TEMPTATION**
Nougat-sellers with brass-and-glass stands are a traditional sight at *festas*. You can taste before you buy.

BATTLE OF THE BANDS

◁ **THE BIG NIGHT**
The village brass band plays outside Hamrun church as a prelude to the sky lighting up with fireworks. Hamrun is famed for its celebrations.

△ **MERRY THRONG**
The streets are choked with locals, meeting, talking, eating and drinking, while tourists are often bussed in from the resorts on special outings.

▽ **HEAD OF THE PARADE**
As the statue is paraded through the streets on the shoulders of selected volunteers, it is heralded by the parish clergy, who ensure that no one forgets this is a religious event.

Every town and village in Malta, and sometimes even every parish, has its very own brass band – or in some cases two.

It all started with the British, who imported their military brass bands for displays of pomp and pageantry. When the locals wanted to start their own bands, the British encouraged them, and officials of the band clubs eventually came to wield political, not just musical power.

Today, bands and their band clubs are highly popular, and during the *festa* every house and car will be playing their band's marches at top volume. In fact, so great is the pride taken in the prowess of local bands that occasionally fights break out in the streets as rival fans and clubs clash. Police and parish priests now monitor the marching routes and try to make bands pass through friendly streets rather than through rival territory.

The music may be up-tempo and rousing, but the bands move at a snail's pace.

SPORT

The Maltese islands have a deservedly high reputation for their watersports,
but there is plenty here to occupy sporting landlovers too

For one of the world's smallest nations, Malta packs in an amazing amount of sporting action – from trotting races, staged on the island since 1868, to computerised ten-pin bowling, to beach volleyball. Watersports fans will discover an impressive range of activities: they can descend to explore the crystal-clear Mediterranean depths with an expert or ascend to parasail around the rugged coastline. They can sail or windsurf, ski or snorkel. Those who prefer their feet on terra firma can attempt their first marathon, play golf or tennis – while those born to spectate will doubtless find that a flutter on the Tote at Marsa racetrack has greater appeal.

Diving delights

The translucent waters that surround the Maltese islands give them special year-round appeal to scuba divers. Nowhere in the Mediterranean can you see so far underwater and nowhere in the Mediterranean can rival Malta's large variety of dive sites, both natural and man-made.

With no rivers depositing sediment and clouding the issue, Malta has it made as a dive destination. Underwater visibility is generally from 6 to 20 metres (19 to 65 ft), but can extend to 50 metres up to 30 metres (164 up to 98 ft) below the surface. Some of the best diving is found off the southern shore of both Malta and Gozo. In the deep water beneath the sheer cliffs, the spectacular rock formations are a diver's delight – among them are arches, caves, buttresses, drop-offs and tunnels.

Dive schools flourish throughout the islands with operators offering tuition, arranging accompanied dives and hiring out equipment.

Taming the seas

Sailing in Malta was given fresh impetus with the revival in 1996, after a 12-year gap, of the

Middle Sea Race for ocean-going yachts. This 1,000-km (600-mile) spectacle, staged each October, starts and ends in Malta's Marsamxett Creek; it encompasses the Italian island of Sicily and takes from three to six days to complete, depending on weather conditions.

Malta's biggest yacht marina is at Msida,

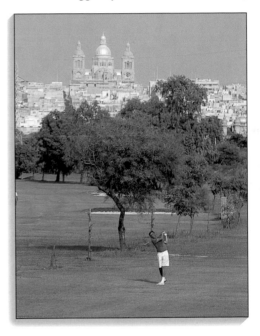

UNDERWATER VIEWING

More than 40 species of fish can be seen around the islands, including grouper, moray, cuttlefish, octopus, flying gurnard, angler fish, barracuda and eagle ray. Sea anemones add their own splash of colour.

World War II also left a rich legacy for today's scuba divers in the form of aircraft and ships scattered about the seabed, mostly in and around the Grand Harbour.

Malta's best-known wreck is that of the destroyer *HMS Maori*, 16 metres (52ft) down off Fort St Angelo. Off Zonqor Point, the lesser-known remains of a Blenheim bomber and a Mosquito aircraft make for equally compelling underwater exploration.

PREDEDING PAGES: yacht race around the island.
LEFT: diving in the pristine waters of the Blue Lagoon.
RIGHT: golf at Marsa.

near Sliema; two other marina projects should be completed soon, on the Three Cities side of Grand Harbour and on the Hilton development at St Julian's.

Windsurfing

Windsurfing came to Malta in the late 1970s and is now a year-round sport which attracts enthusiasts from far and wide. For those who have yet to tread a sailboard, Mellieha Bay is an excellent place to learn. The keenest windsurfers set their sights on the daily wind direction and then speed off to different parts of Malta and Gozo.

Sea conditions can vary from flat calm to

on British racecourses, but trotting meetings that regularly pull in crowds of 4,000 to Marsa racetrack that are held all year round. Trotting for many years remained staunchly male-orientated, but now the spectacle provides exciting entertainment for everybody.

You can bet on the Tote or with independent on-course bookmakers – the stakes are low and the odds not unreasonable. Make your own way to the racetrack rather than take an organised excursion, as tour buses have the infuriating habit of leaving halfway through the meeting.

There are 700 registered horses in Malta, most imported from France and Scandinavia;

choppy when the prevailing *majjistral* sets in from the northwest or the strong *grigal* blows up from the northeast; races are a real test even for very experienced board sailors.

The open expanse of Mellieha Bay also lends itself to waterskiing and snorkelling (Comino's Blue Lagoon is another good spot) and a host of family-orientated activities. Parasailing fans should head for Golden Bay, for a bird's-eye view of Malta's fascinating northwestern tip and striking views across to Comino and Gozo.

Trotting treat

Horse-racing is Malta's most popular spectator sport – not the thoroughbred gallops you see

many are stabled close to the 1,000-metre (3,280-ft) circuit, which was laid down in 1868 but shortened to meet international standards in 1981. Around 500 races are held each year in meetings staged every Sunday afternoon, on alternate Saturdays and on public holidays. It's a full afternoon's entertainment – trotting cards include up to 12 races and can take up to five hours to complete – though you don't have to stay the distance.

Equestrian sport of a less serious kind altogether takes place during the *Mnarja* festival of St Peter and St Paul in Rabat on 29 June each year. Its bareback horse and donkey races on Saqqajja Hill date from the time of the Knights, and winners receive banners to be used in church as altar cloths.

If you want to take the reins yourself, you can visit the Golden Bay Horse Riding School (which is signposted just off Golden Bay beach). It caters for all standards of rider and uses a number of panoramic routes around this part of the coast.

Golf on course

Most Mediterranean holiday countries accept that golf is a big attraction – and Malta is no exception. The island has only the 18-hole Royal Malta Golf Club course at present, but plans are being drawn up for a second course on Malta and one on Gozo.

The Maltese show very little inclination towards golf, leaving visitors to pitch in for the best tee-off times. The Royal Malta, retaining British links in its title (though no-one recalls when, if ever, royal assent was ever given), is a pleasant 5,091-metre (5,567-yard) parkland course that makes few demands on the seasoned club player.

Golf is just one aspect of the Marsa Sports Club complex, Malta's number one sporting venue, which has 17 tennis courts, five squash courts, mini-golf, a cricket ground, billiards room, a freshwater swimming pool and fitness centre. Sports-minded visitors can take out a temporary membership while they are on holiday in Malta.

The long haul

With its equable winter climate and flat topography, there are two notable long-distance sporting events that attract good international fields to the islands. The Malta Marathon is run each February and attracts high-class athletes, including in the past European and Commonwealth champions. The other event is the International Challenge Tour of Malta, a four-day cycle race that covers 320 km (200 miles) of Malta and Gozo in March.

Local favourites

Turn to the sports pages of Malta's newspapers and note the space devoted to football – it dominates the sporting scene throughout the year.

LEFT: Sunday best: trotting for glory at Marsa.
RIGHT: sheltered Mellieha Bay is an ideal place for learning to windsurf.

The football season only excludes the hottest summer months – July and August – otherwise it is a hive of activity throughout the year. Malta's Football Association (MFA) is over 100 years old and one of the oldest in Europe. There are national championships and a national knockout competition (FA Cup), and Malta's national team is active in FIFA's World Cup and UEFA's European Championship, with clubs also taking part in European club competitions. The MFA has a splendid national stadium at Ta' Qali. It will not take long to gather that most Maltese (male and female) are football crazy and are well versed in the fortunes of international clubs.

The Maltese game of *bocci,* similar to the French passion *boules,* but using wooden blocks instead of balls, gets less publicity but is widely popular and is taken seriously by its devotees. Most towns and villages have their own *bocci* club, which becomes a popular social centre on long summer evenings.

Ten-pin bowling is also a serious pursuit and attracts a young crowd to the 20-lane Eden Super Bowl (with fully computerised scoring) at St George's Bay.

The success of Maltese player Tony Drago abroad has given snooker a boost on the island and most sports and band clubs have their own full-size snooker table for patrons. ❑

PLACES

*A detailed guide to the Maltese islands with principal sites
clearly cross-referenced by number to the maps*

Malta may only be a tiny country but it has twice stood at the crossroads of world history and a tour of the island provides some fascinating reminders of its glorious past. It was the Knights of St John who made Malta famous and it is not difficult to find their imprint all over the archipelago. Long before them, however, mysterious temple builders left their marks and 5,000 years later these survive as the world's oldest free-standing structures.

We begin the Places section in Valletta, now one of Europe's tiniest capitals but once the base of the Knights of St John and a fortified city par excellence. Many modern capital city facilities may be lacking but its architectural and historical legacy is superb. Any city would be proud to possess such jewels as the Grand Master's Palace and the Co-Cathedral of St John and we examine these in depth.

A cannon-shot away on the other side of Grand Harbour lies the Three Cities, the original home of the Knights and later the dockyards during British colonial rule. Flattened during World War II, it hides much of its historic pedigree in tranquil streets which see few visitors.

On a plateau in the centre of the island, Mdina, the old capital, is one of the world's finest examples of an enclosed medieval walled city that is still inhabited. Like Valletta, this was a city of the Knights and also features fine domestic architecture and a superb cathedral.

Central Malta is dominated by the great dome of Mosta, but then churches are a Maltese speciality as you will see if you spend time touring this lesser-known area. Sliema, the main residential town, has rapidly developed, along with its satellites, St Julian's and Paceville, into Malta's most important resort area. It is often said of Malta that you love it or hate it. Nowhere is this more true than here.

The north of the island is also known for its brash new resorts, Bugibba and Qawra, and a short distance away are the island's scarce but very pleasant sandy beaches. The south, by contrast, is where Malta's prehistoric temples are to be found.

Before we make the short hop across the water to the islands of Gozo and Comino, we'll tell you more about the British colonial legacy and about Malta's temples. The Places section ends with a suggestion of a short excursion to Sicily.

All the sites of interest are numbered on specially drawn maps to help you find your way round. It's such a small place and car hire is so cheap that it's tempting to use a car for all journeys, but to get the best from the island use the buses and your feet.   ❑

PRECEDING PAGES: tiny wayside chapel surrounded by fields; aerial view of green Gozo; rowing in Grand Harbour; Auberge de Castile, Valletta, with statue of early socialist, Manwel Dimech.
LEFT: St Julian's waterfront.

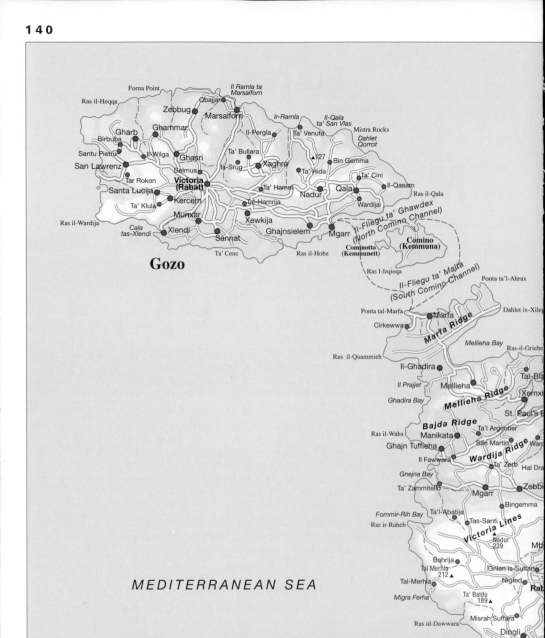

Ras il-Heqqa
Forna Point
Il Ramla ta Marsalforn
Qbajjar
Zebbug
Marsalforn
Ir-Ramla
Il-Qala ta' San Vlas
Mistra Rocks
Dahlet Qorrot
Gharb
Ghammar
Birbuba
Il-Pergla
Ta' Venuta
Bin Gemma
Santu Pietru
Il-Wilga
Ghasri
Ta' Bullara
▲127
San Lawrenz
Gelmus
Is-Srug
Xaghra
Ta' Hida
Ta' Cini
Il-Qasam
Tar Rokon
Victoria (Rabat)
Ta' Hamet
Nadur
Qala
Il-Qasam
Santa Lucija
Ras il-Qala
Ta' Klula
Kercem
Tal-Hamrija
Wardija
Ras il-Wardija
Munxar
Xewkija
Il-Fliegu ta' Ghawdex (North Comino Channel)
Cala tas-Xlendi
Xlendi
Sannat
Ghajnsielem
Mgarr
Comino (Kemmuna)
Ta' Cenc
Ras il-Hobz
Cominotto (Kemmunett)

Gozo

Ras I-Irqieqa
Il-Fliegu ta' Malta (South Comino Channel)
Ponta ta'l-Ahrax
Ponta tal-Marfa
Marfa
Dahlet ix-Xilep
Cirkewwa
Marfa Ridge
Mellieha Bay
Ras-il-Griebe
Ras il-Quammieh
Il-Ghadira
Tal-Bla
Il Prajjet
Mellieha
Xemxi
Ghadira Bay
Mellieha Ridge
St. Paul's B
Bajda Ridge
Ras il-Wahx
Manikata
Ta'l Argentier
Ghajn Tuffieha
San Martin
Ward
Il Fawwara
Wardija Ridge
Gnejna Bay
Ta' Zerb
Hal Dra
Ta' Zammitello
Mgarr
Zebbi
Fommir-Rih Bay
Ta'l-Abatija
Bingemma
Ras ir-Raheb
Tas-Santi
Victoria Lines
Nadur 239
Bahrija
Mta
Tal Merhla ▲212
Gnien is-Sultan
Tal-Merhla
Nigted
Rab
Migra Ferha
Ta' Baldu 189 ▲
Misrah Suffara
Ras id-Dawwara
Dingli
Tal-Pitkal
Tal-Ved
Dingli Cliffs
Bux
Il-Kul

MEDITERRANEAN SEA

N

Maltese Islands

0   3 km
0   3 miles

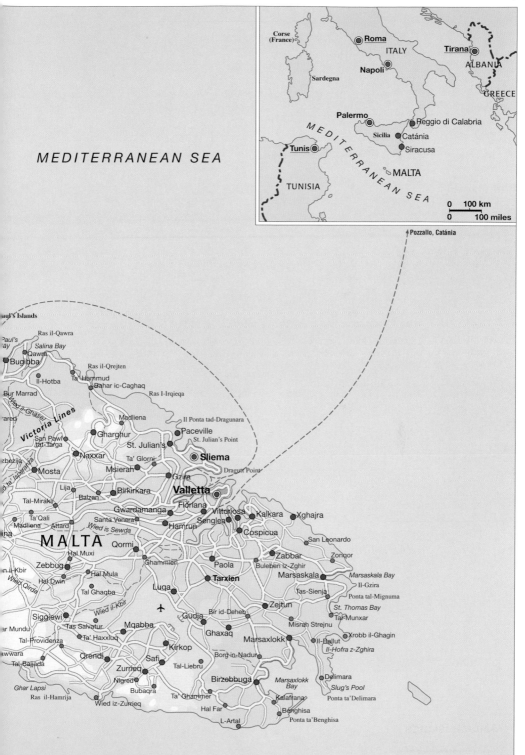

MEDITERRANEAN SEA

Corse
(France)

ITALY

Roma

Tirana

ALBANIA

Napoli

Sardegna

GREECE

MEDITERRANEAN SEA

Palermo

Reggio di Calabria

Sicilia

Catánia

Tunis

Siracusa

MALTA

TUNISIA

0   100 km

0   100 miles

Pozzallo, Catánia

Paul's Islands

Ras il-Qawra

Paul's
ay

Salina Bay

Qawra

Bugibba

Ras il-Qrejten

Il-Hotba

Ta' Hammud

Bahar ic-Caghaq

Bur Marrad

Ras l-Irqieqa

Wied il-Ghasel

Madliena

Il Ponta tad-Dragunara

ared

Victoria Lines

Gharghur

Paceville

San Pawl
tat-Targa

St. Julian's

St. Julian's Point

zbezija

Naxxar

Ta' Glorni

Sliema

Msierah

Gzira

Dragut Point

Mosta

Lija

Birkirkara

Valletta

Tal-MiraklI

Balzan

Floriana

Gwardamanga

Vittoriosa

Kalkara

Xghajra

Ta'Qali

Santa Venera

Senglea

Madliena

Attard

Wied is Sewda

Hamrun

Cospicua

San Leonardo

ina

Qormi

MALTA

Hal Muxi

Zabbar

Zonqor

Zebbug

Ghammieri

Paola

Buleben Iz-Zghir

Marsaskala

an-il-Kbir

Hal Mula

Marsaskala Bay

Wied Qirda

Hal Dwin

Tarxien

Marsaskala

Il-Gzira

Tal Ghaqba

Luqa

Zejtun

Tas-Sienja

Ponta tal-Mignuma

Siggiewi

Wied il-Kbir

Bir id-Deheb

St. Thomas Bay

ar Mundu

Tas Salvatur

Gudja

Misrah Strejnu

Tal-Munxar

Tal-Providenza

Ta' Haxxluq

Mqabba

Ghaxaq

Marsaxlokk

Il-Ballut

Xrobb il-Ghagin

awwara

Tal-Baljada

Qrendi

Safi

Kirkop

Borg in-Nadur

Il-Hofra z-Zghira

Zurrieq

Tal-Liebru

Nigred

Birzebbuga

Marsaxlokk
Bay

Delimara

Ghar Lapsi

Bubaqra

Kalafrana

Slug's Pool

Ras il-Hamrija

Wied iz-Zurrieq

Ta' Ghammier

Hal Far

Benghisa

Ponta ta'Delimara

L-Artal

Ponta ta'Benghisa

VALLETTA

The Knights of St John fashioned Valletta from earth and rock, and created the finest fortified city in Europe. Despite the ravages of time, it is still "a city built by gentlemen for gentlemen"

Emerging bloodied but unbowed after the heroic Great Siege of 1565, the Knights and the inhabitants of Malta realised that in order to be ready for a second Islamic invasion, they had to build a new and better fortified city on Malta. Despite their success, the island still represented the stepping stone to the Christian mainland and they believed that the forces of Islam would not fail to strike again.

The site chosen was virgin territory across from what was then called the Great Harbour (now the Grand Harbour). The high, barren, uninhabited rocky peninsula known as Mount Sceberras, with the tiny fort of St Elmo at its tip, both commanded the entrances to the harbours and dominated the lands on either side. It was from this unguarded superior position that the Turks had managed to rain down their fire with such devastation. The Knights would not make the mistake again of leaving such a strategic position available to the enemy.

A planned city

After much political argument and discussion, plans that had been drawn up by the Vatican architect, Francesco Laparelli, were accepted. One of the most important planned towns of the Renaissance would now be built. Laparelli's Valletta would be a city laid out in a rigid grid plan – that is, with all roads running straight and crossing each other at right angles. There would be main squares and secondary squares.

To make the city beautiful there would be uniformity of house design. Noxious trades would be zoned together to protect the residential quarters. Laparelli planned an imposing space for a Grand Masters' palace to be built "as large as Palazzo Farnese in Rome", and there would be excellent sites for the conventual church and hospital as well as for eight *auberges* for the different *langues* that formed the Order. Since the promontory was so hilly, and since much of it had yet to be levelled, it was impossible to estimate the number of houses that could be built.

On the morning of 28 March 1566, with great pomp, the foundation stone was laid. There, where the chapel of Our Lady of Victory would be built, a richly decorated altar was set up and High Mass celebrated in honour of Santo Spirito. The new city that would rise was christened Valletta after Grand Master Jean Parisot de la Valette, who had been the Great Siege commander and led the Order to victory.

In spite of the enthusiasm and urgency, work was slow and laboured. Hard rock had to be turned into a plateau before building could begin. After a few years Laparelli returned to Rome and the work passed into the hands of a Maltese architect, Gerolamo Cassar.

PRECEDING PAGES: the view to the Three Cities across Grand Harbour. **LEFT:** typical Valletta balconies. **BELOW:** the landmark Carmelite Church soars above the city.

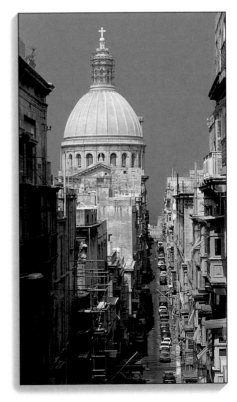

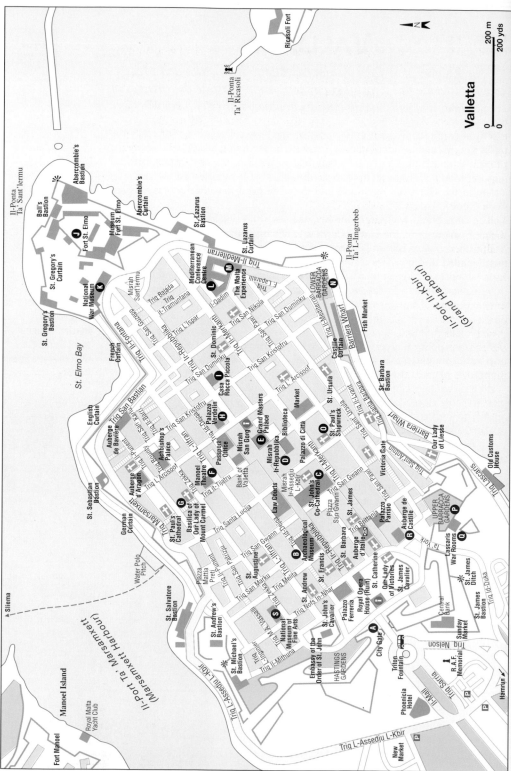

Valletta

Lasting glory

Gerolamo Cassar *(see box, page 112)*, then in his late forties, had worked with Laparelli and, during the Siege, while only a boy, had helped repair fortifications and invent war weapons. He had studied in Rome at the expense of the Order. Slowly but surely the city began to take shape.

Today, although much restored after the damage of World War II, and masked by a plethora of modern shop fronts and advertising hoardings, the city remains a delight, combining Laparelli's original designs and Cassar's magnificent architecture. The dramatic Valletta outline, with its superb bastion walls wrapped protectively around it, and its skyline of rectangular masses varied only by a cupola or church spire, remains one of Europe's great cityscapes.

A walk along Republic Street

Valletta is made for walking. Driving is neither recommended nor practical in the city, so enter on foot from **City Gate Ⓐ** through the busy confusion of Malta's central bus terminus. The waft of frying date and aniseed cakes, the hustle and bustle of business people and tourists, and the grand gate itself make for a memorable entrance to the city.

Immediately ahead is **Triq ir-Repubblika** (Republic Street), the city's main artery, leading from the City Gate (also known as Republic Gate) all the way down to Fort St Elmo at the tip of Valletta's promontory. It is not only the historical focus of the city but is also the main shopping street, with popular boutiques, small shopping malls and old-fashioned cafés. What appears to be a bomb site near the gate is just that. This was where, until World War II, the grand and gracious Royal Opera House stood.

Map on page 146

One of the island's Millennium projects was the building of a cultural and shopping centre on the site of the Royal Opera House. Alas, it never transpired, and St James' Cavalier was refurbished into an arts centre instead.

BELOW: Manoel Theatre, with composer, Charles Camilleri.

All of the government-run museums and temples in Malta have standard opening times (which are liable to change at short notice, so phone ahead or check with the tourist office before making a special journey). "Summer" is 16 June to 30 September, and "winter" 1 October to 15 June.

BELOW: Valletta locals seated in front of the Great Siege monument, carved by Antonio Sciberras (1879–1947).

After about 200 metres/yards, on the corner of narrow Melita Street, is the imposing **Archaeological Museum** ⓑ (open summer daily, 7.45am–2pm; winter Mon–Sat 8.15am–5pm, Sun 8.15am–4.15pm; tel: 2123 9545; entrance fee). This was one of the original Knights' *auberges*, the Auberge de Provence. It was the subject of major restoration work in the mid 1990s, but has since re-opened to the public. It contains collections of prehistoric pottery, sculpture and personal ornaments recovered from the megalithic temples that dot the island, including Malta's famous "Fat Ladies". There are also some typical examples of tomb furniture of the Punic and Roman periods.

To the right, continuing along Republic Street, is **St John's Square** (Piazza San Gwann), with **St John's Co-Cathedral** ⓒ (Mon–Fri 9.30am– 12.30pm and 1.30–4.30pm, Sat 9.30am–12.30pm; Sun for services only; tel: 2122 0536). Although its frontage is somewhat plain, the interior is awe-inspiring in its wealth and detail and it is regarded as one of the most important and remarkable monuments on the islands. The novelist Sir Walter Scott said it was the most striking interior he had ever seen *(see pages 169–73)*.

Heart of the city

Return to Republic Street and further along the main street, to the left, are the **Law Courts**, a modern, post-war building complete with massive pillars. Beyond are the two grand squares that give the city its centre.

The first is **Republic Square** ⓓ (Misrah Ir-Repubblika), until recently known as Queen's Square. Its landmark statue of Queen Victoria is a permanent resting-place for pigeons, and is surrounded by open-air cafés. **Caffè Cordina** is Valletta's best-known café and has a fine reputation for the quality of its food

and coffee, even if service can be slow. As well as being a perennial tourist hang-out, it is the meeting place of businessmen and lawyers who collect there in the late morning beneath the painted ceilings, standing around the bar.

Map on page 146

To the left of the square is the flank of the Grand Master's Palace, but lending its imposing presence as a backdrop is the **Biblioteca**, the National Library (Mon–Fri 8.15am–5.45pm, Sat 8.15am–1.15pm; tel: 2123 6585; free entrance). Dating from 1786, it was the last building of importance erected in Valletta by the Order of St John. There are said to be more that 300,000 books and documents in the building including, in the archives, more than 10,000 priceless manuscripts dating from the 12th to the 19th centuries. Among the letters is the signed bill and accompanying letter in which Henry VIII proclaimed himself the head of the Church of England.

Continue a little way along Republic Street to **Palace Square** (Misrah San Gorg). Regrettably, it now serves as a car park, but it is impossible to diminish the inner splendour of the **Grand Master's Palace ⑤** (open summer Mon–Fri 8am–3.45pm; winter Mon–Wed 8.30am–3.45pm, Thur–Fri 8.30am–4pm; tel 2122 1221; entrance fee), where visitors can tour the Armouries and Royal Apartments. *See pages 161–65 for a full description.*

The national flag flying in Palace Square.

On the opposite side of Palace Square is the **Main Guard**, currently home to the Italian Cultural Centre. This elegant building once housed a ceremonial guard, but originally it was the Chancellery of the Knights. Above its Doric portico is a royal coat of arms, carved in limestone, which was erected by the British and has an inscription dated 1814 recording in Latin the covenant between Malta and Britain. Under the plans for the rehabilitation of the city, this spread of buildings may become government offices.

BELOW:
relaxing *al fresco* in Republic Square.

Running parallel to Republic Street is Strait Street, a landmark for anyone who served in Malta during World War II. Known then as "The Gut", it comprised of nothing but ever-open bars, dance halls and brothels. Today, these establishments have all but disappeared.

BELOW: statue of former Prime Minister Borg Olivier.

The people's theatre

A short distance from the Palace, in **Old Theatre Street** (Triq it-Tijatru), is the **Manoel Theatre** 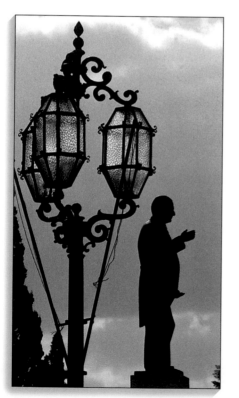, an 18th-century gem with gilded boxes rising in tiers to the ornate ceiling. It is reputed to be the second-oldest theatre still in use in Europe. Built in 1731 by Grand Master Manoel de Vilhena, mostly with money from his own pocket, it was opened "for the honest recreation of the people".

The theatre was a great success for well over a century but with the opening of the Royal Opera House (able to accommodate far larger audiences), the Manoel fell into disrepair. In time, as its fortunes changed, it became a doss-house for beggars, a dance hall and, more recently, a cinema. Then, in response to a public appeal, the theatre was bought by the nation and, after delicate restoration, has been officially declared Malta's National Theatre. It stages plays in both Maltese and English. Some of these are by touring British companies, and concerts with international artists such as Vladimir Ashkenazy and Dame Kiri te Kanawa.

You don't have to attend a performance at the theatre to get a glimpse inside. Tours generally depart Mon–Fri 10.30am and 11.30am, Sat 11.30am only and include entry to the theatre's interesting small museum (Mon–Fri 10am–12.30pm; entrance fee). Free concerts are also given in the theatre's recital room every Wednesday at 12.30pm (tel: 2122 2618).

Adjacent to the theatre, just after the intersection with Old Mint Street (Triq Zekka), is the landmark domed **Basilica of Our Lady of Mount Carmel** ❻. Also known as the Carmelite Church, Cassar's original building (1570) was destroyed during World War II, but was superbly rebuilt and completed in 1958. Its mighty dome is a feature of the Valletta cityscape from wherever it is viewed.

War and peace

Return to Republic Street, and still on Palace Square, on the other side of the Main Guard, is the impressively proportioned **Palazzo Verdelin** ❿, which houses a theatre alternating two audio-visual shows, **Malta George Cross – the Wartime Experience** and the **Valletta Experience** (Mon–Fri 10am–noon, Sat 10am–1pm; tel: 2122 7436; entrance fee). The former is the stirring story of the island's second Great Siege of 1942 and makes for an excellent introduction to the National War Museum.

After sitting through the newsreels of screaming Stuka bombers and island devastation, walk a little way along Republic Street and soothe your nerves at the **Casa Rocca Piccola** ❶ (tours only, Mon–Sat 10am–4pm; tel: 2123 1796; entrance fee). Not a museum, the house is still lived in and has withstood the ravages of time extremely well. The owners are very amiable and give a lively guided tour behind the scenes of the only patrician house in Valletta open to the public.

Fort St Elmo

At the very tip of the peninsula, **Fort St Elmo** ❶, first built in 1488, played a pivotal role in the defence of the islands during the first Great Siege (open Sat 1–5pm, Sun 9am–5pm; tel 2122 2430). Unfortunately, because

Map on page 146

of the high ground which overlooked it, the Turks were able to breach its defences and the Knights suffered devastating losses. With the exception of a handful of Maltese who were able to swim to safety across the harbour, its complement of 600 brave defenders was slaughtered. Look carefully at its outer walls and you can still see the scars of 1565. Guided tours bring the epic tales of the Siege to life and point out lesser-known contemporary secrets of the Fort, such as the grim adjacent barracks where part of the filming for *Midnight Express* took place.

Every other Sunday in summer, weather permitting, a spectacular live re-enactment of a military parade is staged, called In Guardia. It's full of colour, noise and cannon salutes and makes for a very entertaining couple of hours in an atmospheric and historical setting. Guided tours are given after the show (pick up a leaflet from the tourist office for showtimes).

With the creation of Valletta, the land bordering St Elmo was levelled and the fort was repaired and enlarged to form a classical star-shaped fort as part of the defensive bastion walls that encircle the city. During World War II its bastions were manned by the coastal and anti-aircraft batteries of the Royal Malta Artillery. It is therefore appropriate that today part of the fort is devoted to the **National War Museum** Ⓚ (open summer daily 7.45am–2pm; winter Mon–Sat 8.15am–5pm, Sun 8.15am–4.15pm; tel: 2122 2430; entrance fee). The items on display document the island's resistance during World War II and the most treasured exhibit is the actual George Cross medal conferred in 1942.

Memorial outside the Palazzo Verdelin to those killed in the riots of 7 June 1919.

Sacra Infermeria

Just a two-minute walk away along Triq il Mediterran is the **Mediterranean Conference Centre** Ⓛ (tel: 2124 3840/6; Mon–Fri 9.30am–4.30pm, Sat and

BELOW: the steep-stepped street of St John.

The splendid silver plate on which patients were fed at the Sacra Infermeria was mostly looted by Napoleon and melted down to pay for his Egyptian campaign. However, some pieces survived and are on display at the National Museum of Fine Arts (see page 154).

Sun 9.30am–4pm) – an uninspired title for such a fascinating place. For more than two centuries this landmark was the *Sacra Infermeria* (the Holy Infirmary) of the Order of the Knights of St John of Jerusalem. Work on the foundation began in 1574 and extensions were added over the next century. Not only was the nursing of the highest standard, it also featured the world's longest hospital ward, the Long Hall, which, in 1666, was described as one of the "grandest interiors in the world". By 1787 the hospital had a complement of 563 beds which could be increased to 914 in times of emergency. Patients were fed generous portions from silver plates.

Today there is public access to two parts of the building (separate entrances). The most popular is **The Malta Experience** ⓜ (shows each hour Mon–Fri 11am–4pm, Sat and Sun 11am–1pm; tel: 2124 3776; entrance fee). This is a dramatic audio-visual show encapsulating the main events in the islands' history using the latest projection techniques. The other exhibition area is devoted to the **Knights Hospitallers** (Mon–Fri 9.30am–5pm; tel: 2122 4135; entrance fee), which explains the hospitaller aspects of the Knights' work through a series of tableaux. Admission to this exhibition will also enable you to see the Long Hall, as long as no commercial exhibitions are taking place.

Gardens with a view

Continue along Triq il-Mediterran to the **Lower Barracca Gardens** ⓝ for the fine sea views; a neoclassical monument to the first British governor of Malta, Sir Alexander Ball; and the Siege Bell. The latter is dedicated to the victims of the second Great Siege of World War II and was unveiled by Queen Elizabeth II in 1992.

Past the Church of St Ursula turn inland up the steps and then left onto Triq

BELOW: aerial view of Fort St Elmo.

San Pawl to find the church of **St Paul Shipwreck ⓞ**. Often described as Valletta's hidden gem, it has an ornate baroque interior and claims the wristbone of St Paul and half of the column on which he was beheaded in Rome.

Map on page 146

Grand Harbour

Continue along Triq San Pawl and turn left back towards the sea to the **Upper Barracca Gardens ⓟ**. This is the highest point on the 16th-century bastion walls that the Knights of the Order of St John built, and it provides a magnificent panorama of Grand Harbour. From left to right, there is the breakwater entrance to the harbour and, across the water facing Valletta, Fort Ricasoli and Bighi (once well-known as a naval hospital but now used for state housing). Fort St Angelo rises majestically, while directly ahead is the town of Senglea, often dwarfed by the giant supertankers that come in for servicing at the dockyard. To the right are more dockyard workings and a towering grain silo.

Enjoying a beer in the warm Mediterranean sunshine.

The days when the harbour was busy with liners, warships and toiling tugs are long passed. No more the busy activity between ships or the countless numbers of *dghajsa* ferrying people aboard or ashore. The only traffic now is the occasional container ship and some of the Med's finest cruise ships. Tours of Grand Harbour depart regularly from the Strand at Sliema *(see page 207)*.

Just outside the Barracca Gardens entrance is another of Malta's audiovisual shows, **Sacred Island** (shows every 90 mins daily 10am–5pm; tel: 2122 2644; entrance fee), which takes a religious perspective on the archipelago. Close by, signs point to the **Lascaris War Rooms ⓠ** which are burrowed into the solid rock below the Gardens. This underground complex (Mon–Fri 9.30am–4.30pm; tel: 2123 8396; entrance fee) is a honeycomb of

BELOW: one of Valletta's many picturesque small shops.

Map
on page
146

map rooms and planning rooms where Malta's defensive strategy during World War II was plotted. It is a fascinating secret place, well interpreted with models, dioramas and a lively headphones tour.

Auberges and palazzi

Just around the corner from the Barracca Gardens is one of the city's most handsome and most photographed buildings, the **Auberge de Castile** ®. A wonderful example of baroque, it was redesigned under the instructions of Grand Master Pinto in 1741 by Andrea Belli, a Maltese architect from Zejtun. The high doorway, flanked by a pair of cannons, is approached by an elegant flight of steps. The exterior is magnificently decorated with carved stone and inside there is a particularly fine staircase and an attractive paved courtyard.

Abutting Castile Place in Merchants' Street (Triq il Merkanti), just around the corner, is the old **Palazzo Parisio**, now the Ministry of Foreign Affairs. When Napoleon Bonaparte took Malta he used the Palazzo Parisio as his quarters. Opposite is the former post office, also a former Knights' *auberge (see box below)*.

Continue from Castile Place into South Street (Triq Nofs in-Nhar), across Republic Street to the **National Museum of Fine Arts** ⑤ (open summer daily 7.45am–2pm; winter Mon–Sat 8.15am–5pm, Sun 8.15am–4.15pm; tel: 2122 5769; entrance fee), an elegant building that began life as a private palace but was taken over in British times to become Admiralty House. Lord Louis Mountbatten, as Admiral of the Fleet, had his headquarters there. In the museum are Italian and Maltese paintings. Look out in particular for the works of Antoine de Favray and Louis du Cros, whose paintings adeptly capture the flavour of Valletta's past greatness. ❑

BELOW: watching the world from a *gallerija*.
RIGHT: small hole-in-the-wall shops and bars can still be found in the city.

THE KNIGHTS' AUBERGES

Of the eight *auberges* in Valletta designed by Gerolamo Cassar for the various *langues* of the Knights *(see page 46)*, five still stand. The most famous and most imposing is the Auberge de Castile, now the office of the Prime Minister. The others are the Auberge d'Aragon (a government ministry) in Pjazza Independenza, the Auberge d'Italie (the former post office) in Merchant's Street, the Auberge de Provence (the Archaeological Museum) and the Auberge d'Angleterre et Baviere, used as government offices, but currently awaiting new designation. Three *auberges* have disappeared. The d'Allemagne was demolished to make way for St Paul's Anglican Cathedral and two were destroyed in World War II. The Law Courts stand on the former site of the d'Auvergne, while the faceless headquarters of the General Workers Union occupies the site of the old Auberge de France.

The two *auberges* with public access, the former post office and the Archaeological Museum, have been gutted and much altered over the centuries so there is little to remind you of their former function or atmosphere. But if you want to see inside a relatively little-changed *auberge*, make the short trip to Vittoriosa where the Auberge d'Angleterre now functions as the local public library.

THE BRITISH INFLUENCE ON DAILY LIFE

Malta may be an independent nation with Latin traits and Italian and African neighbours, but many of its people still carry a torch for the British

The Maltese islands came under the protection of the British Crown in 1800. This followed a Maltese request for Britain's help in ending the French tyranny that had begun in 1798 when Napoleon Bonaparte, en route to Egypt, evicted the Order of the Knights and seized the islands. For the best part of 200 years, the islands were British and adopted many of Britain's customs and laws. Today, wherever you go there are affectionate reminders of those days.

Most people in Malta speak English, cars travel on the left (unlike in the rest of Continental Europe), British street furniture abounds, and almost every football fan follows the fortunes of British clubs – especially Manchester United – even if they have allegiances to Italian teams such as Juventus or AC Milan. Many British Sunday and Monday newspapers are bought just for the football columns.

Food and drink, too, shows a British influence. Not only do supermarkets stock all the big British brands, many cafés do a plate of sausage, egg and chips. Several of the island's older bars have a pub-like feel, serve archetypal British beers and drinks like Pale Ale and Shandy, and go under British-style pub names.

The British armed forces may have moved on (their barracks are often now used as government housing estates), but as returning visitors they are always welcome. In the old days, *dghajsas* (water taxis) would ply Grand Harbour, offering to ferry servicemen across to Strait Street, Valletta's red-light district. Things may have changed, but the British still manage to bring people out of their homes; if a ship from the Royal Navy enters Grand Harbour, thousands of Maltese still turn out to line the quay, and queue for an opportunity to go on board to see the new technology and talk to the sailors.

◁ RED SENTRY Maltese postal collection times may be unfamiliar to British visitors, but the shape is that of an old friend.

▷ STILL RUNNING Many old British cars from the 1950s and '60s are seen on the roads.

△ PIT STOP During a village *festa* the locals call in at their favourite bar to cool off with a lager or a pale ale.

THE GREAT WALL OF MALTA

The wall known as the Victoria Lines was built by the British between 1870 and 1899 along a natural fault that runs 12 km (8 miles) across Malta from Kuncizzjoni in the west to Madliena. Its purpose was to protect Valletta and the south from a landborne invasion from the north, just as Hadrian's Wall in Britain was built by the Romans to prevent an invasion from the north.

The Victoria Lines links four forts and a number of artillery batteries, but some sceptics still cast doubt as to whether the wall ever really had any military significance. One cherished theory is that it was built simply to keep the British armed forces occupied. In the event, British naval power was such that the defensive line was never properly tested.

These days, the wall is one of Malta's best-kept secrets. To walkers it offers some of the best vantage points for enjoying views over the island's threatened open countryside.

△ RED, WHITE AND BLUE
Modern telephones are everywhere, but the old red boxes have been retained. You see blue British police lamps, too.

▽ GRAND HARBOUR
Ships of the Royal Navy have been largely replaced by cruise liners, but their occasional visits are greeted with enthusiasm.

◁ SIGN OF THE TIMES
Many shops have a name that commemorates a British event of the era when they first opened.

▷ V SIGN
The bust of Churchill in the Upper Barracca Gardens was erected to mark the end of World War II.

THE GRAND MASTER'S PALACE

Map on page 146

At the height of their powers, the Grand Masters of the Order were the equals of European royalty. Their palace preserves the wealth and trappings of this golden age

In 1571, when Valletta's fortifications were considered safe enough to resist a fresh enemy attack, the Order of St John transferred its seat from Fort St Angelo and Birgu (now Vittoriosa) to the new city of Valletta. Work on the Grand Master's Palace **E** was started in earnest the following year under Grand Master La Cassière, with the architect Gerolamo Cassar (1520–92) entrusted with its design and construction.

From the time it was completed, a few years later, until the end of the Order's stay in Malta in 1798, the Palace was used by all successive Grand Masters, and after that, until 1964, by the British governors. Since 1976, it has housed the offices of the President of the Republic.

A military bearing

By profession Cassar was a military architect and became proficient in civic architecture relatively late in life, mostly as a result of his visit to Rome and other Italian cities in 1569. Even so, his style remained, to a considerable extent, severe, no doubt further inspired by the military character of the Order who had become hardened by the steel and fire of battle.

The main facade of the Palace, which opens on to Republic Street, is plain and generally disappointing, and was even more so before the addition of its only decorative elements, the two Doric gateways and the long wooden balconies that were constructed during the time of Grand Master Emanuel Pinto de Fonseca (1741–73). Corner pilasters with ponderous rustications, so characteristic of 16th- and 17th-century Valletta, rise the height of the building, giving it a visual impression of strength.

Upstairs, downstairs

The sumptuous interior of the Palace more than makes up for the unprepossessing aspect of the facade. All state rooms, as was usual in important buildings of the period, are on the first floor, while the ground floor was reserved for stables, coach-houses, kitchens, servants' quarters and stores.

Some fine masonry work in local limestone – the groined cross-vaults, saucer-domes and plain vaulting supported on massive walls – can be seen in most of the ground-floor rooms and corridors, especially in the older sections of the building. An open corridor runs round the main **Neptune Courtyard**; its balustraded arcading, sub-tropical trees, a small flower-garden with a bronze statue of Neptune and a sculptured marble and stone fountain bearing the

PRECEDING PAGES: corridor of power within the Palace.
LEFT: Neptune Courtyard.
BELOW: learning the history of the Tapestry Room.

coat-of-arms of the Aragonese Grand Master, Ramon Perellos (1697–1720), make it one of the finest ensembles of its kind in Malta.

The Armouries

Two large vaults at the rear of the Palace contain the Armouries, which have one of the most important collections of arms and armour in the world.

The Armouries were, from the time of Grand Master Pinto, originally housed in a long hall in the upper floor of the Palace, but were transferred to their present location in 1976, when the hall was converted into the Chamber of Parliament. On permanent exhibition are splendid suits of armour (some of them sumptuously engraved), rapiers, swords, daggers, halberds, pikes and lances, and flintlocks, arquebuses, pistols, mortars and small ordnance. A limited number of Turkish arms and trophies completes the collection.

At the back of another courtyard, named after Prince Alfred to commemorate the first visit to Malta by the second son of Queen Victoria in 1858, stands a high bell-tower with a clock that has been chiming the hours since 1745. Four bronze figures, representing Moorish slaves, strike three gongs with a hammer every quarter of an hour. Its four dials show the hour and minutes, the phases of the moon, the month and the day.

The Grand Master's apartments

The first floor is reached by a winding marble staircase with unusually shallow steps, said to have been purposely constructed for the benefit of old and gout-ridden Knights and Grand Masters. The newel (the staircase's centre pillar) is a hollow masonry cylinder with balustraded openings, while a handrail is carved

Map on page 146

into the wall. The barrel-vaulted ceiling, which follows both the curvature and slope of the stairs, is a rare masterpiece in masonry work and a tribute to Malta's ancient craft of stoneworking.

At the foot of the stairs, a marble slab fixed to the lobby wall gives the names of the Grand Masters of the Order of St John who ruled over Malta between 1530 and 1798; another marble inscription at the top of the staircase lists the British civil commissioners and governors who represented the British Crown when Malta was a British dependency between 1800 and 1964. The two inscriptions provide an admirable exercise in historical continuity.

The first floor, or *piano nobile*, contains the main apartments built round wide corridors overlooking the Neptune Courtyard. The highlights are the **Council Chamber**, also known as the Tapestry Room, and the **Supreme Council Hall** (also called, until a few years ago, the Hall of St Michael and St George). Both halls have superb timber ceilings, with decorated wooden beams of red Sicilian chestnut resting on carved supporting brackets designed to reduce the span. Richly painted and gilded, cross-beams, placed at frequent intervals, provide an elaborate coffered effect.

Stone lion guarding the palace courtyard.

The Council Chamber

The senior members of the Order met regularly in this room to discuss the day-to-day administration of the island. The tradition was continued by the Maltese Parliament, which held its sittings here from 1921 until 1976, when it moved to the former Armouries.

The most striking feature of the room, indeed one of the most memorable treasures of the islands, is a set of **Gobelin tapestries**, donated to the Order by

BELOW: a recent floor mosaic in a Palace corridor.

REPUBBLIKA TA' MALTA

Grand Master Ramón Perellos in 1710. Known as *Les Tentures des Indes*, they depict in vivid colours (subdued by age) jungle scenes recalling the hunting expeditions of a German prince in Brazil, the Caribbean Islands, India and tropical Africa undertaken between 1636 and 1644. A whole menagerie of wild animals, including a striped horse, elephants, a bizarre rhino (apparently drawn from the imagination, rather than sight), forest bulls and ostriches all vie for prominence against a background provided by luscious and exotic flora with a wealth of detail culled from the illustrations of a botanical handbook.

Above the hangings around the four walls of the Chamber is a frieze made of rectangular panels showing galleys of the Order in action against the Turkish fleet. The frieze incorporates allegorical figures representing Faith, Charity, Fortitude, Virtue, Manhood, Vocation, Providence, Munificence, Victory, Hope and Justice. At one end is a large painted crucifix on which Grand Masters and members of the Council took solemn oaths during their deliberations by extending their hand towards it.

The Supreme Council Chamber

The Grand Master summoned his Supreme Council, consisting of the 16 most senior members of the Order, whenever important decisions on domestic affairs or on foreign relations had to be taken. Gianbattista Tiepolo (1693–1770) immortalised one of the sessions of the Grand Council held in the Supreme Council Chamber with a superb painting which hangs in Udine, Italy.

The main chamber frieze depicts the Great Siege of 1565 (*see box below*). At the end of the hall is a modified version of the original throne used by the Grand Masters and later, during the colonial period, by Governors representing the

THE GREAT SIEGE FRIEZE

The main chamber frieze in the Supreme Council Hall is by Matteo Perez d'Aleccio (1547–1628), painter, engraver and probably a pupil of Michelangelo. Painted between 1576 and 1581, the work is unique in being the only reliable pictorial depiction of the Great Siege of 1565. The event was described to the painter by eye-witnesses.

You can follow the dramatic episodes of the arrival of the Turkish armada in May, the landing of the Turkish troops in Marsaxlokk Bay, the epic month-long siege of Fort St Elmo and its fall on the eve of St John's Day. The assault on Fort St Michael and the Posts of Castile and Allemagne at the Borgo, with Grand Master La Valette wounded at the head of his troops, is graphically illustrated with evident feeling. Perez d'Aleccio completes the pictorial history of one of the major events of Malta's history with a vivid panorama of the entire war, the arrival of the Little Relief and later of the Great Relief (sent from Sicily) and the final withdrawal of the Turkish army on 7 September. Separating the Siege panels are allegorical female figures which represent Justice, Happiness, Prudence, Fortitude, Temperance and the three theological virtues of Faith, Hope and Charity. Perez d'Aleccio also painted the fine frieze in the Yellow Room.

British monarchs. At the opposite end of the hall is a singers' gallery, previously in the private chapel of the Grand Master, decorated with scenes from Genesis, said to have been brought by the Order on their flight from Rhodes.

Map on page 146

The State Dining Hall

Adjacent to the Supreme Council Chamber, the State Dining Hall is a room of beautiful proportions in which the Grand Masters and British governors gave sumptuous dinners in honour of important visitors and local dignitaries. The hall originally had a timber ceiling like all the state rooms of the Palace, but this was unfortunately destroyed by aerial bombardment during World War II and replaced by a concrete roof painted with a copy of the original design. Paintings of British royalty adorn the walls: King George III, during whose reign Malta became a part of the British Empire, George IV, Victoria, Edward VII, Alexandra, George VI and Elizabeth II.

The Ambassador's Room

On the other side of the Supreme Council Chamber is the Ambassador's Room, also known as the State Room, where Grand Masters received the credentials of envoys to Malta, a practice retained to this day by the President of the Republic when accepting the credentials of new ambassadors accredited to the islands. The Ambassador's Room is decorated with a high frieze of paintings depicting episodes from the Order's earlier history during its sojourn in Acre, Cyprus, Rhodes and Viterbo, and a splendid series of personages from the Old Testament. Impressive paintings of European monarchs, including Louis XIV, Louis XV and Louis XVI, and Catherine II of Russia, decorate the walls. ❑

The Grand Master's seat of power in the Throne Room.

BELOW: fanciful wild animals in the Tapestry Room.

ST JOHN'S CO-CATHEDRAL

Map on page 146

Despite the military nature of many of the Knights' structures, they were, above all, an essentially religious brotherhood, and the Conventual Church was their most important building

William Makepeace Thackeray wrote of St John's in 1846: "The Church of Saint John, not a handsome structure without, is magnificent within: a noble hall covered with a rich embroidery of gilded carving: it seemed to me a fitting place for this wealthy body of aristocratic soldiers, who made their devotions as it were on parade, and though on their knees, never forgot their epaulets on their quarters of nobility."

Work was begun on the Conventual Church dedicated to St John the Baptist (the patron saint of the Order) in November 1573. Its design and construction were entrusted to the Order's chief architect, Gerolamo Cassar. Originally, it was planned to be sited in lower Valletta, close to the Holy Infirmary, but, realising that the ringing of the bells would disturb the sick, the Grand Master changed the site to its present position at the heart of the city ●.

Valletta

A fortress church

Cassar's training in military architecture explains the austere lines of the facade, which has been described accurately as that of a fortress-church and a continuation, in conception, of Valletta's fortified lines.

The two western towers, quite rare in Renaissance and baroque Italy, set the pattern for future Maltese church architecture, and there is hardly a church on the island without the characteristic twin bell-towers on its front.

But if the facade of St John's is bleak, the interior is an unqualified triumph. The leading art critic Nikolaus Pevsner described it as the first complete example of high baroque anywhere.

Into the darkness

As you leave the sun-lit square and walk through the main portal into the semi-darkness of the cathedral, you are overwhelmed by an almost incredible sense of contrast. The rigid plain lines of the exterior change, as if by a magic wand, into a dazzling blaze of colour and decoration which made Sir Walter Scott exclaim with delight in 1831: "This is the most magnificent place I saw in my life."

For a few moments the eye moves gradually along the richly painted vault, down the arabesque carvings which cover every inch of the walls, and past the multi-coloured marble slabs which cover the floor from end to end. Then slowly but surely a sense of harmony takes over.

The building was completed in 1577, but important additions were made well into the 18th century. The plan of the church is simple: a vast rectangular chamber with an apse at its eastern end, a slightly pointed barrel vault, originally coffered, and chapels at the

PRECEDING PAGES: the frescoed ceiling by Mattia Preti. **LEFT:** High Mass. **BELOW:** the Cathedral clock tower.

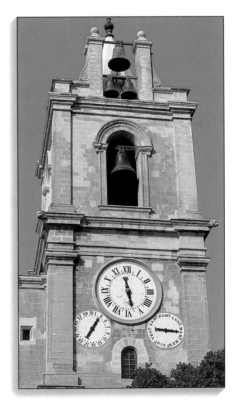

In the crypt are the remains of 12 Grand Masters, including the hero of the Great Siege, Jean Parisot de la Valette. Unfortunately, the crypt is not usually open to the public.

sides behind high arches. Cassar, obviously uncertain of the structural and statical possibilities of the local limestone, used extra-thick walls between the side chapels as supports for the heavy buttresses above, thus counteracting the enormous lateral thrust of the huge vault.

Very narrow doors (opened years after the church was completed) lead from one chapel to the other, each small enough not to interfere with the stability of the supporting walls. The vault is divided into six bays by wide ribs, each resting on the pilasters between the arches of the side chapels. In each bay, an oval window gives light, although the light is somewhat restricted owing to the presence of the buttresses outside.

Enter Preti

For more than 70 years after its completion, St John's remained a vast cavernous stone structure barren of all decoration. Then, in 1661, Grand Master Rafael Cotoner commissioned Mattia Preti to decorate the ceiling. Known as *Il Cavalier Calabrese*, Preti was one of the most outstanding artists of his age. Born in Taverna, Calabria, in 1613, he studied in Rome and Naples, where he came under the influence of the art of Caravaggio and the Venetian Masters of the 16th century, whose main traits characterise all his artistic works.

Preti divided each of the six bays of the vault into three sections by means of painted architectural devices such as balustraded balconies, cornices and elaborately decorated archways, thus creating 18 spaces in which he depicted episodes from the life of John the Baptist. Using surprisingly skilful illusionistic effects, dexterity in the use and combination of colours and, above all, perfect draughtsmanship, he turned the cathedral into his own artistic triumph.

BELOW: corridor and ornamented side chapel.

The Knights and St John

The two Cotoner brothers, Grand Masters Rafael (1660–63) and Nicolas (1663–80), under whose rule the decoration was brought to fruition, are given a place of honour in the large lunette over the main door.

In the vivid colours of the vault is the entire biblical narrative of the life of John the Baptist; from Zachary in the Temple, to John's Birth, his Encounter with Christ in the Desert, Christ's Baptism, John's Preachings in the Wilderness, the Reproval of Herod, the Dance of Salome and the final episode of the Beheading. Figures of saints and heroes of the Order, dramatically illuminated on each side of the oval windows, are considered among the best of Preti's art.

Preti completed his masterpiece in less than five years, while working concurrently on the preparation of drawings for the elaborate full-relief sculptures of the nave and aisles. The plain stone surface of the pilasters, arches, walls and ceilings of the chapels (perfect material for the carver's chisel) was transformed into a riot of gilded flowers, scrolls, shells, winged angels and escutcheons – all the design motifs that are characteristic of baroque ornamentation.

The chapels of the *langues*: right aisle

Each of the eight *langues*, or national sections of the Order, had its own chapel where the Knights prayed and heard Mass. The chapel nearest the entrance on the right is that of Castile, León and Portugal, dedicated to St James. The Portuguese Grand Masters Antonio Manoel de Vilhena (1722–36) and Manuel Pinto de Fonseca (1741–73) are commemorated in two splendid monuments.

The next chapel, dedicated to St George, is that of the *langue* of Aragon, Catalunya and Navarre, whose altarpiece and paintings are also by Preti. The

Map on page 146

Cannons guard the entrance to the Knight's former church.

BELOW: the pavement floor is made up of marble memorial tombstones.

chapel contains two of the most beautiful Grand Masters' mausoleums in St John's: Nicolas Cotoner (1663–80) and Ramón Perellos (1697–1720).

The **Chapel of Auvergne**, with an altarpiece depicting scenes from the life of St Sebastian, comes next. The monument commemorates Grand Master de Chattes Gessan (1660), who died only four months after his election.

The chapels of the *langues*: left aisle

The opening times for the Cathedral and the Museum are Mon–Fri 9.30am–12.30pm and 1.30–4.30pm, Sat 9.30am–12.30pm, Sun, for services only. Entrance fee for museum.

At the end of the left aisle is the **Chapel of the Holy Relics**, with an altarpiece of *St Charles Borromeo*. Next to it is the **Chapel of Provence**, with a contemporary copy of Guido Reni's *St Michael*, and the mausoleums of the two Provençal Grand Masters, de Paule (1623–36) and Lascaris Castellar (1636–57).

Next is the **Chapel of France**, dedicated to St Paul. This chapel was shorn of Preti's sculptural decoration in the 1840s by a short-lived iconoclastic movement that introduced motifs representing the British royal crown, the fleur-de-lys and the eight-pointed cross. The mausoleum of Grand Master de Rohan (1775–97), which was also adversely tampered with, and that of Adrien de Wignacourt (1690–97), are both located here.

Adjoining the Chapel of France is the **Langue of Italy**, with an altarpiece of the *Mystic Marriage of St Catherine*, one of Preti's finest works in Malta. The chapel contains the monument of Grand Master Carafa (1680–90), with a marble relief of the Battle of the Dardanelles fought in 1656 by the galleys of the Order of St John with Carafa as the Captain-General of the fleet.

The last chapel is dedicated to the **Three Kings of the Langue of Germany**, with the monument of Grand Master Zondadari (1720–22), a splendid mausoleum in bronze and black marble.

BELOW: detail of a marble memorial.

Map on page 146

The chancel and choir

The chancel and choir, and indeed the whole of St John's, is dominated by a magnificent marble group representing the *Baptism of Christ* by Giuseppe Mazzuoli (1644–1725), with a gilt bronze *gloria* as background, the work of Giovanni Giardini (1646–1721), an Italian sculptor and silversmith. The **high altar**, certainly the richest in Malta, is made of lapis lazuli and precious marbles and is enriched by a relief of the *Last Supper*, also in gilt bronze, at its centre.

The cathedral museum

The Beheading of St John by Caravaggio (1573–1610), the renowned Italian painter, is undoubtedly the most famous painting in St John's – and, indeed, the Maltese islands. A crucial landmark in the history of European art, it was one of Caravaggio's last works, and certainly considered one of his best. Another of the artist's masterpieces, *St Jerome,* hangs close by.

The museum's other principal treasures are a magnificent set of 14 Flemish **tapestries** by de Vos, made after cartoons by Rubens and Poussin, which portray scenes from the Life of Christ and religious allegories. During June (the festival month of John the Baptist), they are hung in the nave of the church.

Illuminated manuscript from the Cathedral Museum.

Heroes below

The history of the Order, its Knights and admirals, its warriors and heroes, is emblazoned on **marble tombstones** which cover the floor of the nave, aisles and oratory. Latin inscriptions under heraldic coats-of-arms with many quarterings, scrolls and patronymics, resound with brave deeds on the field of battle or at sea, and record names of the most aristocratic European families of the time. ❑

BELOW: Caravaggio's savage masterpiece, *The Beheading of St John.*

THE THREE CITIES

Map on page 178

Once home to the Knights and later the great dockyards that kept the British Mediterranean Navy afloat, today the Three Cities remains one of Malta's most atmospheric areas

When Emperor, Charles V of Spain gave Malta to the homeless Order of St John they settled in the area known as Il Borgo, which was the home of a small but flourishing community. Set deep in the safe reaches of the harbour, its creeks provided shelter for the Knights' galleys.

This spread of land, around the bay from Valletta, consisted of two promontories with dividing flat ground; Birgu (now Vittoriosa) and Isola (now Senglea), with Bormla (now Cospicua) between. Jutting out from Vittoriosa was Fort St Angelo, the only means of defence. Curiously, to this day, the Maltese living in this area cling to the old names handed down from the days of the Knights and call the Three Cities, respectively, Birgu, l'Isla and Bormla. Today's road signs, as if designed to confuse rather than aid, use either.

During the Knights' tenure, considerable sums were spent creating the kind of buildings the Order required, and the whole was wrapped in impregnable defensive bastion walls. Later the British garrison made its own additions.

PRECEDING PAGES: Vittoriosa, home of boats big and small. **LEFT:** *dghasja* racing at Seglea. **BELOW:** Senglea's famous vedette.

Docklands

Above all, this is the location of Malta's famous dockyards, the target of most of the bombing in World War II as the Axis partners tried to destroy the docks and the ships undergoing essential repair. Cospicua and Senglea suffered considerable damage. Houses and streets were reduced to rubble, families were evacuated. Since then the whole district has been totally rebuilt, but much of it hastily. The small amount of historical or architectural interest that remained after the conflict is masked by post-war building and development. It is much neglected and in need of restoration and rehabilitation, but nonethless remains an intriguing place.

Cospicua took the brunt of the bombardment and has been re-established as a commercial centre around the dockyard gates. Its huge church of the **Immaculate Conception**, built in 1637, narrowly escaped total destruction and is worth a look inside. For a general visit, however, Cospicua is the least worthwhile of the Three Cities.

Vittoriosa

Vittoriosa, the least damaged and most fascinating of the Three Cities, is not yet a place for the average tourist as there are few cafés, no restaurants and only tiny local shops to serve the neighbourhood. But for independent explorers this is all to the good.

The church of **St Lawrence**  (San Lawrenz), on the waterfront facing Senglea, is the logical starting point for any Three Cities tour. This was originally the conventual church of the Order of St John and contains many relics of the Knights. Built in 1723 to replace a smaller church erected by Count Roger the Norman, it is a magnificent building in a picturesque corner. In front of it stands the **Freedom Monument**, erected in 1979 to commemorate the withdrawal of the British forces, while behind is the **Church Museum** containing the sword and hat of the most heroic Grand Master, Jean Parisot de la Valette (officially open daily 9am–noon but often closed, so enquire at the tourist office in Valletta before making a special journey).

The Freedom Monument marks not only the site of the British withdrawal, but also the very spot where Nelson's representative landed in 1799 to claim the island for Britain.

Headquarters of the Inquisition

Continue on behind the church to enter **Pjazza Vittoriosa ❸** (Victory Square), the heart of Vittoriosa with its balconied band institute building and its inevitable Victory monument. Just off here (turn right) on Main Gate Street is the **Inquisitor's Palace ❹** (open summer daily 7.45am–2pm; winter Mon–Sat 8.15am–5pm, Sun 8.15am–4.15pm; entrance fee), a 16th-century *palazzo* that once housed the court, residence and prison of the Office of the Inquisition.

As the Pope's delegate, the Inquisitor was accommodated in style. Though its role was to combat heresy and protect the Catholic faith, this Office was not quite as dogmatic when it was first established as the infamous Spanish Inquisition. It was only as the Inquisitor's power base grew stronger that it took on a more ruthless role (though there are no records of torture ever being used here). Two Inquisitors went on to Rome to become popes – Alexander VII (1655–67) and Innocent XII (1676–89). The Office also provided 25 cardinals.

If the exterior is unprepossessing, inside there are fine murals, and the ceiling of the main hall features coats of arms of the 62 Inquisitors carved in wood.

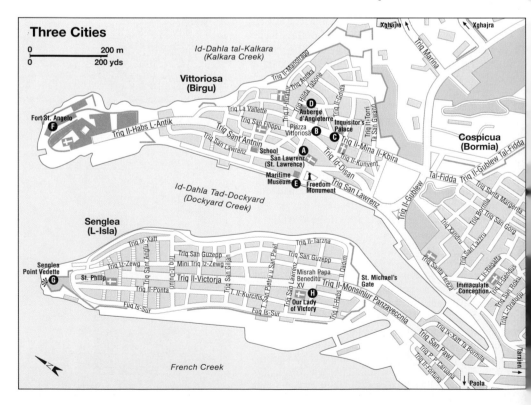

The dreaded Judgement Room is a reminder of the power that the Inquisition so ostentatiously wielded. Its door was made deliberately low so that each prisoner was forced to bow to the presiding Inquisitor on entering. Directly below here are a honeycomb of cells where their victims were incarcerated.

Map on page 178

The *auberges* of Vittoriosa

Walk back to Victory Square and turn right into Triq Hilda Tabone/Britannic Street. This was once the headquarters of the Knights and several *auberges* (Knights' inns) once graced this and surrounding streets. Name plaques recall former sites but the only surviving *auberge* is the **Auberge d'Angleterre ①** on North West/Mistral Street, just off Triq Hilda Tabone. Today, this handsome honey-coloured sandstone building houses a public library but it is not always open to the public so please check on tel: 2166 2166.

Festival banners outside the Inquisitor's Palace.

Along the waterfront

Back past the church to the waterfront and through the grand entrance arch to the old dockside is a splendid colonnaded building which once housed the old naval bakery. It is now home to the **Maritime Museum ②** (open summer daily 7.45am–2pm; winter Mon–Sat 8.15am–5pm, Sun 8.15am–4.15pm; entrance fee), which features collections of model ships, actual Maltese boats and many exhibits dealing with the maritime history of the Maltese islands from the Phoenicians to the British occupation. The building formerly known as Scamp's Palace has been converted into Malta's third casino, the Casino di Venezia.

A short walk along the quay is **Fort St Angelo ②** (Sat 9am–1pm; entrance fee). Acclaimed as a masterpiece of military architecture, it has a long and illus-

BELOW: the walls of Senglea, seen across the creek from Cospicua.

TIP

Try to visit the Three Cities in the afternoon so you can stay on to see the setting sun turning the waterfront buildings gloriously golden.

trious past. According to the records, the fortress was originally established in AD 828 by the Arabs. Before that a Phoenician temple stood here until it was replaced by the Romans, who built a new temple to the goddess Juno. In 1090 Roger the Norman, Count of Sicily, erected a small chapel dedicated to the Blessed Virgin on the spot.

In 1530, when the Order arrived, Grand Master de l'Isle Adam set about converting this high ground into a fortress and during the first Great Siege, St Angelo was the Knights' impregnable command centre and pivot around which the battles were fought.

In 1912 the fortress became HMS St Angelo, headquarters of the British navy, and received another severe pounding during World War II. Today, it is open to the public for one afternoon a week and the views across the Grand Harbour alone make the visit wortwhile.

Senglea

On the opposite side of the water to Vittoriosa, Senglea is named after Grand Master de la Sengle, who fortified the promontory and founded this community in 1554. Despite the massive destruction that rendered it uninhabitable during World War II, it has regained a picturesque charm. Once, during Malta's boom period of the 1970s, it had all the makings of becoming an artists' colony when foreign painters, writers and sculptors moved into the houses and apartments overlooking the harbour. Now, with just a sprinkling of emigrés, it has returned to familiar local life.

BELOW: the Three Cities' dockyards serve some of the world's largest cruise ships and tankers.

Senglea's appeal stems from its excellent view over Grand Harbour. The harbour may not be as busy as once it was, but from the gardens with their

famous **Senglea Point Vedette**  sentry post at the tip of its promontory, both Valletta and Fort St Angelo look absolutely superb, particularly when floodlit at night. Carved onto the vedette are an oversized eye and ear, symbols of vigilance.

Below, ringing Senglea at the water's edge, is a pleasant walkway that heads towards Cospicua. In the cool of the evening, the still waters in the creek take on the appearance of a tranquil lagoon. The imposing 17th-century parish church of **Our Lady of Victory** was rebuilt here after the war. The statue of Our Lady of Victory is paraded through the streets on 8 September – Victory Day – one of Malta's five national holidays.

Kalkara to Fort St Rocco

From Vittoriosa the road winds around Kalkara Creek to **Kalkara**. Many of Malta's traditional boats are repaired here or wintered alongside the few craftsmen who still build the *dghajsa* that were once used to ferry passengers to and from ships berthed in Grand Harbour.

Beyond is **Fort Ricasoli**, built in 1670 to guard the entrance to the Grand Harbour. In the days of the Order it had a complement of 2,000 soldiers.

A short distance away is **Fort St Rocco**, one of the many small forts that were created by the Knights as part of Malta's coastal defence. This area is now the location of the Mediterranean Film Studios, which offer film-makers two of the world's largest water tanks, both overlooking the sea and positioned in such a way as to give the cameras natural sky as their backdrop. One tank is a specially designed deep-water photography tank where scenes can be shot under water in controlled conditions. ❑

Where the Knights' galleys once tied up, now huge container ships drop anchor.

BELOW:
boats moored in Kalkara.

MDINA AND RABAT

The Silent City of Mdina is a time capsule of medieval
palazzi *and a world unto itself, while beneath neighbouring*
Rabat lie fascinating underground discoveries

Map
on page
186

Valletta

The Romans called their town *Melita*, the Arabs *Medina*, and in the early days of the Knights it was known as *Citta Notabile*. When the Knights completed the building of the new city of Valletta, the old capital was rechristened *Citta Vecchia* (Old City) to distinguish it from the new. The Maltese, however, corrupting the Arabic, preferred Mdina and that is the name that stuck.

A strategic location

Because of its commanding position on a high ridge that runs along the southwest of the island, there have been settlements here since the Bronze Age. At over 150 metres (500 ft) above sea level, it has always been easy to defend, while below it is surrounded by fertile fields able to produce abundant vegetables and fruit to satisfy a growing population.

In AD 870, after the Aghlabite Arabs had invaded and taken Malta, these new conquerors began to extend the city's perimeter walls along the plateau ridge to encompass a suburb of dwellings they would call Rabat. Then, in 1090, when Roger the Norman, Count of Sicily, conquered the islands, he decreed that a cathedral would be built within the walls to make the city fit for Christians. It was erected on the ruins of a small sanctuary where the house of Publius, the first Bishop of Malta had once stood.

Mdina's Golden Age

As the years passed and Malta fell into different hands, so the city flourished. Beautiful palaces gave the city a remarkable patrician air. In 1429, when the Saracens attempted to conquer Malta, Mdina stood firm because, as legend has it, St Paul appeared riding a white charger and brandishing a flaming sword to exhort the Maltese defenders. In recognition of this bravery, Alfonso V of Aragon, into whose hands the islands had now passed, gave the city the soubriquet of *Citta Notabile* ("Noble City").

Over a century later, during the first Great Siege, the city once again acquitted itself with honours and possibly changed the whole fate of Christendom. Its cavalry garrison attacked the Turkish base camp just when victory was within enemy grasp. The Turks pulled back and the tide of war was turned.

The Silent City

As the capital, Mdina was the seat of power of the ecclesiastical, military and civil authorities. It was – and still is – the home of the oldest Maltese families. Within its boundaries are grand *palazzi*, monasteries, churches, cathedrals and museums.

For many years it has been known as the Silent City because its narrow streets are unsuitable for traffic

PRECEDING PAGES:
Mdina's triumphal
Main Gate.
LEFT: the walled
city of Mdina from
the air.
BELOW: ceiling of
Mdina's Carmelite
Church.

and its use has been purely residential. But nowadays Mdina is not so silent since residents with permits may drive in with cars, and restaurants, bars, cafés and tourist attractions have been opened in the historical buildings.

The streets were built deliberately narrow and angled so that the limited space would be used to best advantage and cooling draughts of air would be circulated. The tall cool stone buildings would cast shadows on each other and so keep them cooler still in the hot summer.

The city walls

Mdina is one of the world's finest examples of a medieval walled city that is still inhabited. The city's fortifications were completed after the Great Siege and as the Order built Valletta, so they repaired Mdina and gave it the bastion walls that ring it today.

There are three entrances to the city. The Main Gate leads from the gardens of Rabat outside the walls, the Greek Gate opens below into the moat's wide

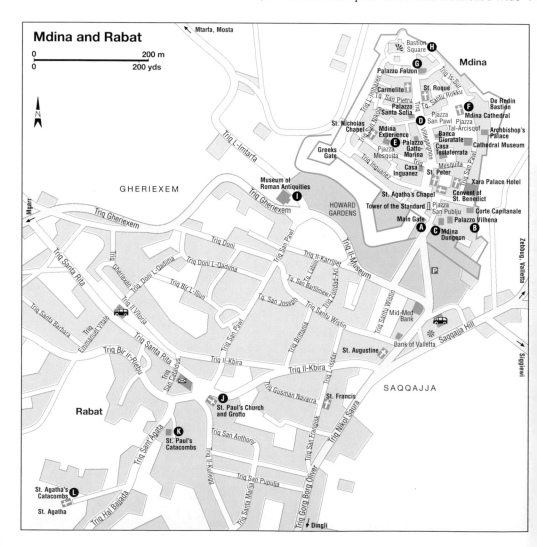

Mdina and Rabat

ditch and takes its name from the colony that lived in that area; and the "Hole in the Wall" is exactly that. It was cut into Mdina's walls when Malta's steam railway was in operation and the citizens demanded easier access to the station below on the road leading to Mtarfa.

Map on page 186

Entering the city

The **Main Gate** Ⓐ was constructed in 1724 on the instructions of Grand Master de Vilhena. A baroque triumphal archway with imposing pillars, rich carving and an ornate superstructure, it was reached by drawbridge across a dry moat. This gate replaced an earlier, simple gate still visible in the outside walls to the right. On the inside are the arms of Antonio de Inguanez, which were removed during the short occupation by French forces in 1798 and replaced by a statue of Liberty. The present arms were placed there in 1886 by order of the British governor.

Inside, to the left of the plaza (St Publius Square), is the **Tower of the Standard**, currently the police station but dating back to the 16th century. It was on the top of this tower that bonfires were lit to warn the population that corsairs had landed or that the island had been invaded.

Facing the tower is the Magisterial Palace, the **Palazzo Vilhena** Ⓑ, dating from 1733. Now it houses the worthy but dull National Museum of Natural History (open summer daily 7.45am–2pm; winter Mon–Sat 8.15am–5pm, Sun 8.15am–4.15pm; entrance fee), with its collection of stuffed animals and birds, as well as rocks and minerals.

Opposite here, the **Mdina Dungeon** Ⓒ (daily 9.30am–5pm; tel: 2145 0267; entrance fee) is anything but dull. It occupies a real dungeon and offers a grisly

BELOW:
a fine house on
St Paul's Square.

trawl through the horrors of sickness, death, torture and executions that plagued the islands in medieval times. It's best left to sensation-seeking teenagers and is definitely not for young children.

Triq Villegaignon

Imposing door knocker on the stately Casa Inguanez in Mdina.

Straight ahead and to the left is Mdina's main thoroughfare, **Triq Villegaignon** **D** (Villegaignon Street). Along its length are Malta's finest houses, preserved by the island's ancient families. Many have private art treasures that would be warmly welcomed by museums in any country. At No. 6, **Casa Inguanez** dates to 1350 and has been in the family's hands since then. The Inguanezs are the oldest of the Mdina families; the Governorship of Malta was held by a Baron Inguanez until supplanted by the Order of St John in 1530.

On the corner of Casa Inguanez is Triq Mesquita, leading to Triq Gatto Murina with the **Palazzo Gatto-Murina**. The building has grace and style and is a fine example of 14th-century workmanship. Continue along Triq Mesquita to the **Mdina Experience** **E** (Mon–Fri 10.30am–4pm; tel: 2145 4322; entrance fee), a multimedia extravaganza that combines an opportunity to learn about the history of the city with a chance to examine a Maltese patrician's house.

Return to Villegaignon Street and turn left to St Paul's Square, the spacious forecourt to **Mdina Cathedral** **F** *(see pages 192–95)*. Continuing along the main street, other buildings of note include: the **Banca Giuratale**, built by Grand Master de Vilhena to house the University; the **Palazzo Santa Sofia**, on the corner of Holy Cross Street, reputed to be the oldest house in Mdina with its ground floor dating from the 13th century; and the **Carmelite Church**, with a fine interior, built in 1659.

BELOW:
courtyard of the
Palazzo Falzon.

A few yards further along from the Carmelite Church is **Palazzo Falzon** , also known as the Norman House (viewing by appointment only; tel: 2145 4512; entrance fee). Originally built in the 14th century, and added to in the 15th, it has been beautifully restored to reflect the domestic style of Mdina's 16th-century Golden Age.

Triq Villegaignon ends at Pjazza Tas-Sur, much better known as **Bastion Square** , where there is a magnificent view of almost the whole of northern Malta. The great dome of Mosta appears a mere stone's throw away. By far the best way to take in the panorama is relaxing at a table at either of the two cafés that sit on the ramparts. The cakes at the Fontanella are excellent.

Rabat

Immediately outside Mdina's fortified walls is the suburb of Rabat, separated from the city to which it was attached in Roman times. The Arabs, who wanted to give wealthy Mdina more strategic protection, first made the distinction. They cut a ditch into the plateau to isolate the city and shaped its outer perimeter to make scaling its walls a hazardous venture. Centuries later, the Knights built the dry moat and the steep impregnable bastion walls that still ring the city. Nowadays, Rabat is the commercial centre of this rural part of the island, with banks, offices, shops, a market and inexpensive restaurants.

On the perimeter road that separates Rabat from Mdina is the most important of the Roman remains found in this area. Once the house of a wealthy citizen, today it is the **Museum of Roman Antiquities** (open daily 9am 4.30pm; tel: 2145 4125; entrance fee), also called the Roman Villa Museum (though in fact it was never a villa).

The plundering of Mdina's Carmelite Church by French troops in 1798 was the final straw for the islanders and triggered their uprising against Napoleon.

BELOW: a quiet narrow side street of the Silent City.

Its foundations were discovered in 1881 and over its mosaic flooring has been built a small museum of Roman antiquities, with a collection of the relics and statuary found nearby.

Remembering St Paul

From the Roman museum, Triq St Paul leads straight into the heart of Rabat, to **St Paul's Church**, which is reputed to be the first recognised parish church on the Maltese islands. Below it is **St Paul's Grotto ❿**, where the saint is believed to have spent some time after his shipwreck. Legend has it that its walls have miraculous properties and that scrapings from them will cure the sick if kept by their beds. For centuries visiting pilgrims have scraped pieces off the walls and yet (miraculously?) the grotto has stayed the very same size. In 1990, Pope John Paul II came here to pay his respects to St Paul.

The church itself was built in 1675 at the expense of a noble woman, Cosmana Navarra, and above its high altar is a painting of St Paul's shipwreck by Stefano Erardi. The adjoining **Church of St Publius** was built as an act of piety by Giovanni Beneguas, a Spanish nobleman who lived for some time as a hermit in the Grotto. The crypt contains a marble statue of St Paul and traces of frescoes. In the inner room are a marble statue given by Grand Master Pinto, lamps donated by Pope Paul VI and a Christian temple with an *agape* table (on which food was prepared by Christians celebrating the Last Supper).

Down to the catacombs

In Roman times it was customary for the bodies of the dead to be cremated, and burial on open ground was forbidden throughout the Roman Empire. In Malta,

There is a theory that St Paul was held captive in the grotto in Rabat that bears his name. The holes in the wall are said to have held securing rings for chains and irons.

BELOW: mazey mosaic floor left behind by the Romans at Rabat.

particularly, burial would have posed a problem, due to the lack of topsoil. Elsewhere in the empire Palestinian Jews, who did not believe in cremation, adapted to the laws by introducing burial in subterranean vaults, and this practice was adopted by Christians. Soon these catacombs would also serve as refuges in times of persecution: places where Christians could hold their religious services in comparative safety.

It is believed that underground churches and catacombs abound in Malta, some known but buried under later buildings and others, so it is said, currently in use, with tiled floors and whitewashed walls, as household cellars. Beneath the streets of Rabat alone there are said to be several miles of catacombs and in St Agatha Street two are open to visitors. Both comprise eerie, vaulted tunnels with stone-cut tombs, niches, canopies and *agape* tables.

St Paul's Catacombs ❿ (open summer 7.45am–2pm; winter Mon–Sat 8.15am–5pm, Sun 8.15am–4.15pm; tel: 2145 4562; entrance fee) were in use until the arrival of the Arabs, but were discovered only in 1894. The tunnels are very dark and unless you have a torch it can be quite disconcerting. Ask for a map before you descend into this mini labyrinth.

A few yards along the street are **St Agatha's Catacombs** ⓛ (guided tours only, hourly Mon–Fri 9am–noon and 1–4pm, Sat 9am–1pm; tel: 2145 4503; entrance fee). Local tradition holds that St Agatha was in Malta and hid in Rabat's catacombs but later returned home to Sicily only to be tortured and die a martyr rather than marry the Roman governor of Catania. The principal feature of the catacombs are its many superbly coloured frescoes, most of which are medieval, but some date to before the Arab invasion. Sadly all have been defaced. Above the catacombs is the church of **St Agatha** and a small museum. ❑

Map on page 186

St Agatha, above the catacombs in which she sought sanctuary.

BELOW: an altar and the rich frescoes in the Catacombs of St Agatha.

Map
on page
186

Valletta

MDINA CATHEDRAL

*In a city of high patrician architectural standards the
baroque cathedral dominates the skyline and
is the jewel in Mdina's crown*

The closing years of the 17th century heralded a new and exciting architectural period for the island. Self-assured and vital, it was baroque in nature, Italian and Sicilian in origin, but with a character distinctly its own. Mdina cathedral is probably the finest example of this Maltese baroque style.

The site on which the cathedral was built, is, according to hallowed tradition, the site of the house of Publius, the chief man of the island, who, as related in Acts: XXVIII, lay sick with fever and was healed by St Paul in AD 60. He later became first Bishop of Malta. St Luke also visited the island, and in the side chapel dedicated to the Blessed Sacrament is an icon of the Virgin said to have been painted by the saint.

The old cathedral

There were other churches on this site but the first documented cathedral dates back to the late 12th to the early 13th century. It is depicted in two frescoes painted by Matteo Perez d'Aleccio in the Palace of the Grand Masters in Valletta and appears to have been built in the south Italian Romanesque style, with a single nave, a high-pitched timber roof and a squat bell-tower to one side.

In January 1693 the old cathedral was destroyed by a great earthquake which

BELOW:
a richly ornamented
side chapel.

shook the whole of the central Mediterranean. Only the apse at the back of the cathedral survived, a credit to the renowned Maltese architect Lorenzo Gafa' (1639–1702) who, while rebuilding it a few years earlier in 1681, decided to strengthen its structure.

Gafa's masterpiece

Gafa' was again commissioned to design and supervise the new building which he commenced in 1697. He was then 58 and, having benefited from the work of other Maltese pioneers and with a wealth of experience in church-building behind him, he had reached full architectural maturity.

The monumental facade, with its interplay of balanced vertical and horizontal lines in the true spirit of the Roman baroque, is constructed with two superimposed orders, the Corinthian in the lower level and the Composite above. The central feature projects a little forward and carries a fine square-headed portal surmounted by a broken pediment containing the crest of the head of the diocese and the Maltese national emblem in heraldic symbols of red and white. It is flanked by the coats of arms of Grand Master Ramón Perellos (1697–1720) and of Bishop Cocco Palmieri (1684–1713). The slightly recessed side bays carry two towers with richly ornamented spires containing six bells, the oldest of which was cast in Venice in 1370.

The plan of the cathedral is in the form of a Latin cross, with a central vaulted nave and two aisles with small side chapels. The transepts, chancel and choir are of generous proportions, while the two small chapels on each side of the chancel are small gems of architecture. The floor is a superb patchwork of inlaid multicoloured marble slabs, some macabre, some gaudy. They commemorate lead-

The two cannons outside the cathedral date from the early 17th century and were once taken to London for display at the Artillery Museum in Woolwich. In 1888 they were returned with many others, at the request of Malta's governor.

BELOW: the patron saints of the cathedral, Peter and Paul.

ing Maltese ecclesiastics, bishops, prelates, monsignors and canons, as well as prominent laymen, most of whom belonged to Maltese nobility and aristocratic families.

For decoration, the cathedral has a frescoed nave ceiling dating from 1794 and featuring scenes from the life of St Paul, to whom the cathedral is dedicated. It was executed by the two Sicilian brothers, Antonio and Vincenzo Manno. The interior of the dome was painted as recently as 1955.

Mattia Preti (1613–99), who is responsible for much of Malta's glory, is the author of the altar-piece of the choir, the apse above and the two lateral panels, all depicting various episodes in the life of Malta's patron, St Paul. The royal arms of Spain take pride of place in the centre of the arch surrounding the apse and recall the munificence of Holy Roman Emperor Charles V, who donated the islands to the Order of St John in 1530.

Two interesting relics which survived the earthquake that demolished the earlier cathedral are the marble baptismal font (1495) and the Irish oak sacristy door – a marvel of wood carving (1520). Both bear the national emblem – a shield divided vertically in the traditional red and white Maltese colours.

Gafa's architectural masterpiece, however, and the culmination of all his artistic work, is undoubtedly the cathedral's magnificent baroque dome. Bold and dynamic, more sculptural than architectural, seen from a distance it rises high above the hill of Mdina and dominates the surrounding countryside for miles. The striking profile of the old city's skyline is one of the island's most famous silhouettes.

The Cathedral Museum

Not to be overlooked is the fine **Cathedral Museum** housed in the former seminary (Mon–Sat 9am–1pm and 1.30pm–4.30pm; tel: 2145 4697; entrance fee). In addition to the usual ecclesiastical objects, it holds Italian and Maltese paintings, several fine engravings (some by Goya), and a comprehensive collection of woodcuts by Albrecht Dürer. Other highlights are Byzantine enamel miniatures for celebrating Mass on ship and magnificent 11th-century illuminated hymn books. ❏

RIGHT: the facade of Lorenzo Gafa's cathedral, rated as the finest domed church on the islands.

Map
on pages
210–11

Valletta

PRECEDING PAGES:
Mosta Dome is
an unmistakable
landmark.
BELOW: the
geometric
patterned interior
of the dome.

CENTRAL MALTA

An extraordinary dome, an outstanding palazzo, *fine churches, gardens and handicrafts await visitors touring the less visited central part of the island*

The best view of Malta, and particularly of the central part of the island, is from a helicopter. If you imagine it as a dartboard then the bull's-eye is the great rotund dome of the church of **Mosta ❶**. If you cannot get up this high then a good substitute is the bastion walls of Mdina, from where the immensity of this great building can also be appreciated.

The miracle of Mosta

Mosta Dome or, to give its full title, the Church of Santa Marija Assunta, can be seen from almost any vantage point in Malta. The islanders take great pride in its impressive scale. At 40 metres (130 ft) in diameter it "out-domes" St Paul's Cathedral in London by 6.7 metres (22 ft), and is reputed to be either the third or the fourth largest unsupported dome in the world, surpassed only by St Peter's in Rome, St Sophia in Istanbul and (though Mosta Dome officials are not much amused by this recent addition) the church at Xewkija in Gozo. Controversy still rages on this issue and unless you are prepared for an argument it's best not to get too engaged in such local disputes.

Whatever its size ranking, the Mosta Dome is a remarkable church with an elegant interior, built to the design of Giorgio Grognet de Vasse with almost total voluntary labour drawn from the parish. The first stone was laid in 1833, and it took 27 years to complete the main structure. Its generous size came about because it was erected around a church already existing on the site. The original one had become too small for the growing parish but could not be demolished until an alternative was available.

A true miracle occurred in the church during World War II, when a bomb pierced the dome while the church was crammed full of parishioners. It grazed the interior wall, skidded across the floor but did not explode. A replica is now on display in the church.

Naxxar

Just north of Mosta, and now virtually connected to it by continuous strip development, lies the town of **Naxxar ❷** (pronounced *Nash-shar*). Like Mosta, it has a parish church of prodigious size: Our Lady of Victory was completed in 1616 by Tomasso Dingli, a prolific boy-wonder architect who distinguished himself with several notable churches in this part of the island. It is certainly worth a visit, if you can negotiate the traffic screaming all around it.

Opposite here is the **Palazzo Parisio** (guided tours only, Tues, Thur and Fri 9am–1pm on the hour; entrance fee). This is named after the same Parisio family whose principal house in Valletta was commandeered by Napoleon. The Naxxar house was

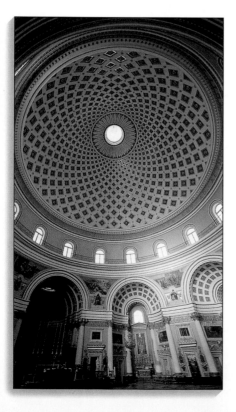

rebuilt to its present state in 1898 for the banker and philanthropist, Giuseppe Scicluna, though he only enjoyed it for a year before his death in 1907.

The Palazzo Parisio is an outstanding example of a Maltese stately home, and the finest of its kind open to the public. It is said that its construction and furnishings set new standards for the island, and certainly its carved Lombardy furniture, brilliant stucco friezes, inspired painted ceilings and its Carrara marbles are remarkable. The great marble coping stone over the balustrade is the longest single piece on the island. It is said to have been transported by countless mules, but if you want the full story you will have to ask your guide.

Naxxar is also renowned as the venue for Malta's International Fair, a large trade gathering which takes place each July, in grounds immediately behind the Palazzo Parisio.

A replica of the famous unexploded bomb in Mosta Dome.

The Three Villages

From Naxxar take the road to **Balzan**, which, along with **Lija** and **Attard**, make up the "Three Villages". Despite the promising olde-worlde title, don't expect to see villages in the conventional sense. Indeed, you will be very hard pressed even to distinguish one community from the other. In recent years the three have grown into one virtually amorphous mass with their boundary lines known only to the residents.

Of more concern to those who live here is the fact that for centuries the Three Villages has been a very desirable address – where property prices are constantly high and where there are superb patrician houses that date back to the 17th century. Many wealthy aristocratic families came to live here as peace returned to the islands after the Great Siege and as Valletta became overcrowded.

BELOW: ballroom of the Palazzo Parisio in Naxxar.

PARISH CHURCHES

The central region of the island holds some of Malta's largest parish churches. The first of these, built to accommodate expanding parish boundaries with their fast-growing populations, were St George at Qormi and St Philip, Zebbug. They were erected to show village wealth as much as the visible face of the church. But it is Attard's parish church, dedicated to Santa Marija, that heralds the splendours to come. It was designed by Tommaso Dingli (1591–1666) in 1613 when he was just 22 years old.

This young man went on to become one of the island's most prolific architects and is probably best known for his work on the parish church of Santa Marija in Birkirkara, a triumph of indigenous design and sculpture, and a fine example of a Maltese Renaissance church. Later, he went on to design the parish churches of Naxxar, Gharghur, Gudja and Zabbar. Not that they all remain, like Attard, as he envisaged them. As the parishes grew, alterations were made since many proved too small for their growing congregations. In fact, Dingli's Birkirkara church was never completed because even then they knew it would be too small. And Our Lady of Graces in Zabbar was not only expanded but also given a new dome as the original was damaged by French cannon fire.

BELOW:
a peaceful corner of San Anton Palace Gardens in Attard.

Attard

As if to underscore the exclusivity of the Three Villages, the President's official residence is in Attard, at San Anton Palace. This elegant and stately house was the country residence of the Grand Masters from the early 17th century. Grand Master Antoine de Paule (1623–36) was the first to install himself and indulged in the decadent type of lifestyle that was to become the Knights' hallmark after the first Great Siege. Over 600 guests could be entertained at one time; this lavish living incurred the displeasure of the Inquisition. In the British colonial era it was used as the governor's residence; it has been occupied by the Maltese president since 1974. The palace is closed to visitors but the **San Anton Palace Gardens ❸** are open daily dawn until dusk (free entrance).

The gardens are a favourite of expats and older visitors and feature a surprising variety of sub-tropical plants. There is some nice statuary and aviaries to add interest but the gardens' famous camel departed some while ago, along with other residents of its so-called zoo. Disappointingly, there are no refreshment facilities inside the gardens, but by the gate furthest away from the palace you will find a pub, and perhaps an ice-cream van.

In the centre of Attard is the Renaissance jewel of the church of **Santa Marija** *(see box on page 199)*, designed by Tomasso Dingli. The detailed carvings in the stonework repay a close look, and it is interesting to note that since the temple-like facade could not support a tower, in 1718 a bell-tower was placed above the northern transept.

There is little else of sightseeing interest in the Three Villages, though if you are in the area on 6 August, Lija is renowned for the celebrations and superb fireworks at its *festa*.

Birkirkara

From Balzan it is a five-minute detour to the densely populated town of Birkirkara ❹, (road signs abbreviate this to B'kara). It's worth the trip, however, to see the church of **St Helena**, an outstanding example of the Maltese baroque style. The church was designed by Domenicho Cachia (1710–90) and replaced Tomasso Dingli's earlier church. The Knights so liked Cachia's powerfully proportioned design and his rich interior of frescoes, paintings and carvings that they awarded him the commission for Valletta's prestigious Auberge de Castile – a job that he performed magnificently.

Two winding steps lead up to the platform on which the church stands. Aside from the twin-towered facade, the aisle screens and the entablature are striking features of a building which has been described as the finest parish church on the island.

Ta' Qali Crafts Village

Just outside Attard there are signs to **Ta' Qali Crafts Village** ❺ (Mon–Fri 8am–4pm). Built on the old World War II airfield, it's not the most attractive of places, with many of the huts and workrooms clearly still dating from this era. But if you want to see people making a wide variety of Maltese crafts then this is probably still the best place to come. Visit early or late to avoid the coach tours.

Pottery, lace-making, weaving, silver-working and glass-blowing are just some of the indigenous skills on show. Mdina glass is the best known and largest business of its kind, and it is fascinating to watch the glass-blowing and forming processes. Prices here are lower than in city shops.   ❑

Map on pages 210–11

BELOW: glass blowers at Ta' Qali Crafts Village.

SLIEMA AND ST JULIAN'S

The construction sites have more sand than the beaches and the thunder of traffic drowns the lap of the waves, but at least there are great views across to Valletta. Welcome to touristic Malta

Map on page 206

Valletta

There has been a shift in the centre of tourism in the last decade or so, away from the long-established resort areas of Sliema and St Julian's, to the new purpose-built resorts of Bugibba and Qawra in the north. Nonetheless, this large holiday conurbation, which runs from Msida, just outside Valletta, to St George's Bay, is still the island's most popular hotspot.

The shaping of Sliema

Sliema is not only Malta's major holiday area, it is also the main residential area. This is where prestigious apartments sell to the upwardly mobile at what by local standards are exorbitant prices. It is also where Malta's wealthy middle classes reside, where children can walk safely to and from friends' houses in the evenings, and where there are many fashionable boutiques in which to shop. There may be a plethora of hotels, bars and restaurants in the area, but the core remains residential.

Sliema was originally planned as a small resort for the residents of Valletta. With its pleasant coastline indented with small coves and its smooth white rocky beaches facing the clear blue sea, this was where they would come in summer to swim and take the fresh air. There used to be a little fishing community, some smallholdings and a military presence in Fort Tigne, which was built in 1761 by Grand Master Pinto.

Gradually, as the wealth and size of the population within the city of Valletta increased, so Sliema began to take shape. Families moved out of the city, villas and refined houses were built, land was developed, and it became an elegant place to live.

By the early 20th century fine domestic architecture in cream limestone gave Sliema a subtle grace and elegance of its own. While Valletta remained the capital and business centre, those families who had not already decamped to the desirable residences of the Three Villages, now moved to Sliema. A Sliema address now implied a certain social status.

Sliema today

Although much remains the same as it was, there have been significant changes, designed to accommodate the new wealthy Maltese, as well as the tourist. Today's generations have begun to settle in the villages ouside Sliema. Property prices in central Sliema are the highest on the islands and the young cannot afford the new apartments.

But, for every one ready to move out, there are two or more ready to move in: people for whom the status of being able to say they live in Sliema counts. The people on the south of the islands refer to Sliema people as *tal pepe*, "the snobs".

PRECEDING PAGES: Marsamxett Harbour and Manoel Island. **LEFT:** waterfront at St Julian's. **BELOW:** small craft in Spinola Bay.

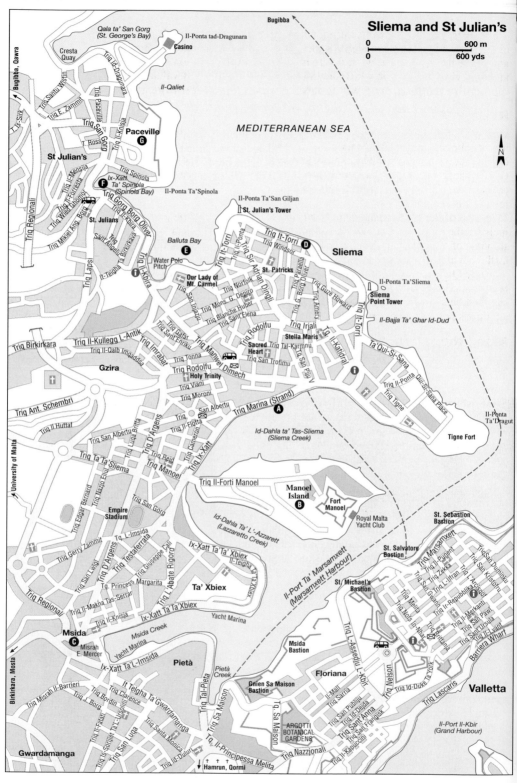

Sliema and St Julian's

MEDITERRANEAN SEA

Sliema is, as everyone will confirm, not the place that it once was. In a matter of a few recent years the wonderful seafront houses that created an elegant vista and made the promenade what it was have gone. In the creation of such an idealised vista, the land on which they stood became increasingly valuable and coveted. In their place are towering faceless blocks of flats and large hotels.

Map on page 206

Holiday Sliema

Of course, none of this is evident to first-time visitors. The main focus of activity is on the **Strand** Ⓐ (Triq Marina), where a ferry connects to Valletta and boat cruises set off around Grand Harbour, and head further afield to Comino and Gozo. The front buzzes with cafés serving snacks like *pastizzi* or *timpana*, cream cakes, ice cream, cold drinks and cappuccino. There are some good restaurants along here, too.

The tip of the Sliema peninsula is known as **Tigne**, a quiet quarter which includes the Crowne Plaza and Fortina hotels. Opposite the Fortina is the classic view of Valletta with the Carmelite Church rising like London's St Paul's Cathedral at the centre of an unforgettable cityscape.

Along **Qui-si-Sana** waterfront (its name means the healthy place) there are beach concessions with pools, bars and changing facilities. Most of **Fort Tigne** has long been government housing, but it is currently being converted into an ambitious holiday complex.

Most visitors to St Julian's and Sliema come to Malta for guaranteed sunshine.

Along the seafront

Opposite the ferries a roadbridge connects the Strand to **Manoel Island** Ⓑ. The Knights' quarantine hospital used to be located here and Fort Manoel was

BELOW: the view of St Julian's Bay from the fashionable restaurants by the waterfront.

built in 1730 to protect the harbour. During World War I the Knights' hospital was revived to care for wounded soldiers, earning Malta the nickname of "Nurse of the Mediterranean".

Today the island is somewhat forlorn, home to shipyards used for yacht repairs and the Royal Malta Yacht Club. But, together with Tigne, it is soon to be transformed into an upmarket tourist complex and extended yacht marina.

The road continues around Lazzaretto Creek to Ta' Xbiex (pronounced *tash-b-yesh*), an exclusive residential quarter where many embassies are based, and onto **Msida ●**. This is the biggest marina in Malta, capable of holding over 1,000 vessels at a time. Permanently moored is the *Black Pearl*, once a star in the film *Popeye (see page 219)*, now a floating restaurant.

Along The Front

From the Strand **Triq It-Torri ●** cuts a congested swathe through to the other side of the Sliema peninsula. At the top of the hill it meets **Bisazza Street**. Together these are Sliema's two major shopping streets.

Along **The Front** – as locals refer to this stretch of Tower Road – there are more hotels, restaurants and (public) rocky beaches where both Sliema folk and tourists swim. In the evening it becomes a busy promenade. Generations of Maltese have enjoyed the *passegiata* here, walking, talking and socialising. This is where boy meets girl. There are ice-cream sellers, soft-drinks kiosks and men with baskets of roasted almonds, hazelnuts and peanuts.

The road continues along the seafront to **Balluta Bay ●**, where there is a pocket handkerchief-sized sandy beach and some very well-tended gardens. Out of season or late in the day you may well be able to stake a claim on the

BELOW:
sunbathing on the rocks is a popular choice at Sliema.

sand. If not, then you will surely find some room along the flat rocks, which make excellent sunbathing platforms at the bottom of the gardens. Balluta Bay is also home to one of the island's best water-polo teams, Neptunes, whose club and poolside lido are on the front.

Map
on page
206

St Julian's

Balluta Bay runs almost seamlessly into St Julian's, and at **Spinola Bay** ❻ (Ix-Xatt ta' Spinola) the road reaches its busiest junction, with constant traffic congestion and aggravation. This is a great pity as this was once a simple corner where fishermen would land their catches in the evening – some still do.

This is certainly one of Malta's most picturesque corners and features a clutch of fine restaurants which enjoy a romantic setting. Right on the front, the San Giuliano and the Raffael occupy the former boathouses of the **Spinola Palace**. The palace, built in 1688, is still there, set in lovely grounds on the hill directly above; it too is now occupied by a luxury restaurant.

At this point you are entering the heart of the package-holiday and nightlife part of St Julian's, with bars and restaurants coming thick and fast. This area comes alive only at night, when the epicentre of the action is the quarter known as **Paceville** ❼. During the summer, impatient traffic jams build at 2 or 3am, while a surging mass of bodies pack the streets, overflowing from the high-decibel bars and clubs that are the lifeblood of this tawdry area.

Uncomfortably close to Paceville, but tucked quietly away on a private promontory, is the Westin Dragonara Hotel, with its beach club (open to day visitors) and casino; and within walking distance the Hilton complex, with its "high tower" and yacht marina. ❑

There are many island excursions to choose from.

BELOW: one of the most enduring watering holes in St Julian's.

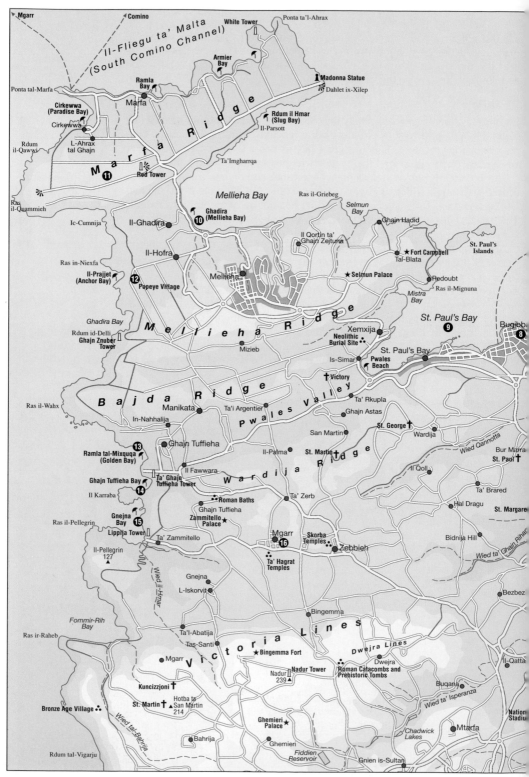

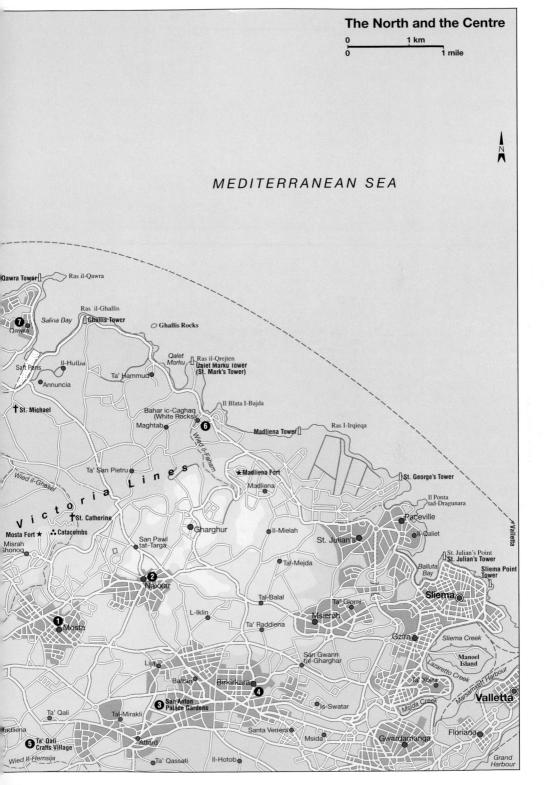

MEDITERRANEAN SEA

Qawra Tower Ras il-Qawra

Ras il-Ghallis
7 Salina Bay Ghallis Tower
Qawra Ghallis Rocks

Salt Pans Il-Hulba Qalet Ras il-Qrejten
Marku Qalet Marku Tower
(St. Mark's Tower)
Annuncia Ta' Hammud

† St. Michael Il Blata l-Bajda
Bahar ic-Caghaq
(White Rocks)
Maghtab **6** Madliena Tower Ras l-Irqieqa

Ta' San Pietru ★ Madliena Fort ⌐ St. George's Tower
Madliena

V Wied il-Ghasel † St. Catherine Il Ponta
i San Pawl Il-Mielah tad-Dragunara
c Mosta Fort ★ .: Catacombs tat-Targa Gharghur Paceville
t St. Julian's Il-Qaliet
Misrah **o**
Ghonoq **r** Tal-Mejda St. Julian's Point
i St. Julian's Tower
a Sliema Point
2 Tal-Balal Balluta Tower
L Naxxar Bay
i L-Iklin Ta' Giorni Sliema
n Ta' Raddiena Msierah
1 Mosta **e** Gzira
s Tal-Mirakli Sliema Creek

Lija San Gwann Manoel
Balzan tal-Gharghar Island
Birkirkara **4** Ta' Xbiex Lazaretto Creek
3 San Anton
Palace Gardens Is-Swatar Msida Creek Valletta
Ta' Qali
Madliena Santa Venera Floriana
5 Ta' Qali Msida
Crafts Village Attard Gwardamanga
Wied ll-Hemsija Ta' Qassati Il-Hotob Grand
Harbour

N

→ Valletta

THE NORTH

With its crowded golden sands, tourist complexes and entertainments, the north is primarily for holidaymakers. But there are quieter parts too, where you can escape from the crowds

Map on pages 210–11

Valletta

The road sweeps north from Sliema out of the crowded suburbs heading for the beaches and coastline of the north. But a beach to a Maltese sunseeker doesn't necessarily mean a nice bit of sand, or even a foreshore of pebbles or stones. It can mean any stretch by the sea that gives access to the water and if it comprises great slabs and boulders of rock just a metre or two from a busy main road, then this is "beach" too.

It is this coast road, from Sliema to Qawra, that the Maltese find particularly appealing; at weekends they will drive from miles away to park their cars in one long ribbon from end to end. Then they will stay until late at night, picnicking and barbecuing, and the return journey south can be excruciatingly slow.

Family fun

The road meets the coastline again at Bahar-ic-Caghaq. As this is a bit of a tongue-twister for most visitors (it is pronounced *bah-har i tchark*), it is better known as **White Rocks ❻**. Sharing a site here are three family attractions: the **Splash and Fun Water Park** (open daily summer only; entrance fee); **Mediterraneo Marine World** (open daily 1 Apr–30 Sept; entrance fee) and a dinosaur-themed playground (open daily; free entrance). Splash and Fun claims the largest seawater swimming pool on the island, and its water slides are always popular. It's best to come early in the day, however, as it is only a small facility and soon gets very busy.

Mediterraneo Marine World is also a small-scale park, although it does manage to put on reasonably entertaining dolphin and seal displays. The dolphins hail from the Black Sea and were rescued from a bankrupt water park in the former Soviet Union. Whether they are truly happy here is anyone's guess, but they seem to be enjoying themselves and are certainly in a better position than they were.

Alongside the complex are the white rocks that give this area its name. Add a bright red and yellow parasol to the deep blue Mediterranean background and it's not to hard to see why so many Maltese families like this stretch of coast.

Qawra and Bugibba

After another 3 km (2 miles) is **Salina Bay**, named after the local salt pans that have been worked since the days of the Knights. You will probably smell them before you see them. The bay marks the start of the largest purpose-built tourist complex on Malta, which was completed in just under 10 years.

Straight across the bay is **Qawra ❼** (pronounced *Ow-rah*) with its impressive Sol Suncrest Hotel and lidos facing onto Salina Bay. This is the quieter, slightly

PRECEDING PAGES: sailing around St Paul's Island. **LEFT:** Sunday crowds at Golden Bay. **BELOW:** the rocky shore of peaceful Ghajn Hadid.

more upmarket part of the development. The road continues around the peninsula, marked at its end by Qawra Tower before it turns into St Paul's Bay. Once this stretch of coast was fortified by the Knights, but there is nothing of historical or cultural interest here today.

Bugibba  is the main town of the area. To impartial viewers it may look like a faceless sprawl of tacky, ugly concrete, but to many thousands each year this is holiday heaven. There is no beach (in the conventional sense of the word) but it's a popular resort with both overseas visitors and the Maltese themselves, and at weekends the latter pack out the local restaurants and the Oracle Casino.

St Paul's Bay

The only attractive part of Bugibba is its jetty, where pleasure boats make an enjoyable trip around **St Paul's Bay** ❾. Out here are **St Paul's Islands**, the site of the Apostle's legendary shipwreck in AD 60. It has been remarked that if this happened today St Paul might be tempted to dive back in the water and try his luck elsewhere. However, the settlement of St Paul's Bay is no Bugibba or Qawra. This is a real community where Maltese live and work and have fished the waters for centuries. Nonetheless it has suffered major overbuilding.

At the head of the bay is Pwales Beach, though like Bugibba and Qawra, St Paul's Bay is also sandless. Continue around the coast road past **Xemxija**. On the hillside there is a Neolithic burial site (not signposted), where the dead were buried in womb-like tombs cut into the rock, suggesting a return to Mother Earth.

The road snakes upwards and just before Mellieha is a turn to the **Selmun Palace**. The Knights would no doubt approve that this handsome 17th-century

At Burmarrad, 2 km (1½ miles) south of Bugibba, is the Church of San Pawl Milqi, which means "St Paul welcomed". The apostle is believed to have spent his first few days on Malta here. The present church dates from the 17th century and is now a museum (open daily).

BELOW: seafront lido at Bugibba.

fortress is now home to a French restaurant, while at the rear is a luxury hotel complex. Nearby **Ghajn Hadid Bay** offers a little-known small sandy beach.

Map on pages 210–11

Mellieha Bay

Superbly positioned on a high ridge with its parish church of Our Lady of Victory on a spur, **Mellieha** has some good restaurants and shops. These cater to both the residents of the village and the luxury estates below, and also to visitors, many of whom self-cater in nearby apartments.

Down the long winding hill below the village is the longest sandy beach on Malta. Its proper name is Ghadira (pronounced *aa-dee-ra*) but to visitors it is better known as **Mellieha Bay ❿**. Unsurprisingly, the beach is extremely popular and its facilities improve each year. There are cafés, beach establishments and all the facilities for renting windsurfing equipment and canoes, as well as waterskiing and parascending. It is very crowded at weekends, when families arrive early to select the best positions for their parasols.

All the fun of the seaside at Bugibba.

Marfa Ridge

The best vantage point from which to survey Mellieha and its beach is from **Marfa Ridge ⓫**, the tall ridge of land that on the map looks like a fishtail on the end of Malta. To get there, continue on the main road past the beach and as you ascend the steep hill, take a sharp turn left. A short way along this track is the **Red Tower** (occasionally open to the public), built by the Knights in 1649. It takes its name from its distinctive red paint, and has been recently renovated. Immediately below, you can look down to the small lakes of the **Ghadira Bird Reserve** (Jan and Dec Sat and Sun 9.30am–3.30pm; Feb–May, Oct and Nov Sat

BELOW: St Paul's Bay is also home to the yachting crowd.

and Sun 10.30am–4.30pm; closed June–Sep; guided tours only), one of the very few places on the islands where birds can rest in safety. If you drive or walk a little further on past the tower, you will be greeted with marvellous views over to the Gozo Channel. It's odds-on that you will see the ferry steaming between Mgarr on Gozo and Cirkewwa on Malta.

The Marfa Ridge has a wild beauty with rocky outcrops, fertile fields, plantations of acacia and the remains of many a *girna* – a small round stone hut, only slightly higher than a man, dating back to the Bronze Age. Don't confuse these with recent stone shelters on the ridge that are used by modern-day hunters.

Marfa Ridge beaches

At the northern end of the ridge are some pleasant beaches. The small, attractive **Ramla Bay** is dominated by its large hotel, well known for its beach and sports facilities (the hotel is open to non-residents using the restaurant or café). Alongside is a small, free stretch of sand suitable for family picnics.

Paradise Bay, 2 km (1 mile) west at **Cirkewwa** near the Gozo ferry terminal, is another attractive option, with a pleasant beach reached by narrow steps. It is usually sandy, but in some years there is a lot of shingle. Paradise Bay is very popular with Maltese villagers for their coach outings, and can become particularly crowded at weekends. Kiosks serve simple refreshments.

Armier and **Little Armier** are small, flat, unsophisticated sandy bays facing towards Comino – not "smart" beaches but nonetheless popular. They have inexpensive beach cafés and simple facilities, and are good for children.

Slug Bay (Rdum il Hmar), further along the rough road leading to the eastern tip of Marfa Ridge, faces Mellieha rather than the Gozo channel. To clamber

TIP

The male population of Malta indulges in the controversial habit of shooting migrating birds. Marfa Ridge is one of the places that they do this. Whatever your feelings on the issue, do not confront hunters directly.

BELOW: a great view of Mellieha and its bay, from Marfa Ridge.

down to it, there is a winding footpath whose small entrance is concealed in a car park and picnic area among the acacia and eucalyptus trees. Try to park your car where it can be seen from the main track, no matter how tempting it is to leave the car in the cool shade of the trees on a hot day: cars are often broken into here.

The shore is starkly pretty, with room for just a few people on the patch of sand in its tiny bay. Many prefer to swim off the flat rocks around the entrance, although most are sharp and can make getting out of the water difficult. It is a remote and private place and, because of its ruggedness, never crowded.

Popeye Village

By Mellieha Beach on the approach road down from Mellieha, there is a roundabout with a sign to Anchor Bay and **Popeye Village ⑫** (Il Prajet; open daily; entrance fee). The former name comes from days long ago when a number of anchors were to be found on the beach in this pretty little sandy bay.

The latter is much more recent. In 1980, *Popeye* the movie (with Robin Williams in the starring role) was filmed in Malta, and Anchor Bay was chosen as the location for the rustic Newfoundland-style fishing village of Sweethaven.

Nineteen wooden structures made up the original fictitious village, though two burnt down in 1982, and all the special wood shingles used in the construction of the roof tops were specially imported from Canada. The rest of the wood was shipped from Holland and the village took more than seven months to complete, using a 165-man construction crew, armed with some 8 tons of nails and more than 9,000 litres (2,000 gallons) of paint. It is said that the village was only built to last a few months, but it has stood the test of time much

Map on pages 210–11

Scuba diving is a popular sport at Golden Bay.

BELOW: there are exhilirating views of both sides of the island from Marfa Ridge.

An excellent way to get off the beaten track and explore the headlands surrounding Ghajn Tuffieha and Golden Bay is to go horse riding. You can arrange this at the Golden Bay horse riding stables, tel: 2157 3360.

BELOW: Popeye Village, an unlikely but perennially popular attraction.

better than the film (which was a turkey) and is now one of the island's most popular attractions. That said, there's little to do here except stare at, and take photographs of, the film-set buildings. Nonetheless, it is an intriguing and picturesque sight.

Ghajn Tuffieha Bay and Golden Bay

A road cuts through the Pwales Valley from St Paul's Bay to two of Malta's most popular sandy beaches, Ghajn Tuffieha Bay and Golden Bay. Both are in a dramatic setting, each surrounded by flat-topped, golden-and-brown-coloured rocky cliffs with excellent stretches of fine sand.

Golden Bay ⑬ is the more accessible of the two, with an attendant-run car park close to the sand and a smart new café-restaurant with a viewing platform looking down onto the beach. The Golden Sands Hotel is currently undergoing a total redevelopment, but there are other small beach facilities with plenty of refreshments, as well as the opportunity to rent a windsurfing board, pedalo or canoe. Don't swim if the red flag is flying as there are undercurrents here.

Ghajn Tuffieha Bay ⑭ (pronounced *eye-n-toof-ee-ha*), whose strange-sounding name has the intriguing translation of "the apple spring", is much the prettier of the two beaches. There is no building in its backdrop, just a hillside planted with struggling tamarisk and acacia where for centuries goatherds have brought their animals to pasture. It is a delightful place, accessible only by a long staggered staircase down the side of the steep hill to the sands. The climb inevitably means that the beach gets less crowded than its neighbour.

At the far end of Ghajn Tuffieha beach is a high and treacherous narrow clay ridge; below it, on the far side, is a tempting, smooth, cream-coloured rock

promontory. On the other side of this ridge is another popular beach, **Gnejna Bay ⓯** (pronounced *j-nay-na*). The sand here is mixed with shingle and to accommodate all tastes there is even a short stretch of smooth white rock for sunbathing on. On the left of the bay are boathouses cut into the rock. Refreshments are provided by mobile kiosks or vans.

Map on pages 210–11

Mgarr

If you don't fancy getting to Gnejna Bay by scrambling over the rocks from Ghajn Tuffieha, then you will have to go the long way round via the village of **Mgarr ⓰**. As in so many of Malta's villages, the village square is dominated by a handsome, oversized church. Dedicated to the Virgin Mary, it has a dome which is curious not only for its silver patina but its oval shape *(see margin note, right)*. Mgarr is known for its two village-square restaurants, drawing custom from near and far to join its *fenkata* (rabbit-feast) evenings.

In and around Mgarr are some of Malta's oldest temple remains. Just 200 metres/yards off the square, heading back towards Valletta, is **Ta' Hagrat** temple. It's easy to miss as it is only signposted in one direction, and when you do find it you will wonder whether it was worth the effort. To the untrained eye this small tatty clump of stones is indecipherable and the site it occupies has been fenced off (keys available from the Archaeological Museum in Valletta).

A couple of kilometres east at Zebbieh are the **Skorba** temples, the site of the earliest known settlement in Malta, perhaps going back as far as 3,800 BC. There are signs of two temples and a number of houses, indicating that a flourishing fishing and farming settlement must have been here at some time. However, as at Ta' Hagrat, the site is unfathomable to the average visitor. ❑

Mgarr's parish church is nicknamed the Egg Church because the roof was paid for by locals whose main source of income was eggs. Its dome was designed as a tribute to this versatile foodstuff.

BELOW: walking to Gnejna Bay from Ghajn Tuffieha.

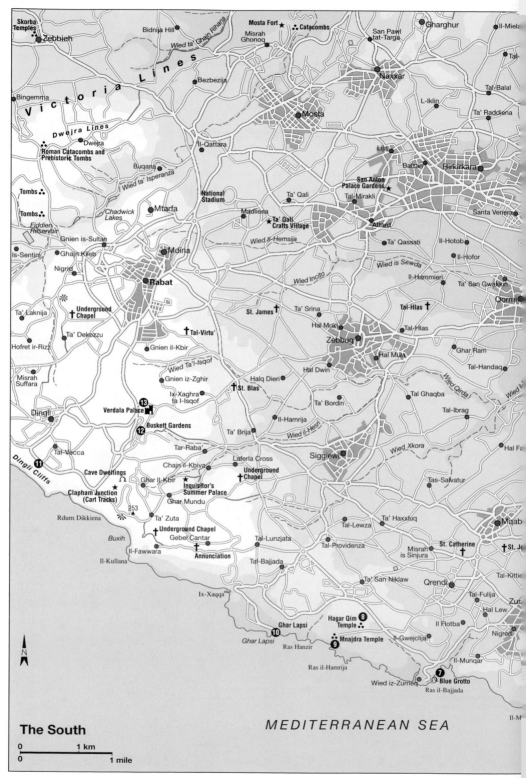

Skorba Temples
Zebbieh
Bidnija Hill
Wied ta' Ghajn Rihana
Mosta Fort
Catacombs
Misrah Ghonoq
San Pawl tat-Targa
Gharghur
Il-Miela

Victoria Lines
Bezbezija
Naxxar
Tal-

Bingemma
Mosta
Tal-Balal

Dwejra Lines
Il-Qattara
Lija
Ta' Raddiena

Roman Catacombs and Prehistoric Tombs
Dwejra
Buqana
Wied ta' Isperanza
Balzan
Birkirkara

Tombs
National Stadium
Ta' Qali
San Anton Palace Gardens
Tal-Mirakli
Santa Venera

Tombs
Chadwick Lakes
Mtarfa
Madliena
Ta' Qali Crafts Village
Attard
Ta' Qassati
Il-Hotob

Fiddien Reservoir
Gnien is-Sultan
Wied Il-Hemsija
Ta' Qassati
Il-Hofor

Is-Sentin
Ghajn Kileb
Mdina
Wied is Sewda
Il-Hammieri
Ta' San Gwakkin

Nigriet
Rabat
Wied Incito
Il-Hammieri
Qormi

Ta' Laknija
Underground Chapel
St. James
Ta' Srina
Tal-Hlas
Ghar Ram

Ta' Dekozzu
Tal-Virtu'
Hal Muxi
Tal-Hlas
Tal-Handaq

Hofret ir-Rizz
Gnien il-Kbir
Zebbug
Hal Mula

Misrah Suffara
Wied Ta'l-Isqof
Gnien iz-Zghir
Halq Dieri
Hal Dwin
Tal Ghaqba

Dingli
Ix-Xaghra ta l-Isqof
St. Blas
Ta' Bordin
Tal-Ibrag

13
Verdala Palace
Il-Hamrija
Wied Qirda

12
Buskett Gardens
Ta' Brija
Wied il-Hesri
Wied Xkora
Hal

11
Dingli Cliffs
Tal-Vecca
Tar-Raba'
Laferla Cross
Siggiewi
Tas-Salvatur

Cave Dwellings
Chajn il-Kbiva
Underground Chapel
Mqab

Clapham Junction (Cart Tracks)
Ghar Il-Kbir
Inquisitor's Summer Palace
Ghar Mundu

253
Rdum Dikkiena
Ta' Zuta
Underground Chapel
Gebel Cantar
Tal-Lunzjata
Tal-Lewza
Ta' Haxxluq
Misrah is Sinjura
St. Catherine
St. Jo

Buxih
Il-Fawwara
Annunciation
Tal-Bajjada
Tal-Providenza
Tal-Kittie

Il-Kullana
Ta' San Niklaw
Qrendi
Tal-Fulija

Ix-Xaqqa
Hal Lew

Hagar Qim Temple
8
Il Flotba
Nigred

Ghar Lapsi
10
9
Mnajdra Temple
Ghar Lapsi
Il-Gwejclija
Il-Munqar

Ghar Lapsi
Ras Hanzir
Ras il-Hamrija
Wied iz-Zurrieq
7
Blue Grotto
Ras il-Bajjada
Il-M

N

The South

0 — 1 km
0 — 1 mile

MEDITERRANEAN SEA

Il-M

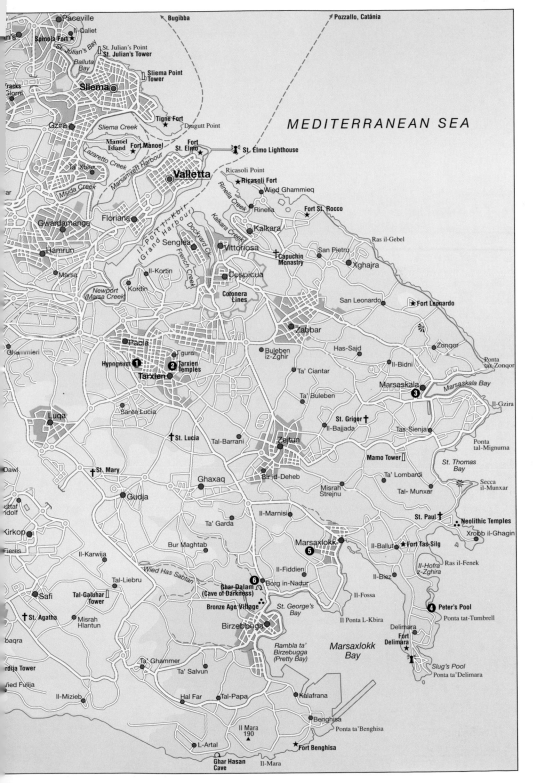

MEDITERRANEAN SEA

THE SOUTH

Some of the world's oldest temples, Malta's most picturesque fishing village, dramatic sea caves, towering cliffs and shady woods are the highlights of the south of the island

Map on pages 222–23

The most fascinating of Malta's many temples is actually the closest to Valletta – the **Hypogeum ❶** at Paola. It is also known as the Hal-Saflieni Hypogeum after the name of the immediate locality, Hypogeum means underground chamber and its subterranean nature sets it apart from the archipelago's other temples. In fact it was only discovered accidentally in 1902, when workmen were preparing house foundations.

The Hypogeum was dug out of the rock in around 3000 BC by people using flint and hard rocks. They created a network of corridors and deep chambers on three levels. At the deepest level there appears to be a secret granary, which is reached by seven uneven angled steps that turn sharply to the right and have a sheer drop into a narrow chamber on their left. This deliberate drop is said to be a device to trap would-be thieves as they approached in the enveloping darkness.

Echoes of the past

The Hypogeum was a place for both ritual and burial. When discovered, it was full of fragments of bone and pottery, of which only a little has been retained. An estimated 7,000 bodies were interred here. The chambers are finely finished on a well-proportioned scale. The most impressive, commonly referred to as the "Holy of Holies", has pillars and lintels that are architecturally remarkable. The room was probably used for the sacrifice of animals.

There are patterns and symbols on the walls and there is an oracle chamber where a square niche was cut into a wall so that the priest's voice would echo around the temple. When the deep voice of a man speaks into the niche, the sound reverberates around the chamber; when a woman speaks into it, nothing happens. Two *Sleeping Lady* figurines were found in the middle chambers but, unlike the other artifacts from the Hypogeum, these are now displayed in the Museum of Archaeology in Valletta.

The Hypogeum was closed for much of the 1990s for restoration, and there were rumours that it would never re-open as the very breath of visitors damages the soft limestone. It has now re-opened, but check with the tourist office in Valletta (tel: 9973 0000) early in your holiday as visitor numbers are limited and there is sometimes a waiting list.

Tarxien

A short distance by car, still in the suburb of Paola, are the **Tarxien Temples ❷** (pronounced *tar-sheen*), which were discovered in 1914 and excavated with great care (open summer daily 7.45am–2pm; winter Mon–Sat 8.15am–5pm, Sun 8.15am–4.15pm; tel: 2169 5578; entrance fee).

PRECEDING PAGES: casting a line at Marsaxlokk. **LEFT:** Marsaxlokk harbour and *luzzus*. **BELOW:** fruit and vegetables for sale.

TIP

There is little interpretation on-site at Tarxien. To learn more you will either have to buy one of their guide books or ask the custodian to give you a guided tour. There is no charge for this but a tip is always appreciated. *See also Temple Vision, pages 236–37.*

BELOW:
sophisticated stonework on the temples at Tarxien.

This group of four temples is remarkable for the quality of its carvings, which include not only subtle decorative spirals but also friezes of farm animals, among them a bull, representing virility, and a suckling sow, denoting fertility.

Of considerable historical importance was the discovery here of the large base of a monumental statue to Mother Earth. It indicates that these early people had created the first-known free-standing statue of a deity. Had it survived, it would have been at least 2.5 metres (8 ft) high.

Certain walls and floors of the temples are discoloured with a curious dark patina which experts believe was caused in the late Bronze Age by the funeral pyres of a new people arriving at the temples. These latter folk cremated their dead, while the the original dwellers interred bodies.

The south east corner

Leave behind the faceless suburbs of Paola and head west to **Zabbar**, which is entered via the Hompesch Arch, dedicated to the very last Grand Master of the Order in Malta, Ferdinand von Hompesch (1797–98). In the centre of Zabbar the Church of Our Lady of Graces, known locally as Ta Grazzia, is a masterpiece of local church architecture. It was designed by the acclaimed local architect Tomasso Dingli, but took on its present appearance in 1737, when a new facade was added.

Marsaskala ❸ was once a quiet fishing village. Today, it has been taken over by hundreds of apartment buildings and is a popular locals' holiday resort, if not the sort of place where overseas visitors come. Its large bay cuts a pretty picture nonetheless, with its flotilla of fishing boats and pleasure craft and a tall Italianate campanile as a backdrop.

Map
on pages
222–23

Follow the coast road south to St Thomas Bay, a scruffy sort of place where fisherman's boats and broken huts litter the foreshore in a less than picturesque way. There is, however, that rare commodity, a sandy beach and plenty of rocky slabs on which to sunbathe. If it is crowded here, as is often the case, then a better alternative is **Peter's Pool ❹**, just south of here on the main road.

The path down to the pool is well trodden. There is no sand, not even a shore, but if you want to swim in a glorious natural lido then this is the place to come. Just jump or dive into the deep clear blue water from the rocky shelving and watch where the locals get out. But stay away from the currents, which swirl under the rocky outcrops at the pool's end. If swimming is not your thing there are some good coastal paths to explore and it's easy to find your way.

A word of caution: thieves operate in this region and will casually break your car windows to gain access. The best defence is to leave the windows open and leave nothing in your car.

*Taking to the waters
on the south coast.*

Marsaxlokk

Marsaxlokk ❺ – which, for the benefit of tongue-tied visitors, is pronounced *Marsa-shlock* – is quite simply the prettiest fishing village on the islands. It also holds Malta's largest fishing fleet, and the harbour, with its multitude of colourful *luzzus* (traditional fishing boats), is a photographer's dream.

A market is held on the quay daily with fruit and vegetables for the locals and lace and knick-knacks for the coach parties that descend on the village. Most visitors enjoy a meal of freshly caught fish on the quayside, before returning to their coach. Despite its many day-trippers, however, the basic structure of the village is still largely untouched. Sadly, the same could not be said for Marsaxlokk

BELOW: the bay
of Marsaskala.

Bay. It was here that the Turkish fleet anchored prior to the Great Siege of 1565, and the bay was also used by the invading French in 1798. In the late 20th century it was defaced by a large, obtrusive power station.

The Cave of Darkness

Continue on the coast road around St George's Bay and, just before you get into Birzebugga, signs indicate the route a little way inland to **Ghar Dalam** ❻ (open summer daily 7.45am–2pm; winter Mon–Sat 8.15am–5pm, Sun 8.15am–4.15pm; tel: 2165 0165; entrance fee). Its name means Cave of Darkness and it is a natural formation some 200 metres (600 ft) long carved out by a subterranean river and only re-discovered in 1865.

Its upper rock stratum yielded bones of humans and animals dating from the Phoenician period (1st century BC); the second stratum dated to Neolithic times (5200–4500 BC) and contained fragments of pottery with animal patterns, imported pieces of obsidian from Lipari and Pantelleria, and the remains of domestic animals. But it was a third layer of rock that yielded the most exciting finds: this dated from the Pleistocene era (1.8 million–11,000 years ago) and contained the fossilised skeletons, antlers and teeth of deer, bears, dwarf elephants and hippopotami (on display in a refurbished exhibition next to the cave).

BELOW: despite the advent of tourism, fishing is still an important part of the local economy.

Several similar fossils have also been discovered on Sicily and have fuelled speculation that the islands once formed part of a land bridge between the African and European continents, between present-day Sicily and Libya or Tunisia. Another theory is that a major earthquake broke up the land and caused severe flooding; this created the Maltese archipelago and separated the two continents.

From Bronze Age to Industrial Age

Close to Ghar Dalam is another ancient site, the scant remains of the Bronze Age site of **Borg in-Nadur** (open any time; free entrance). However, there is no interpretation here and only the archaeologically inclined will get anything out of a visit. Of more general interest is the monument on the coast road which commemorates the summit between George Bush and Mikhail Gorbachev which marked the end of the Cold War on 23 December 1989. This was held on a cruiser moored in Marsaxlokk Bay, and sea conditions were so rough that the meeting was nicknamed The Seasick Summit.

Signs along this road point invitingly to **Pretty Bay** and, sure enough, around the Birzebbuga headland is a sandy beach which, indeed, must have been pretty once upon a time. The panorama now, however, is dominated by the giant Kalafrana freeport container terminal, almost within swimming distance of the beach. This is one of Malta's most important sources of income after tourism and here the two clash in a spectacular visual juxtaposition.

The road winds inland past the disused airfield of Hal Far while the container port spreads itself thickly over this area, turning it into one giant industrial estate. Just past the airfield, look for the minor road signposted to Zurrieq. If you miss it, continue towards Luqa, then pick up the Zurrieq signs.

The Blue Grotto

There is little to detain you in Zurrieq but just south is the tiny picturesque rocky inlet of **Wied-iz-Zurrieq**. Here, traditional Maltese fishing boats are moored in the water in great numbers or hauled ashore to be repainted in fine colours. It is a spectacular drive into Wied-iz-Zurrieq along the cliffs. From its jetty beneath the simple cafés and souvenir shops, small boats taking eight passengers at a time ferry visitors to the famous **Blue Grotto** ❼. The best time to go is in the early morning, when the light reflected through the caves brings out the colour. Don't worry about being cheated on the price of a trip. A few years ago this was a concern, but nowadays these are government-regulated and clearly marked with a bona-fide ticket booth. Boats start running at around 8am and finish at 4pm every day in summer.

More temples

Continue on the same road to the famous temples of Hagar Qim and Mnajdra (open summer daily Mon–Sat, 7.45am–2pm; winter Mon–Sat, 8.15am–5pm, Sun 8.15am–4.15pm; tel: 2142 4231; entrance fee).

Hagar Qim ❽, pronounced *adge-are eem*, means Standing Stones. It is at the top of the hill (by the car park) and is almost completely surrounded by a curtain wall, with three massive standing stones set into it. When the site was discovered in 1839, the *Maltese Venus*, the statue of the *Seated Woman* and several other female figurines were all found here. They now reside at the Archaeological Museum in Valletta. The monumental facade is very impressive and gives a good impression of the huge scale of these megalithic structures. Originally, they had wooden roofs but these have long since rotted away.

Map on pages 222–23

The design of luzzus dates back to the Phoenicians.

BELOW: cave discoveries are throwing new light on Malta's ancient history.

Between Ghar Lapsi and Dingli Cliffs is the small settlement of Tal-Providenza. This is home to the Madonna Tal-Providenza, one of Malta's best baroque churches.

A corridor leads to the interior that is made up of a series of round chambers, almost all of which have their own entrance. Both Hagar Qim and Mnajdra were used for sacrifices, with libations of milk and blood presented at the altars. The latter are mushroom-shaped, possibly to stop the sacrificial blood from dripping off the edge. They were shrines to Mother Earth and it was probably believed that the dead returned to her womb only if sacrifices were offered. In the chambers there are decorated stones, libation altars and tie holes where curtains were hung in order to conceal the priestesses.

The site of **Mnajdra ❾** (pronounced *im-na-eed-rah*), a five-minute walk down the steep hillside with the broad blue sea and the tiny island of Filfla as a backdrop, is much more romantic than that of Hagar Qim. The temples here have been dated to around 3700 BC, predating Hagar Qim by some 900 years. The badly reconstructed eastern temple consists of just one chamber and is thought to be the oldest; the two-chambered temple attached to it is probably the most recent section. The southern complex is the second oldest.

A calendar in stone

According to a recent theory, the temples at Mnajdra, like the circle at Stonehenge in Britain, fulfilled some kind of calendar function. The main entrance faces east, and during the spring and autumn solstice the first ray of sunlight falls on a stone slab on the rear wall of the second kidney-shaped chamber. Then, during the winter and summer solstice, the first ray touches the corners of two stone pillars in the section connecting the two stone chambers.

The first chamber to the left of this connecting section contains a niche which is decorated with a carefully executed pitted pattern – a distinctive feature of

BELOW: an early-morning boat trip to the Blue Grotto can be a magical experience.

Mnajdra. One chamber in the outer wall to the right of the entrance contains a particularly attractive pillared altar; the small holes connecting with the main room can be closed off, and probably served some oracular purpose.

The two kidney-shaped chambers at the main entrance and in the connecting section were created with particular care. Today we talk of the precision of watchmakers; 5,000 years ago the precision of the "calendar people" of Malta may have been just as famous.

The tiny island of **Filfla** is also thought to be somehow connected to the temples. Because of the mysterious way the rock stands in the water and the way the setting midsummer sun catches it, Filfla may have been an integral part of temple ritual and the reason why the temples were built in this exposed position.

More recently, the island was used for target practice by British warships. Local lore has it that two-tailed lizards live here among the unexploded shells. Filfla has been declared a nature reserve but law-breakers, instead of landing, now pass by on boats to shoot the resting migratory birds.

Just west of the temples is **Ghar Lapsi ⑩**, a popular locals' bathing spot. After a hot day of temple-watching it is an excellent place to take a dip. There is no foreshore, but the locals have contrived to make this into a natural lido, with iron steps provided to make the cool clear waters easily accessible. Scuba divers also find its underwater world beautiful.

Dingli Cliffs

From Ghar Lapsi turn inland towards Siggiewi, head briefly towards Rabat, then south back towards the coast and **Dingli Cliffs ⑪**, Malta's highest point. Eventually the road heading north runs out of asphalt. It's a good idea to stretch

Malta's temples have been receiving visitors for centuries.

BELOW: an aerial view of the complex chambers of Hagar Qim.

TIP

December and
January is a good time
for a stroll in Buskett
Gardens as this is
when the oranges
are picked and their
sweet scent
permeates the air.

your legs at this point. There are stunning views down some 250 metres (800 ft) to the waves below, and also far out to sea. This is one of the island's favourite walking spots. Close to the cliffs is the enigmatic **Clapham Junction**, where the sharp-eyed may see the best examples of Malta's famous cart tracks.

Also close by, along a country road down the lush valley to Siggiewi, is the **Inquisitor's Summer Palace**. A remarkable and beautiful house concealed on the side of the hill, it was built in 1625 by the Inquisitor, Horatus Visconti, as his summer residence. The elegant building is only one room deep, with all rooms interconnecting. There is a small chapel at one end and beneath its terrace apron are deep caves where the Inquisitor's staff are said to have lived. For years the palace lay abandoned, prey to vandals. Now it has been renovated and is used by the Prime Minister as his summer residence (closed to visitors).

Buskett Gardens

Buskett Gardens ⓬ is Malta's largest wooded area – a delightful spot, cool and shady in summer, ripe with oranges in winter. The name "gardens" is something of a misnomer as this is essentially a wood comprising fir, oak, olive trees and citrus groves and gets its name from the Italian, *boschetto*, meaning "a place where aromatic firs grow."

Buskett is particularly popular with picnickers, and for more than 300 years, on 29 June, one of the most popular *festas* in Malta, *Mnarja* – the feast day of St Peter and St Paul – has been celebrated here. Its name comes from the Latin word *illuminaria*, used originally by the clergy to describe the lighting up of the churches of Mdina and Rabat in honour of the two saints.

The day traditionally starts with horse and donkey races on a road that leads

BELOW: terraced
fields on the edge
of Dingli Cliffs
make for scenic
farming.

up to the Saqqija hill entrance into Rabat. Here, there is a stone balcony on which successive Grand Masters and governors sat to watch the races, and later present banners to the winners. These were then taken by the winners to adorn their parish church. Today crowds gather in Buskett Gardens to cook rabbit, drink wine, and sing and dance well into the night.

Map on pages 222–23

Verdala Palace

On the northern outskirts of Buskett Gardens, on elevated ground surrounded by woodland, is **Verdala Palace ⓭**, a silent, romantic castle, which is half-villa and half-fort (viewing by appointment only; tel: 9973 0000; entrance fee).

Designed by Gerolamo Cassar in 1586 for Grand Master Fra Hugues de Verdale, Verdala may look like a traditional medieval castle, but it was never designed to withstand serious assault. However, its four corner towers are positioned to afford excellent musket fire should it ever be required. The castle has been enlarged and embellished over the centuries – with the British in their later years installing plumbing and sanitation as they converted it into the Governor's family's summer residence.

Spring is a delightful time to see the island's carpets of wild flowers.

It has a quiet grandeur, with frescoes in the main room depicting highlights from the life of Grand Master Verdale. There is a fine staircase to one side leading to the roof, from which there is a superb view of the countryside. Within its stone walls is a concealed chamber with rings in the floor and wall where it is said that prisoners were chained and tortured.

The Chapel of St Anthony the Abbot, built in the 16th century, is in the grounds. Viewed, from Buskett Gardens below, note the *trompe l'oeil* windows painted to create the impression of symmetry. ❏

BELOW: Verdala Palace, glimpsed through the orange groves of Buskett Gardens.

THE SECRETS OF MALTA'S TEMPLES

The island's temples have been jointly declared a UNESCO *World Heritage Site. A little insight into their history will enhance your enjoyment of them*

Between 3600 and 2500 BC there was a building boom in Malta. Prehistoric farmers with no tools but flint, obsidian and bone built well over 50 massive temples, of which 33 survive in various states of preservation.

All of them began with the same basic design: a corridor slicing through two kidney-shaped chambers to reach a small altar apse at the far end, with a Herculean outer shell of hard grey limestone. Their entrances are massive uprights of softer, golden stone with equally massive lintels.

The great blocks, many of them over 5 metres (16 ft) long and weighing up to 20 tons, were moved around on the stone rollers, shaped like cannon balls, which still lie around most sites. As more temples were added, the outer walls, corbelled in towards the top, were extended to incorporate them. They were probably roofed over with beams, brushwood and clay.

The earliest interiors were plastered and painted with red ochre. All were decorated with intricately carved spirals on steps and altars, friezes of farm animals, snakes and fish, and a simple pattern of pitted dots. Still evident are sockets for wooden barriers or curtains and niches for rituals.

▽ **PORTHOLE DOORS**
Doorways cut through great slabs of golden stone, like this one at Hagar Qim, were a feature of later temples.

◁ SEA VIEWS
The most bewitching of all the temples for its location, Mnajdra gazes out to the tiny island of Filfla – with which it may have been ritually linked.

▽ HOLY STONES
Oracle holes at Ggantija. Look, too, for sockets for wooden barriers or curtain rails, inner sanctums, sunken hearths and places of animal sacrifice.

FAT LADIES AND FERTILITY

Statues of grossly overweight figures are found in all Maltese temples. Their pleated skirts, generous thighs and surprisingly small hands and feet led them to being called "Fat Ladies". But they are of indeterminate sex, and, furthermore, it has been noticed that the "ladies" have no breasts. As a result, their name has been revised to the more accurate (and politically correct) term of "Obese Figures".

However, certain figurines, such as the *Sleeping Lady* (above) and the *Malta Venus* (below), show that Neolithic women were well endowed. Meanwhile, pleats are a unisex feature, since statuettes exist of men in skirts with neatly bobbed hair or pigtails.

Fertility, in its widest sense, appears to have been what people worshipped. The male dominance of temple culture is left in no doubt by carved enshrined phalluses.

◁ THE HYPOGEUM
Of all the Neolithic remains this is the most astonishing: a labyrinth of burial chambers with ritual rooms carved out of the rock in precise imitation of the temples above ground.

▷ SPIRAL DECORATION
Spirals are thought to have had ritual significance. Pictured here is an altar front from Tarxien that held a secret drawer in which a flint knife and animal remains were discovered.

△ GOLDEN WONDER
Hagar Qim is entirely golden, as no grey stone was available. Its precise masonry is matched by that at Tarxien.

A wealth of very fine pottery has also been found on all of Malta's temple sites, some of which now rests in the Archaeological Museum in Valletta.

GOZO

While Gozo is just a small island, there is plenty to see.
It is worth more than just a day trip from Malta.

Tradition has it that Gozo is Homer's Ogygia, the island where the nymph Calypso held the Greek hero Odysseus captive for seven years. There may be other contenders for the honour, but there is certainly a strange enchantment about the place.

The Arabs named the island Ghawdex, which meant "joy", and when the Spanish came, they translated joy into Castilian, which is *gozo*. For some reason, however, the local population still preferred Ghawdex (pronounced *Ow-desh*), to which they have remained steadfastly loyal ever since.

The island's tightly packed hilltop villages and the little fortress farmhouses that dot the countryside are a legacy of cruel invasions: the marauding Turks and those feared sea-wolves of the Mediterranean who sailed these waters, the Barbary pirates. In the island's blackest hour, in 1551, pirates devastated Gozo, carrying off almost the entire population of 5,000 into slavery. Fortunately, a few hundred islanders disappeared into the countryside and within a century the population was back to half its strength. No matter what history has thrown at them, the Gozitans appear to have adapted and then proceeded to carry on much as before.

In Malta the Gozitans are known as a strong, resilient people who have the disconcerting habit of walking away with the nation's top jobs. Indeed, there have been more Gozitan presidents, archbishops and chief justices than the Maltese would care to count.

Only one-third of the size of Malta, Gozo is still a land of farmers and fishermen, and adheres to the solid values of those who live by the elements. With an area of only 67 sq. km (26 sq. miles) and a population of 25,000, it is possible to stroll along Gozo's country lanes and goat tracks for an hour or more and see only a young boy herding his goats and sheep, or a farmer hoeing his fields.

In the countryside, flat-topped hills rise out of valley floors, drystone walls contour every gradient and church domes crest the skyline. The outcrops of limestone range in colour from imperious grey through glowing russet to gold as rich as whipped butter.

In summer the hot sun bakes any ground that is not devoutly worked, but in spring it is a gaudy patchwork. Tiny fields of lush green wheat and barley jostle chrome-yellow daisies and spreads of crimson-flowered lucerne. Carpets of miniature wild flowers sprout from apparently solid rock, thyme and wild fennel scent the air and, as far distant as one can see, there is the cobalt sea and sky.   ❑

PRECEDING PAGES: the rural way of life is still evident on the island; *festa* time.
LEFT: nimble fingers engage in lacework, but craftswomen like this old lady are a dying breed.

VICTORIA

The pint-sized capital of Gozo has a quiet charm that is best appreciated in the morning, or late afternoon when it wakes from its siesta. Its ancient citadel is the hub and heart of the island

Map on page 248

Queen Victoria gave her name to Gozo's capital and elevated it to city status as part of her Golden Jubilee celebrations in 1887. The Gozitans politely installed a fountain and commemorative plaque in the Cathedral Square, then went back to using the ancient name of Rabat (which means "suburb"). Like Rabat on Malta, which sprawls outside the fortress walls of Mdina, Gozo's suburb nestles beneath the protective bastions of its citadel, a romantic mass of sheer rock faces, curtain walls, ravelins and bell towers that dominates the skyline from almost every approach road.

Origins

The ridge on which the city stands has been inhabited at least since the Bronze Age. The Carthaginians left behind a Punic inscription thanking the *prl whds 'm gwl* (the people of Gozo) for helping to restore three temples. A quick tally of Victoria's churches today indicates that, in the religious sphere at least, not a lot has changed. The town was fortified under the Romans and one of the present-day crossroads, Triq Putirjal (Main Gate Street), and three elegant stone crosses mark the limits of the old walls.

The Arabs appear to have spurned the lower town and established themselves on the more easily defended heights of the hill. In the Middle Ages both suburb and citadel were thriving, close-packed communities. Few of the medieval houses have survived, but the narrow twisting lanes and alleyways remain.

Republic Street

Triq ir-Repubblika  (Republic Street) is the town's main thoroughfare, a pleasant mixture of shops and balconied houses which slices through Victoria from east to west. It accommodates banks, a police station, a post office, two opera houses and the Bishop of Gozo's 19th-century palace. On the feasts of the Assumption (15 August, known locally as Santa Marija) and of St George (the third weekend in July), it still lives up to its old name of Racecourse Street, when everyone turns out to cheer a medley of thoroughbred trotting ponies and gasping hacks as they pelt uphill towards a lavish carrot – a stupendous array of silver cups and salvers.

The colourful **Villa Rundle Gardens** (Gnien Rundle), at the bottom of the hill, are also taken over for the celebrations of Santa Marija by a jolly agricultural and industrial show, which is just as much fun for people-watchers as sheep and onion fanciers.

The fact that Victoria has two opera houses is wonderfully Gozitan. The whole thing began modestly enough a hundred years ago, with the founding of two

PRECEDING PAGES: the view into Cathedral Square, Victoria. **LEFT:** the Citadel rises above the town. **BELOW:** waiting for customers.

band clubs to provide music for the saint's day processions of the cathedral and St George's Basilica respectively. Then, in the 1960s, the St George's club built the Astra Theatre. The cathedral club, not to be outdone, moved premises to the Aurora Theatre, and since then there has been a tit-for-tat rivalry over everything from facades to discos and opera productions. Since even the Gozitans haven't found a way of financing operas, the theatres also act as cinemas.

The meeting place

The official title of Victoria's main square is **Pjazza Independenza** ❸ (Independence Square) – but it is going to be a long time before this name catches on. Surrounded by tall clipped ficus trees, cafés and busy little shops and market stalls, it has been known locally as **It-Tokk** for as long as the Gozitans can remember. It means "meeting place" and this is exactly what the square has been throughout its many incarnations.

The square is graced, on the right, by the **Banca Giuratale**, a semi-circular baroque confection built in 1733 as the council chambers of Gozo's governing Jurats. It now houses various government departments including the tourist information office. On the left is the small church of **St James the Apostle** (1740), which has been rebuilt following the collapse of its foundations in the 1980s. The vigorous use of its bells to drown out political meetings in the square is said to have contributed to the delay in the issuing of a restoration permit.

The old town

Pjazza San Gorg, which lies immediately behind the main square, is dominated by the imposing **St George's Basilica** ❸. The present building dates from

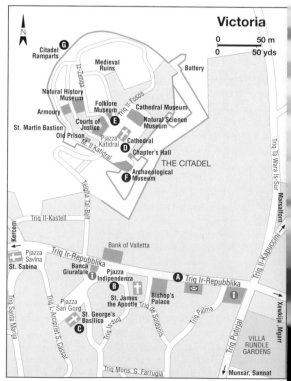

1678, though it has been much extended, and the facade was rebuilt in 1818. The paintings on the gilded ceiling and dome were completed between 1949 and 1964, and the striking bronze altar canopy, executed in 1967, is a copy of Bernini's in St Peter's, Rome. The main altar-piece, a glowing triumphant St George, was painted by Mattia Preti (1613–99) of Valletta cathedral fame.

Spreading out behind St George's is the old part of the town, **Il Borgo**, a maze of little streets and alleys designed to baffle invaders and deflect the flight of arrows and shot. Old stone balconies and religious niches are the things to look for here.

Cross back over Republic Street and on the corner, just as you start to walk uphill to the citadel is the Citadel Theatre showing **Gozo 360 degrees** (shows every half hour Mon–Sat 10.30am–3.30pm, Sun 10.30am–1pm; entrance fee). This entertaining audio-visual introduction to the history, geography and culture of Calypso's Isle does for Gozo what the acclaimed Malta Experience does for the big island. It's certainly easier to understand than its gimmicky rival, Gozo Heritage, at Ghajnsielem.

The citadel

The massive golden-coloured citadel bastions, which rise above the town, date from the first years of the 17th century. It is thought that Francesco Laparelli, papal engineer, architect of Valletta and one-time assistant to Michelangelo, drew up the plans for them in 1567, two years after the Great Siege, but it was another 32 years before building commenced. King Philip II of Spain paid a significant sum towards their cost, and the Gozitans provided the rest by way of donations and taxes on wine, oil and agricultural exports.

Map on page 248

BELOW: aerial view of Victoria and the citadel.

The effectiveness of these splendid fortifications was never tested. By the time they were finished, the Ottoman Turks had been driven out of the western Mediterranean. For a few more years the upper town retained its importance because, by law, every Gozitan was bound to sleep there. But when this restriction was lifted in 1637, the population began to drift away to more convenient locations in the countryside. In 1693 an earthquake reduced many of the abandoned buildings to rubble.

The citadel reborn

Today, the Knights' impressive bastions are being restored and what remains of the old town is being revived. It takes some imagination to picture it in its medieval heyday, with its small palaces, chapels and warren of crowded alleys, but it is still well worth a visit.

To the left of the **Cathedral Square** (Pjazza Katidral), viewed from the great entrance arch, is the early 17th-century Palace of the Governors of Gozo, with the "fat" mouldings that distinguished Maltese architecture in the previous century. It is now part of the adjoining **Law Courts**. On the right are the parish offices and the **Chapter's Hall**, built in 1899. The huddle of domestic dwellings that once filled the square was demolished in the 1860s.

The Cathedral

Built at the turn of the 17th century, on a site previously occupied by at least three churches and two pagan temples, the **Cathedral**  is the work of the Maltese architect Lorenzo Gafa', who also designed Mdina's cathedral. It has his usual lightness and grace, though since funds ran dry the dome he intended

BELOW: religious artefacts for sale.

Map
on page
248

for it was never completed. This deficiency has cleverly been turned into an asset by a *trompe l'oeil* substitute, painted by Antonio Manuele of Messina in 1739. From the nave this artful sham soars skywards in perfect symmetry; viewed from near the altar steps, however, it shoots off at an alarming angle. The cathedral floor is paved with the colourful marble tombstones of bishops and priests.

Just around the corner, occupying part of the cathedral's vestry, the **Cathedral Museum** (Mon–Sat 10am–1pm and 1.30–4.30pm; tel: 2155 6087; entrance fee) features Ionic columns from the temple of Juno, a bishop's landau from the late 1860s, church silver and much more in its collection.

Citadel museums

All of the capital's small museums are clustered here in the upper town, in buildings which are as important as the collections they hold (all open 1 Oct–31 Mar Mon–Sat 8.30am–4.30pm, Sun 8.30am–3pm; 1 Apr–30 Sep Mon–Sat 8.45am–4.30pm, Sun 8.30am–3pm; closed public holidays; entrance fee).

The three houses that form the **Folklore Museum**  date from around 1500. As an architectural group they are unique in the Maltese islands, admired for the simple delicacy of the stonework and their "Norman" windows. Don't be deterred by the folklore label; the collection is a fascinating look at rural Gozitan life and its bygones.

Choosing a route.

The **Archaeological Museum** ● is housed in the fortress's last surviving private palace. The design of the sumptuously ornate balcony was reconstructed from the shattered remnants of the original. The exhibits range from Neolithic times to the Middle Ages and among them the 12th-century tombstone of a young Muslim girl, Majmuna, is particularly touching.

High on a wall opposite, a little further up the hill, is an inscription marking the house of the Sicilian soldier, Bernardo DeOpuo *(Audacis Militi)*, a hero of the 1551 attack. Preferring death to slavery, he killed his wife and two daughters, then dispatched several Turks before he himself was felled.

BELOW: fun on a gun in the Citadel.

The **Natural History Museum** forms part of a cluster of 16th-century houses and has a good display of fossils, flora and fauna. Across the alleyway a former 17th-century granary is now the **Armoury**, home to helmets, cannonballs, an old carriage and a couple of 19th-century hearses.

Prisons and ramparts

It is also worth checking if the **Old Prisons** lower down the street, are open. The inmates, incarcerated in the tiny cells here between around 1600 and the 1880s, left poignant carvings of ships on the walls. Attractive little shops selling local crafts line the small street leading to the early 17th-century storehouses and restrooms of the Knights. From the 1880s right up until 1964 these were the island's "New Prisons". Today, they are used to display handicrafts.

For all the intrinsic interest of the citadel, however, the most enduring memory is the view from the **ramparts** ●, a panorama of rolling valleys, strange, decapitated hills and just in the distance a glimpse of the big island of Malta. ❏

AROUND GOZO

Map
on page
256

*This tiny island includes the world's oldest free-standing temple,
unspoilt villages and near-biblical landscapes. A tour around it will
show you why UNESCO wants to make Gozo a World Heritage Site*

Valletta

T here is a brisk year-round helicopter link between Malta and Gozo, but most
visitors still arrive on Calypso's island, like Ulysses, by boat. It is a 25-
minute trip by car ferry from Cirkewwa at the northern tip of Malta. In summer, another ferry service runs between Sliema on Malta and Mgarr on Gozo.

Whatever means of transport you take, en route you are sure to have a fine
view of Comino. It was once a troublesome pirate's lair and the haunt of invading Turks, which explains its impressive 17th-century fort and gun battery *(see
page 269)*. The flashes of limpid, turquoise sea are its famous Blue Lagoon.

First impressions

Sailing into Gozo's only port, **Mgarr ❶**, gives a concentrated view of all that
makes the island special: chapel, church spire and fort line the horizon, small
flat-topped houses, tiny fields and greenery rise to meet them, while at the
water's edge bob gaily painted fishing boats with Christian shrines amidships
and the pagan eye of Osiris on their bows. Only the mock-Gothic church on
the skyline is out of character. This cathedral-sized building was started in 1924,
delayed for lack of funds, then finished at a gallop in the 1970s after the priest
in charge won the National Lottery.

Fort Chambray, adjacent, was also built with
prize money, the loot accumulated by the last great
admiral of the Order of St John, Knight Grand Cross
Jacques de Chambray. Having retired from active service in 1749, and disgusted by the Order's peace-
time lack of vigour, the old sea dog became Governor
of Gozo and spent his last years fortifying Mgarr
harbour at his own expense.

Fifty years on, when Napoleon's troops arrived on
the island, the old warrior's ramparts, manned by
Knights and Gozitans, gave the French force a good
deal more trouble than they had bargained for. Since
then, the fort has been both a British garrison and
a mental hospital. It now awaits development as a
luxury hotel complex.

The road to Victoria

Most traffic passes through Ghajnsielem ("The Spring
of Peace"), a straggling, newish village whose main
claim to fame these days is **Gozo Heritage** (daily
9am–5pm; tel: 2155 1475; entrance fee), based in a
fine old farmhouse. A series of tableaux, booming
disembodied voices and special effects provide a
somewhat confusing trot through more than 5,000
years of the island's history.

Around the next bend in the road, the great round
church of the **Xewkija Rotunda ❷** (also known as
the Xewkija Dome) rises across the fields to the left.

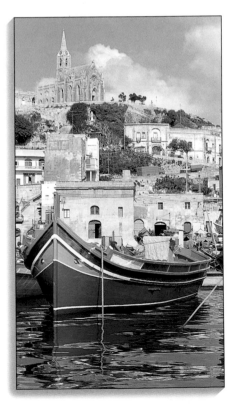

PRECEDING PAGES:
salt pans at Qbajjar,
near Marsalforn.
LEFT: in the cool of
the evening, Qbajjar.
BELOW: first sight of
Gozo: landfall at
Mgarr harbour.

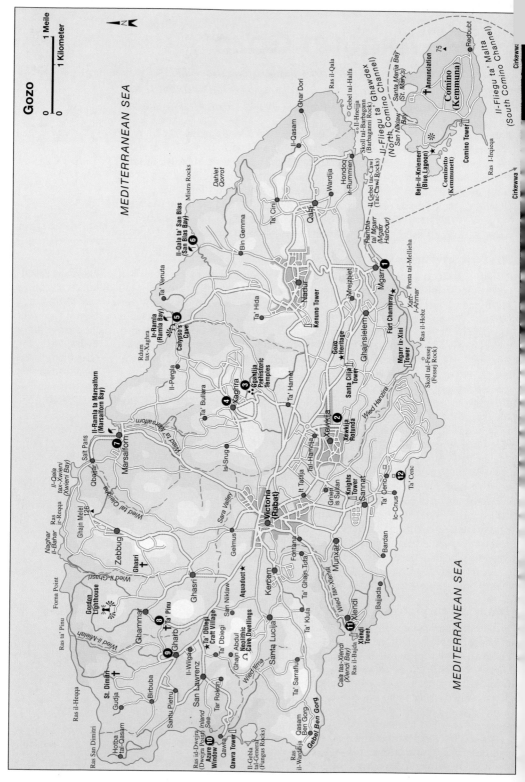

Gozo's fourth-largest community, Xewkija has disjointed the noses of every other parish by building the biggest church. The dome is said to be the third largest unsupported church dome in Europe, bigger even than the Mosta Dome on Malta *(see page 198)*. Based on the design of Santa Maria della Salute in Venice, the church was begun in 1952 and a bell tower was added later.

Remarkably, the whole of this great enterprise was financed by a population of under 3,000 (helped by donations from Xewkijans abroad) and built by willing local labour. Some of the choicest pieces of carved stone from the attractive early 17th-century church which the Rotunda replaced are displayed in a side chapel. The carvings are thought to be the work of two renegade Sicilians who sought sanctuary in the church from the laws of their own country.

A gigantic temple

High on a hill 3 km (2 miles) due north, on the edge of the ancient village of Xaghra, is a much earlier and, in its way, an even bigger monument – the Stone Age complex of **Ggantija Prehistoric Temples ❸** (Mon–Sat 8.30am–4.30pm in winter, 8.30am–6.30pm in summer; Sun 8.30am–3pm all all year round; tel: 2155 3194; entrance fee).

Hunting is a popular sport on Gozo.

Constructed from 3,600–3,000 BC, this is the oldest free-standing stone building known to man, pre-dating Egypt's pyramids and Britain's Stonehenge by over 1,000 years. And of all Malta's Neolithic remains, this is the largest and the best preserved. The two temples cover 1,000 sq. metres (10,800 sq. ft), and their astonishing rear wall still rises 6 metres (20 ft) and contains megaliths weighing in at 40–50 tons – the most gigantic blocks used in any of the archipelago's herculean structures.

BELOW: the slow pace of island life.

TIP

The Oleander restaurant (tel: 2155 7230) in the centre of Xaghra is one of the best places on the island to sample Gozitan home cooking. A meal here is also excellent value.

Xaghra

At the entrance to the village of **Xaghra** ❹ (pronounced shur-rah), just a short walk away from Ggantija, stands the superbly restored **Ta' Kola Windmill** (same admission ticket and details as Ggantija). This is one of the few Maltese windmills still with its sails and original wooden machinery intact. Built in 1725, it contains a forge, ancient tools and living quarters decorated with old country furniture and local fabrics.

Xaghra's main square is one of the most attractive on Gozo, with old-fashioned shops, a good restaurant and a café-bar. Just off here (signposted) are three more small visitor attractions, two caves and a wonderful toy museum. Caves seem to be a speciality of Xaghra, with two choices: **Xerri's Grotto** and **Ninu's Cave** (both open daily 8.30am–6pm; small entrance fee). It is certainly a novel experience to walk through the front door of an ordinary family home and be shown into a basement which displays weird and wonderful stalactites and stalagmites.

There's one more pleasant surprise in store in Xaghra, the **Pomskizillious Toy Museum**. Full of old-fashioned toys and mechanical automata, this is a delight for children who have never grown up. And why the strange name? It derives from the famous English nonsense poet Edward Lear who visited Gozo and described it as "pomskizillious and gromphiberous, being as no words can describe its magnificence". A wax model of Lear himself is a prize exhibit.

The legend of Calypso

Take the road heading north out of Xaghra to Ramla Bay, and within a few minutes you will come to the island's most mythical spot, **Calypso's Cave**. Set

BELOW: spring flowers bloom over Ggantija, as they have for some 5,000 years.

high in the cliff face at the northeast corner of the Xaghra plateau, it is reputed to be a labyrinth, reaching down to sea level in some places. It is here, if we are to believe local legend, and the works of Homer and Callimachus, that the Greek hero Odysseus (Ulysses to the Romans) was washed ashore and into the arms of the golden-haired temptress, Calypso, on his epic return from Troy.

Following a rock fall, the cave can no longer be explored but, for a coin or two, local entrepreneurs will take you as far as you can go into the rocky cleft. However, it is not the cave but the view from the adjacent platform that makes a visit worthwhile.

Best beaches

Looking down from Calypso's Cave there is a splendid vista of the former domain of the sea nymph: tumbling rocks, a wide, fertile valley and the red-gold sweep of **Ramla Bay ❺**, Gozo's finest beach.

A lucky Roman once had a villa in the dunes behind the bay. Since then it has been a no-go area for the building trade. Except for a few bamboo huts serving drinks and snacks in summer, it is as uncommercialised as it was when Calypso ruled the land. However, nymph-like nudity is not appreciated nowadays. There used to be notices advising swimmers to put on a raincoat when they left Gozo's beaches. Now there are more liberal placards which *would* read "NO TOPLESS BATHING" if young jokers did not delight in erasing the negative.

The island's second-best beach, **San Blas ❻**, is also close by – a mere 1.5 km (1 mile) due east as the crow flies, some 6 km (4 miles) via Nadur, as the roads go. If you want to walk it, take a good local map. San Blas is a delightful little cove with just enough sand for a few families to share, so try to get there early.

BELOW: Fungus Rock, highly prized by the Knights.

TIP

Ta' Pinu has a dress code which is strictly enforced. Men must wear long trousers (even long shorts are not permitted) and women must wear a long skirt and cover their shoulders.

Marsalforn

By contrast to San Blas, **Marsalforn** ❼, a few kilometres west along the north coast from Ramla Bay, is a proper seaside resort; indeed, it is the largest on the island, though on Gozo large is always a relative term. It's a cheerful if somewhat bland place, pulsing with life in the summer and just as much a playground for the Gozitans and Maltese as for foreign tourists.

On summer evenings family groups stroll like a tide, back and forth, around the bay. There is one main hotel, several smaller hostelries, wall-to-wall restaurants and snack-bars, along with souvenir shops piled high with hand-knitted sweaters, which have ousted lace as the favoured local craft. The bay has a tiny fishing harbour tucked under one of its arms and a choice of rock, shingle and sand for swimmers.

Salt pans, in use since Roman times, are dotted all along this stretch of coast: glittering little troughs and reservoirs cut into ledges of gold-coloured rock. The most impressive are just past Qbajjar, on the coast road that leads to Ghasri. Not only are they highly photogenic, they also produce tons of prime sea salt a year.

Going west

Malta's national shrine, **Ta' Pinu** ❽ stands on a plateau off the road between Victoria and Gharb. It was near here in 1883 that a local peasant woman, returning from her fields, heard a voice calling to her. A friend confided that he too had heard the voice and together they prayed for the woman's critically sick mother, who miracously recovered. From then on miracle cures multiplied and the little chapel became a place of pilgrimage. To accommodate the thousands of devotees a huge neo-Romanesque church was built in the 1920s,

BELOW:
the island's finest sands at Ramla Bay.
RIGHT: Gharb.

though the original chapel is tucked into it, behind the main altar. In a corridor to the rear is a display of naïve votive paintings, baby clothes and crutches which poignantly attest to cures and escapes from peril.

A short distance west the village of **Gharb** ❾ features a flamboyant 17th-century baroque church. The **Church of the Visitation** was built between 1679 and 1729 and its yellow butterfly facade is one of the finest and most original church fronts in the entire archipelago. The bell towers flanking it to the west are typically Maltese. The medieval market cross makes a splendid contrast with the red telephone box and blue police lamp of Gharb police station, and is a favourite island photograph. Gharb also has some fine old houses alongside the church and a delightful **Folklore Museum** (Mon–Sat 10am–4pm, Sun 10am–noon; tel: 2156 1929; entrance fee) in a rambling house on the square. An old printing press, carriages, costumes and a mass of intriguing rural items are on show.

By backtracking to the main road and heading for San Lawrenz, you will soon reach the **Ta' Dbiegi Craft Village**, where knitwear, lace, leather-work, pottery and other island crafts are on sale.

Dwejra

By the church of San Lawrenz, the road dips down to the geological curiosities of **Dwejra Point** ❿. The tarmac finishes here and to the right is a stunning natural rock arch – the **Azure Window**. Beside it, over a small hill, the **Inland Sea** is a crater into which the sea flows through a cavernous fissure in the cliffs. Little boats ply through the gap on sightseeing trips.

To the left is **Fungus Rock**, once much prized by the Knights for the odd red plant that grows on top of it. Partly because of its colour they used it to treat

A lace tablecloth is an archetypal Gozo souvenir.

BELOW: dramatic cliffs of Ta' Cenc.

blood diseases, to staunch wounds and for other medicinal purposes. Its phallic shape encouraged them to apply it to other parts too. To protect the crop they made this a knightly preserve, shaved down its sides to deter poachers, and placed a sentry on the rope-and-pulley bridge which was erected to reach it. Entry was forbidden to the locals and punishable by death.

The Knights even sent samples of the fungus as princely gifts to the monarchs of Europe. Recently, however, it was sadly discovered that the plant has no medicinal properties whatsoever and isn't even a fungus. It's a rare kind of parasite which attaches itself to other plants' roots and only comes up for air during its short flowering season.

South of Victoria

The road south from Victoria passes downhill through **Fontana** where there is a cavernous 17th-century public wash-house, still used by the locals. On the right is a spring-fed valley planted by the Knights for use as a private game reserve. On the last stretch down to the sea is *the* meeting-place of the summer, La Grotta, an open-air disco set in a lovely terraced garden.

At the seafront the tiny resort of **Xlendi** ⓫ looks onto what is said to be the smallest bay on the island. It resembles a grey-cliffed mini-fjord with a protective tower at its entrance and colourful fishing boats anchored off the small sandy strip of beach. Although it has been much built up in recent years, with banks of holiday apartments, it still has charm. Tamarisks and pastel-painted buildings line the small promenade and there are restaurants, bars and souvenir sellers. Try to stay a night here, for when the day trippers have gone the tiny village regains its small-time atmosphere.

Due west of Xlendi, on bumpy minor roads, is the village of Sannat and, nearby, the wonderfully wild cliffs of **Ta' Cenc** ⓬ – a 150-metre (500-ft) sheer drop to the sea. This area is the home of nesting birds and rare plants as well as Stone Age remains and the most unostentatious luxury hotel on the islands, called Ta' Cenc. Behind the hotel is a neolithic necropolis and other prehistoric remains, including an intact dolmen and some of Malta's mysterious cart tracks, though they are not easy to spot. ❑

RIGHT: the natural wonder of the Azure Window at Dwejra Point, formed by the forces of wind and sea.

COMINO

Map
on page
256

*Once a pirates' haven, this tiny rock is now inhabited by sun-
worshippers and water sports enthusiasts who come for peace,
quiet and the delights of Comino's famous Blue Lagoon*

I f Malta is the busy island, and Gozo the quiet island, then Comino is surely
the great escape island; where indolence and sports are the only staple items
on the day's menu. Lying mid-way between Malta and Gozo, Comino is all
of 2.5 sq. km (1 sq. mile) in size. The island is too minute for it to attract any
serious large-scale development, and so is likely to remain what it has always
been: a barren, rocky wilderness with a variegated coastline of jagged cliffs
interspersed by two small sandy beaches, lots of pretty coves and creeks, arches,
stacks, rock tunnels and, of course, the gorgeous **Blue Lagoon**.

The colours of the waters surrounding the island are breathtaking: deep-water
indigo and navy, sky and turquoise blue in the sandy bays, peaking to the
sparkling azure and emerald of the Blue Lagoon which lies between Comino and
Cominotto. This is the Mediterranean at its best, and as if to reinforce the point
there are even playful dolphins which bob up and down in the deep sea channels between the islands. Clearly they like it here too.

The nearest point to Comino is Mgarr in Gozo, 3 km (2 miles) away. The
Gozitans have always affectionately regarded Comino as their own. And the
Maltese, who think they own Gozo anyway, have never raised any serious
objections to this happy state of affairs.

PRECEDING PAGES:
thrill-riding on the
Oki-Koki speed-
boats; chillin' out in
the Blue Lagoon.
LEFT: looking out
over the Comino
straits, guarded by
a watchtower.
BELOW: mermaid
detail on a *luzzu*.

Spice and game

In ancient times, Ptolemy referred to the island as
Cosyra but the name that stuck is Comino, from the
spice cumin, which used to be grown in vast quantities
here. Cumin still grows wild in clumps all over the
island, but it is the pink and mauve wild-flowering
thyme that hits the eye and scents the air, especially in
spring when the bees start buzzing to produce what is
arguably the region's best honey.

It is said that when the Knights of St John arrived in
the 16th century, the island was teeming with wild
boar and hares. The vegetation also attracted pelicans
and quail. Successive Grand Masters kept Comino as
a private game reserve.

They were very serious about it, too. In 1695 an
edict stated in no uncertain terms: "Admission is
strictly forbidden to subjects of any class or condition,
armed with gun, dog, ferret, net or any device intended
for game; under penalty of the galley for three years
without pay, if the trespasser is an ordinary person;
or a fine of forty ounces of gold, if a cleric or a member
of the learned professions; and if a minor, of banish-
ment from the dominions of the Prince during His
Highness's pleasure."

But the island was far from a paradise, or even
peaceful. Throughout the Middle Ages, both Malta
and Gozo were constantly attacked by Saracen pirates

who used Comino as a base. In 1416, the Maltese petitioned the Viceroy of Sicily to improve their defences. Two years later a tax on wine was introduced to raise the money with which to finance the building of a fortified tower on Comino; but the Maltese were swindled by King Alfonso V of Spain, who used the money for his many adventures elsewhere. Comino remained unprotected and towerless for the next 200 years.

A fortified island

So it was not until 1618 that Grand Master Alof de Wignacourt, feeling the need to protect the Malta Channel more efficiently, arranged the erection of **St Mary's Tower** on Comino. Of the many such towers which were built around the islands at this time, St Mary's was the most expensive and was equipped and manned by 30 soldiers. A century later more forts were constructed, including a battery on the southeast corner of Comino to guard the Channel, as well as a redoubt at **St Mary's Bay**. In 1722, in preparation for an expected attack, **St Mary's Battery**, also know as Perellos Battery, was complete and ready for action. But as no Turkish forces appeared, the fortifications were never seriously tested.

With the tower in place, a small agricultural community of about 200 people eked out a living, growing cumin, cotton and producing honey. But it was an impoverished existence with little hope of economic improvement, and the population inexorably declined. Today, you can count the number of people who live here all year round on the fingers of one hand.

In World War I, the British built an isolation hospital on the island for serious cases of infection. This military-style compound of stone buildings around a

BELOW: pool with a view at the Hotel Comino.

central square can still be seen. **Liberty Square**, as it was called, acted as a kind of village centre with a grocery shop, post-office box and even a bar. Two well-trodden paths named Battery Street and Congreve Street lead to it.

Not far away, at St Mary's Bay, is the only chapel on Comino. It is said to be of great antiquity, predating the fort.

Modern times

Comino entered the 20th century with the tourist boom which followed Malta's independence in 1964. And when its hotel got its act together and was functioning properly, this little island was at last ready to carve out a name for itself within the upper echelons of Europe's tourist markets.

With the arrival of Swiss management came considerable improvements and additional amenities and services. The expanded watersports centre now includes a surf centre, a first-rate diving base and a diving school, all staffed by qualified instructors. The tennis centre has eight Covasco sand courts, three of which are floodlit, and a resident tennis coach.

Progress, if unchecked, does have its price however. The new landing stage in the Blue Lagoon attracts hordes of day trippers on pleasure cruisers. Fast open day-boats piled high with tourists dart in and out of the pretty coves and inlets like landing craft about to disgorge invading mariners.

Fortunately for its residents, the hotel is out of carshot of most of the hubbub and the crowds go home early anyway. An air of calm and orderliness returns and Comino's few but precious natural resources – unspoilt terrain, pristine waters and superb climate – can be enjoyed again. The result is very much the idyll hailed by the advertisements as the last jewel of the Mediterranean. ❏

Map on page 256

TIP

Day visitors to Comino may be able to use the sports facilities of the Hotel Comino, subject to resident demand; tel: 2152 9821.

BELOW: yachts at rest moored just off the island.

GOING TO SEA

*Although Malta has relatively few beaches, its blue skies
and blue waters are the envy of the Mediterranean. An
excellent way of enjoying both is to weigh anchor*

The Maltese are understandably proud of their surrounding sea. In contrast
with the waters of most other countries that border the Mediterranean,
those around Malta, Gozo and Comino are clear, blue and unpolluted. In
the Blue Lagoon, you don't need a snorkel and mask to watch a coin sink to
30 metres (100 ft). The grim sea pollution, annually condemned in other resort
areas by the European Union for failing to meet health standards, does not
exist here. Sometimes there might be a jellyfish or two. So it is little wonder
that so much of Maltese life revolves around the sea, both above and below
its shimmering surface.

Visitors in search of boat trips are well catered for in Malta. Things have pro-
gressed remarkably since the heady, romantic days when the only way to have
a day out was by finding, and bargaining with, a willing fisherman with a *luzzu*.

Grand Harbour cruise

The most popular boat trip, and the one that no visitor to Malta should miss, is
the Grand Harbour cruise. From Sliema, the boat crosses Marsamxett Harbour,
with Valletta as its backdrop, then passes Manoel Island and the Msida Yacht
Marina before heading out to sea and turning through the breakwaters into the
Grand Harbour. This is the way to see Valletta, Fort
St Elmo, Fort St Angelo and the Three Cities as sea-
farers have done, for centuries. In fact, it is only from
this perspective that you can truly start to appreciate
the scale of Malta's sea defences. Deep within the
harbour the modern dockyards and commercial enter-
prises bring Malta's maritime history up to date.

The tour is accompanied by a commentary which
intersperses an insightful historical narrative with
humorous anecdotes and some interesting nuggets
of information.

Days out

The biggest choice of pleasure cruises is to be found
along the Strand in Sliema. The largest company is
Captain Morgan (tel: 2134 3373/2133 1961), with an
ever-growing fleet of distinctive red-and-white boats
and which also operates out of Bugibba. The price of
a day cruise generally includes a buffet lunch with
local wine, constant refreshments and, should it be
required, door-to-door service by minibus.

The most comprehensive sightseeing trip is the
Round the Islands cruise, which takes in the whole
archipelago; alternatively, there is a Round Malta
cruise and a Round Gozo cruise. All the cruise companies run boats to the most popular destination for
visitors, Comino's Blue Lagoon. However, because
of its popularity, this can mean that the lagoon seems

PRECEDING PAGES:
sailing the old-
fashioned way.
LEFT: Comino's
pristine coastline.
BELOW: catamarans,
the quick way to
get further afield.

overcrowded and short on the tranquil, turquoise charm that it once had. An alternative is the Oki-koki speedboat, which picks up passengers from excursion boats at anchor in the lagoon, then roars off at Miami-Vice velocity into the smaller channels and sea caves where larger vessels are unable to go.

Different vessels

Most pleasure cruisers are fairly functional, unremarkable vessels, but there are exceptions. A romantic, schooner-rigged Turkish *gulet*, all wooden boards and gleaming brass, and the *Charlotte Louise*, a square-sail gaff-rigged schooner, both ply the route to Gozo, Comino and the Blue Lagoon.

Modern rigged catamarans also sail the Maltese waters and by night the *Spirit of Malta* turns into a party craft – although, with its reggae music and rum rations, it is actually much more Spirit of the Caribbean.

The most unusual vessel is the *MV Seabelow*. It has a large observation keel below the water line, where passengers eagerly scan the depths for marine life. In truth there's not a lot to see down here. The most unusual sight is a golden statue of Christ, placed on the sea-bed in St Paul's Bay in May 1990 to commemorate the visit of Pope John Paul II. His Holiness stayed above the waves, sailing by on a high-speed catamaran to bless it. The statue has now been moved to Qawra, to a spot where three young Maltese divers lost their lives when they were trapped in an underwater cave.

Plain sailing

Here are a few tips to make sure you have an enjoyable day out. Firstly, make sure you know where you are going. That may sound silly, but many a round-

BELOW: a large traditional *luzzu*, converted for carrying passengers.

the-islands excursion has turned into a Blue Lagoon trip at the last moment because of weather conditions, and the passengers are the last to be told. Don't forget your sunblock and sunhat (sunburn at sea is much more likely than on land because of reflection from the water). Finally, if you're not a good sailor beware the longer cruises, where the swell can be a little rough.

If you only want to dip your toe in the water, metaphorically speaking, try the **Blue Grotto**, or Gozo's **Inland Sea**. The latter is a surprisingly lively small-scale adventure, particularly good for children.

Serious sailing

The main island of Malta alone has an indented coastline of some 200 km (320 miles) of clear water where bays and coves provide secure anchorage for the night. With more than 1,000 sheltered berths on offer, Malta is making its mark as an attractive international yachting centre. The Msida Marina Yachting Centre is the largest facility, though even little Gozo has a marina of its own. You can charter craft from here or through Captain Morgan.

For really serious sailors the two highlights of the calendar are the Syracuse–Malta and Rimini–Malta–Rimini races. Another strenuous annual event is the single-handed, round-Malta race. The Valletta Yacht Club on Manoel Island has full details of these and also organises island regattas.

In the winter months, the winds are usually northeasterly *(grigal)*, which cause surges and can reach storm conditions that last an average of three days; the worst are in January. The prevailing wind, however, is the northwesterly *(majjistral,* or mistral) and can blow up to force nine. Spring and autumn winds are mostly southerly and humid *(xlokk,* or sirocco). ❑

TIP

Yachties will no doubt enjoy the Malta International Boat Show, held annually from late February to early March. Some 60 exhibitors participate, with exhibits both ashore and afloat.

BELOW: a Captain Morgan cruiser and the *Black Pearl* at Msida marina.

Map
on pages
140–41

A TRIP TO SICILY

*With its rich Greek and Roman legacy, the sophistication
of Taormina and the pure drama of Mount Etna, the Italian island
of Sicily makes an alluring excursion from Malta*

J ust 90 km (60 miles) north of Malta, the Mediterranean's largest island is a simple day trip away. Sign on with Virtu Ferries, jump aboard their catamaran (referred to as a high-speed ferry), and within 90 minutes you can set foot on Sicilian soil at Pozzallo. After passport formalities are completed, luxury air-conditioned double-decker buses will whisk you north to Etna and Taormina. If you don't mind whistle-stop packages, if you are short of time and/or money, then this is the way to go. However, be warned that you have to get up very early in the morning to catch the catamaran and that the 90-minute journey out can be a stomach-churning experience.

Independent travellers can also take the same catamaran route to Pozzallo, hire a car and make the long drive north (around 4 hours to Etna). A quicker alternative is to take the catamaran to Catania (crossing time: 3 hours), which is only some 25 km (16 miles) south of Taormina and Etna.

BELOW: the view
from Taormina
towards Mount
Etna.

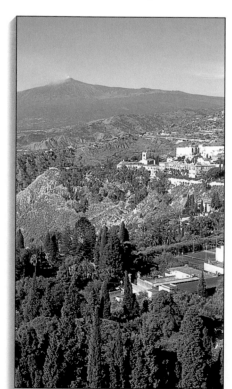

North from Pozzallo

Don't expect an immediate change in topography. After all, long ago these two countries were one landmass and this part of southern Sicily, like Malta, is also mostly barren and flat. After an hour or so, however, the landscape begins to rise and fall. It becomes lush and promising, even in summer, and you will pass over two of Europe's highest road bridges while looking down to the ancient town of **Modica**. The historic town of **Ragusa** lies just a few kilometres further north.

Mount Etna

Rising above the plain of Catania to a height of over 3,300 metres (11,000 ft), **Mount Etna** is the highest and the most active volcano in Europe. In 1669, lava reached as far afield as Catania, and in 1928 the city of Mascali was devastated. The mountain also blew in 1971, 1983, 1998 and 2001. As you ascend the slopes you will see the legacy of this destruction, including houses wrecked and buried up to their rooftops in lava following the 1983 and 2001 eruptions.

Yet, tempting fate, the locals continue to inhabit its slopes and, as a reward, harvest its rich benefits. Etna's fertile soil produces wonderful fruit and vegetables, including the island's best wines and some of the finest olive oil in the world.

Most itineraries stop at the **Sylvester Craters**, created in the 1892 eruption. The craters are a spectacular lunar-like landscape with massive panoramic views down the slopes. Dotted here and there, far below, are smaller, earlier volcanic cones, many now cloaked in mature greenery. The higher the mountain climbs, the darker the colours become; greenery disappears, reds and purples dominate, then in turn give way to greys and blacks. Then, in the cooler months, pure white snow caps the volcano, which is transformed into a popular ski resort.

Taormina

Taormina is Sicily's most dramatic resort, a stirring place celebrated by poets and literary figures from Classical times onwards. Today, it would still figure highly in any Mediterranean beauty contest, not least for its magnificent hill-top setting. Critics point out that this is a safe, sophisicated un-Sicilian pocket, that it is a Sicilian St Tropez, but in a place this beautiful, few visitors care.

The jewel in Taormina's crown is its **Teatro Greco**, originally built by the Greeks and then rebuilt by the Romans when Taormina enjoyed considerable status and prosperity. Constructed on the very crest of the old town and hewn out of the hillside, this is one of the most spectacularly sited ancient amphitheatres in the world. Views plunge down to the coastline in three directions, overlooking the aptly named Isola Bella and the mouthwatering beach resort of **Giardini Naxos**, which was the site of the very first Sicilian colony, founded by Greek settlers. On a clear spring or winter's day, with snow-capped Etna in the background, the scene is truly breathtaking.

A walk along Corso Umberto

Most of Taormina's sights lie on or just off its pedestrianised main street, **Corso Umberto**. Here, former *palazzi* and other venerable buildings, dating from late Medieval times onwards, have been turned into chic shops, romantic restaurants and chi-chi cafés. Luxury food emporia show off bottled peppers, candied fruits and fresh kumquats. Majolica tiles, leather goods and traditional puppets vie for window space with chandeliers and reproductions of Classical statuary. After the relative paucity of Malta's shopping, it is like stumbling into Aladdin's Cave. Prices, of course, reflect the setting.

Start your visit at the corner of Piazza Emanuele and Corso Umberto, where you will find the **Palazzo Corvaja**, a handsome 15th-century structure, formerly home to the Sicilian parliament. The upper part houses an excellent small historical museum (free admission), while below is the tourist office. Head straight for the Teatro Greco (well signposted) then return to the Corso Umberto and walk its whole length. There's lots to admire including the **Torre dell'Orologio** (Clock Tower), half-way along the street, and near the very end, the **Duomo** (Cathedral).

Try to make time to visit the lush, tiered town gardens, the **Giardino Pubblico** (a 5–10-minute walk, signposted from the Teatro Greco). They were bequeathed to the town by an eccentric Englishwoman in the 1920s and feature a number of follies. The largest of these – the Villa Communale – has become synonymous with the gardens.

The return to Malta is usually calmer than the incoming journey. Also, prepare youself for an extremely long day on the move as you won't return to Valletta until late evening. ❏

TIP

Beware of the Italian custom that a drink taken seated at the table is much more expensive than one taken standing at the bar. But wherever you eat or drink in Taormina it is likely to be expensive.

BELOW: the magnificently sited Greco-Roman Theatre at Taormina.
OVERLEAF: Maltese watchtower.

ⵣ INSIGHT GUIDES

Travel Tips

CONTENTS

Getting Acquainted

The Place.............................284
The Climate 284
The Economy 284
Government 284

Planning the Trip

When to Visit........................285
What to Bring.......................285
Getting There 285
Pets 285
Maps 285
Visas & Passports 286
Public Holidays & Festivals....286
Customs 286
Health 286
Money Matters......................286
Tourist Offices......................287

Practical Tips

Media 287
Post & Telecommunications ..288
Local Tourist Offices..............288
Embassies in Malta...............288
Disabled Travellers................288
Security & Crime...................288
Business Travellers 288
Students 289
Medical Treatment 289
Business Hours 289
Etiquette 290
Tipping 290
Religious Services.................290

Getting Around

Orientation...........................290
By Bus 290
Between Islands....................290
By Taxi 291
Driving 291
Car Hire 291
Cycles and Motorbikes 292

Where to Stay

Hotels & Hotel Listings 292
Youth Hostels 294
Farmhouses in Gozo..............294
Holiday Complexes................295

Where to Eat

Restaurant Listings 295
Café Life 296
Fenkata................................297

Culture

Theatre & Museum Times 299
Cinema & Nightlife 299
Special Events & Casinos 299

Sport

Participant Sports..................300
Sporting Events.....................300
Spectator Sports...................300
Other Activities 300

Shopping

What to Buy 301
Crafts and Markets 301

Children

What to do 301

Language

Pronunciation Tips 302
Place Names.........................302

Further Reading

History 302
Architecture 303
Art 303
Fiction..................................303

Getting Acquainted

The Place

Situation: 95 km (60 miles) south of Sicily and around 300 km (180 miles) north and east from the North African coast.
Area: *Malta*: 320 sq km/124 sq miles. *Gozo*: 67 sq km/26 sq miles. *Comino*: 2.5 sq km/1 sq mile.
Capital: Valletta.
Population: 400,000.
Language: Maltese and English.
Religion: Roman Catholic.
Time Zone: GMT + 1 hour. From the last Sunday in March until the last Sunday in October, clocks are a further hour ahead of GMT.
Currency: Maltese Lira.
Weights and Measures: Metric.
Electricity: 220/240-volt and 110 for shavers. Electricity is expensive. Visitors from the UK may use their normal three-pin plug items. Visitors from elsewhere may need an adaptor.
International dialling code: 356.

The Climate

The climate of Malta has been the nation's fortune. Even in winter the temperature rarely drops below 12°C (54°F). Snows or frosts are unknown and rain is likely to fall only between November and February. During the summer months it can top 43°C (109°F), although 29°C (84°F) is more usual. Between April and September, there is virtually non-stop sunshine and soaring temperatures.

Geography

There are no mountains, rivers or lakes on Malta's islands, and the land appears rocky and barren, with only a thin layer of topsoil. Despite this apparent barrenness, the cultivation of vegetables and vines is prolific.

Centuries ago, Malta's dense woodland was razed and the only trees to remain are the carob, pine, citrus, ficus and tamarisk.

The coastline is predominantly rocky, with very occasional sandy stretches. The eastern side of Malta is indented with numerous bays which make for deep natural harbours, while sheer cliffs drop 250 metres (820 ft) to the sea in the southern part of the island.

The Economy

Tourism accounts for more than one-quarter of Malta's gross national product. During the last decade there has been heavy investment in a number of five-star hotels and tourist projects. One of these is the development of Grand Harbour's Pinto Wharf into a cruise liner terminal.

Other main sources of income are manufacturing, financial services, technology and telecommunications, and agriculture. Manufacturing has veered away from traditional textile production to the technological and light engineering sector. ST Microelectronics – the world's fourth-largest semiconductor group – has a major plant at Kirkop employing over 2,000 people. It is Malta's largest private employer and produces 60 percent of the country's domestic exports. The Mosta Technopark has a cluster of light-engineering and electronic firms, and much encouragement is being given to the establishment of small and medium-sized industries.

Legislation has helped the development of financial centre status in the insurance, investment, banking and general finances sectors. A stock exchange was established in 1992 and now registers over 100,000 stockholders. Current privatisation plans include the sale of presently government-controlled entities such as the Malta Freeport, popular state lotteries and gambling venues. Malta became a member of the European Union in 2004.

Government

After a history dominated by the presence of other nations, the Maltese islands gained their independence from Britain on 21 September 1964. The Independence Constitution established a parliamentary democracy, guarding the fundamental rights of citizens and guaranteeing the separation of the executive powers. General and local elections are held by universal suffrage with proportional representation. Malta has always retained its status as a member of the Commonwealth.

On 13 December 1974, Malta became an independent republic with a Maltese president as the head of state, replacing the British monarch and the representative governor-general. Executive power lies with the elected prime minister and the cabinet. The role of the president is largely nominal and ceremonial: while the president assents to bills and can prorogue and dissolve parliament, this is only in accordance with the prime minister.

On 31 March 1979, Malta's agreements with Britain and NATO came to an end and, for the first time in their history, the islands were entirely free of a foreign military presence.

In the present parliament there are 65 members, excluding the speaker, who may be appointed from within or from outside the House of Representatives. In 1987, after an earlier distorted general election result, an amendment to the constitution was passed, guaranteeing that the party polling the majority of the popular vote would govern, if necessary through added seats. Central government is still all-powerful in Malta, but the last decade has seen the introduction of local councils, initially accepted suspiciously by voters but now seen as a valid tool of local and regional improvement.

Planning the Trip

When to Visit

April and May are delightful, although some people will not find the sea warm enough for swimming: flowers are in full bloom, temperatures are balmy, and the crowds have not yet arrived. Summer starts in early June, warms up until August and cools down to October. This is when the sea is at its best. Avoid July and August if you want to miss the crowds. September and October are also great – the flowers are not as abundant, but the warm seas can compensate. December is also pleasant; after the short rainy season, buttercups and mustard plants form a yellow carpet over much of the island.

What to Bring

In summer it can be very hot, so bring only loose, cotton clothing. Sunglasses and a hat with a brim are essential. If travelling between October and May, bring a raincoat or umbrella; during winter months, add a heavy sweater and strong shoes. Men need to wear a jacket and tie only in the most exclusive restaurants, though not in August, which is the hottest month.

Getting There

By Air

All schedule and charter flights arrive at Malta International Airport at Gudja. There is also a heliport terminal on Gozo to service private planes as well as the regular 20-seater helicopter service that flies between Gozo and Malta's international airport.

Malta's national airline, Air Malta, operates from many European cities and some North African ones. In the UK, for enquiries, tel: 0845 6073710 or check out www.airmalta.com. Air Malta flies from Heathrow, Gatwick, Birmingham, Manchester and Glasgow airports in Britain. In Europe, it flies from Athens, Frankfurt, Paris, Rome, Milan, Catania, Munich, Geneva and Copenhagen. Many other airlines also operate scheduled services to Malta.

Flying time from the UK is about 3 hrs 15 mins.

Travel to and from the Airport

There is a No. 39 bus service linking Malta's airport terminal with the capital and neighbouring villages. There are also taxis – usually in the form of white Mercedes. To avoid having to haggle with taxi drivers it is best to pay a fixed rate at a desk within the arrivals terminal and then present the taxi driver with your pre-paid voucher.

Transit/Transfer to Gozo

If your final destination is not Malta, but the nearby islands of Gozo or Comino, the tourist information office within the airport concourse will be able to advise you of your best onward journey if you are not using the helicopter link.

Taxis from the airport or, in the daylight hours, a bus service from Valletta will be able to take you on to the port of Cirkewwa for the ferry to Gozo. For transfers to Comino, contact the Comino Hotel, which runs a ferry service from Cirkewwa to the island, tel: 2152 9821.

By Sea

Many cruise ships call in at Malta's Grand Harbour with tourists on day visits. But, for independent travellers, the only means of getting to the islands by sea is by car ferry (www.virtuferries.com) or catamaran from Sicily. Both services leave Pozzallo, the southernmost point of Sicily. The timetables change constantly and the catamaran car

Pets

Malta is free of rabies, so no animal may be imported from any country where rabies is endemic. Cats and dogs may be brought from the UK but have to undergo a three-week quarantine period. From elsewhere, the quarantine period is six months.

A formal application to import any animal should be made before arrival to: The Director of Agriculture, Department of Agriculture, 14 Mickel Anton Vassallo Street, Valletta, Malta, tel: 2143 5898.

ferry runs only in the summer months when there is good weather. There is also a three-hour catamaran passenger-only service from Catania, Sicily, in good weather.

In Italy most travel agents will be able to book a car passage for you, or call Malta: tel: SMS 2123 2211 or 2133 7133.

By Car

Arriving with a car does not require a permit, but the car must have "Green Card" insurance specific to Malta. Cars may be imported to the islands for a period of up to three months (the maximum permitted stay for a tourist); any longer will require special police permission.

On arrival, the car's engine- and chassis-numbers are logged by customs officers. This is to ensure that the same items reappear for departure and are not sold as spare parts or exchanged on the local market. The same officials examine the cars for goods on which duty is payable.

Maps

Banks and hotels often provide free basic maps for orientation and to help you get around the islands. HSBC's map, for example, gives a clear street plan of Valletta with all important locations listed (including their branches for exchanging money, of course) and a simple orientation map that not only identifies the main towns and villages but also the beaches and other places of interest.

If you are driving, however, a *bona fide* detailed map is essential since the islands' road system is more complicated than it seems. This can be bought at any bookshop or good newsagents.

Visas & Passports

EU visitors require a valid passport or identity card. Members of the Commonwealth require a valid passport or a visitor's passport. This entitles them to a maximum stay of three months as a tourist. This also applies to visitors from British dependencies, Japan and the US. Should you wish to extend your stay beyond three months, or perhaps to take up temporary residence, apply to the Immigration Police at Police Headquarters, Calcedonius Street, Floriana, tel: 2122 4002.

Most other nationals require visas. No visitors may take up employment without a work permit.

Malta is represented by an ambassador, high commissioner or consulate in most major cities throughout the world, with offices where information or advice on passport and visa queries can be obtained. Where Air Malta is represented, its offices can offer assistance too.

In Britain, the Malta High Commission is at 36–38 Piccadilly, London W1J OLE, tel: 020 7292 4800.

Customs

When travelling between EU countries, personal effects intended for one's own use are not subject to any duty. Travellers from outside the EU may bring into Malta, duty-free, either 200 cigarettes, 50 cigars, or 250g in loose tobacco. In addition, 1 litre of spirits (or fortified/sparkling wine) and 2 litres of still wine are permitted. Perfume is limited to 50 grams and eau de toilette to 250 ml.

Health

Inoculations
For visitors arriving from the US, Canada, Australia and Europe, no inoculations are required, though it is a good idea to check when you last had a tetanus booster.

Sun
The Maltese islands are bathed in sunshine virtually year round. In the summer, don't underestimate the intensity of the sun's rays. Take precautions: the wearing of a hat in the middle of the day is recommended for everyone, especially the elderly and the very young. Begin with a high SPF factor suncream or total sun-block until your skin has acclimatised to the sun's rays. Popular brands of sun-tanning creams are always available in Malta.

Pests
As with any Mediterranean country, the usual troupe of gnats, mosquitoes and cockroaches may be resident. Insect repellent creams and sprays are readily available. Malta has a few snakes but happily they are not poisonous. Sometimes the odd jellyfish lurks in the island's clear waters.

Drinking Water
Tap water is quite safe to drink but fountain water must be avoided as it may not come directly from the mains supply.

Money Matters

The Maltese currency is the Lira (Liri), sometimes referred to as the Maltese pound (written as Lm).

Public Holidays & Festivals

There are several public holidays commemorating patron saints' feast days. Every parish celebrates its own as well as those that are national. On these days, shops, businesses and schools are closed, though restaurants and bars will most likely remain open.

Below is a guide to the national public holidays. On New Year's Day and Christmas Day, buses stop between noon–3pm to allow everyone time with their families.

1 January: New Year's Day.
10 February: St Paul's Shipwreck.
19 March: Feast of St Joseph.
31 March: Freedom Day.
March or April: Good Friday.
1 May: St Joseph the Worker.

7 June: Commemoration of 7 June 1919.
29 June: Feast of St Peter and St Paul. *Mnarja* harvest festival.
15 August: Feast of the Assumption.
8 September: Feast of Our Lady of the Victories.
21 September: Independence Day.
8 December: Feast of the Immaculate Conception.
13 December: Republic Day.
25 December: Christmas Day.

The harvest festival of *Mnarja* takes place on the night of 29 June at Buskett Gardens near Rabat and Mdina, and continues into the next day. Folkloric celebration and an all-night picnic are followed the next

morning by horse races through the streets below Rabat.

The weekend before Lent is **Carnival**. Floats, dancing and masked parades fill the streets of Valletta with the islands' biggest show while merry-making in Nadur is worth experiencing too. Village *festi* are held throughout the summer and combine religious celebration of the parish patron saint with fireworks and band parades.

Good Friday is a public and religious holiday, with solemn processions held in many localities.

A full calendar of religious and secular events is available from tourist information centres.

Each lira is divided into 100 cents. Denominations are:
Notes: Lm2, Lm5, Lm10, Lm20, Lm50. *Coins*: 1c, 2c, 5c, 10c, 25c, 50c, Lm1. The Euro is not expected to replace the Lira before 2007.

Changing Money

Sterling travellers' cheques are recommended, though it is just as easy to change US dollar cheques. When changing travellers' cheques, remember to take your passport for identification. Hotels accept travellers' cheques, but restaurants and shops will take only cash or credit cards. However, you will probably find a better rate of exchange at banks than at hotels.

The maximum amount of Maltese currency you are allowed to bring into Malta is Lm50. On departure, you may take out no more than Lm25. To change Liri back to foreign currency you will need all exchange receipts to prove foreign currency was brought in initially.

Credit Cards

Visa and MasterCard are widely accepted, even by the women who sell their lace table cloths on the village waterfront; American Express is also widely accepted. American Express card members needing assistance may call at the representative's offices at 14 Zachary Street, Valletta, tel: 2123 2141.

ATMS are available at most localities and accept major credit and debit cards.

Banking Hours

Opening hours vary but are usually Mon–Fri 8.30am–12.45pm; Sat 8.30am–noon. There is a 24-hour, seven days a week service available at Malta International Airport. Certain foreign exchange bureaux are open after normal banking hours, while others are closed in winter. Both the Bank of Valletta and HSBC publish maps of Malta with complete lists of their branches and opening times. They are available from the banks and from tourist information centres.

Tourist Offices Abroad

France:
Office du Tourisme de Malte,
9 Cite Trevise,
75009 Paris
Tel: (33) 1 48 00 03 79
Fax: (33) 1 48 00 04 41

Ireland:
Plunkett Communications,
46 St James Place,
Dublin 2
Tel: (353) 1 662 0332
Fax: (353) 1 639 8933

Italy:
Ente per il Turismo di Malta,
Via M Gonzaga 7,
20123 Milan
Tel: (39) 0286 7376
Fax: (39) 0287 4687

Netherlands:
Verkeersbureau Malta,
Singel 540, 4th Floor,
1017 AZ Amsterdam
Tel: (31) 20 6270 223
Fax: (31) 20 6207 233

United Kingdom:
Malta Tourist Office,
Unit C, Park House,
14 Northfields,
London SW18 1DD
Tel: (44) 020 8877 6990
Fax: (44) 020 8874 9416

United States and Canada:
Malta Tourist Office.
65 Broadway Suite 823,
New York NY 10006
Tel: (1) 212 430 3799
Fax: (1) 425 795 3425

Practical Tips

Media

Newspapers

Most European daily newspapers arrive in Malta on the day of publication, with newsagents stocking everything from *Le Monde*, *Die Welt*, *La Repubblica*, London's *Times* and *Sun* to the *International Herald Tribune*. An up-to-date supply of international magazines and journals is also widely available.

There are two English-language newspapers: *The Times*, which takes a pro-establishment stance, and *The Malta Independent*, which purports to take an independent line but is equally establishment-biased. There are three English-language Sunday newspapers: *The Sunday Times, The Malta Independent* and *Malta Today*. There are also a number of dailies and Sundays in Maltese.

Radio & Television

TVM is the national public television station, with local programmes shown in Maltese and imported ones in English.

Radio Malta 1, on 999khz medium wave, and Radio Malta 2, on 93.7 VHF/FM, broadcast popular music and general news, mainly in Maltese. There are also 18 commercial radio stations, three of them broadcasting in English. The output is mainly pop music. It is possible to pick up the BBC World Service on short-wave, though the reception is variable. See the local newspapers for frequencies. In addition, both satellite and cable TV are widely available.

There are also five independent television stations which broadcast in Maltese but have some English programmes.

Post & Telecommunications

Post

Post offices are found in most towns and villages. Hours of business are Mon–Sat 7.45am–1pm. Stamps are obtainable from post offices, hotels, newsagents and some souvenir shops in tourist areas. You'll find postboxes in the red British pillar-box style or built into walls.

The main post offices are:
Malta: The General Post Office, 305, Triq Qormi, Marsa.
Gozo: Main Post Office, 129 Triq ir-Repubblika, Victoria. Open Mon–Sat 7.30am–5.15pm.

A *poste restante* service is available. Write in advance to The Postmaster General at the General Post Office address in Marsa listed above. A passport or identity card may be necessary as identification when collecting post.

Telephone

The telephone system has been upgraded in recent years to include the Internet, e-mail, etc. It is now possible to dial any country on the international direct dialling system if you know the prefix.

For internal directory enquiries dial: 1182. International calls should prove no problem, but for overseas operators' help, or prefix number enquiries, dial Freecall: 1152. For faults on the line: tel: 133.

Call boxes throughout the Maltese islands almost exclusively take phonecards, which are on sale at stationer's shops. It is possible to rent mobile telephones; call Vodaphone, tel: 1189, or Go Mobile, tel: 1187.

Fax/Telex

Faxes and telexes may be sent from Maltacom offices located at:
Malta International Airport:
tel: 2124 9382/3. Open: 7am–7pm daily.
Valletta: South Street, tel: 2124 1409 or 2122 4131. Open: 7am–7pm daily.

St Julian's: St George's Road, tel: 2131 0980. Open: 24 hours.
St Paul's Bay: St Paul's Street, tel: 2158 0511.
Sliema: Bisazza Street (in the Plaza Shopping Centre), tel: 2133 5501.
Victoria (Gozo): Triq ir-Repubblika, tel: 2156 3590.
Many stationer's shops will send and receive faxes too.

Local Tourist Offices

The address of the main tourist office is: **Malta Tourism Authority**, Auberge d'Italie, Merchants Street, Valetta, tel: 2291 5000, www.tourism.org.mt/ This office is not open to personal callers. Walk-in tourist information offices are located at:
Malta, Freedom Square, Valletta, tel: 2123 7747; Spinola Palace, St Julian's, tel: 2138 1392.
Malta International Airport, Gudja, tel: 2369 6073.
Gozo, Independence Square, Victoria, tel: 2156 1419.
Mgarr Harbour, tel: 2155 3343.

Embassies in Malta

US Embassy: Development House, St Anne Street, Floriana; tel: 2561 4000.
Australian High Commission: Villa Fiorentino, Rampa Ta' Xbiex, tel: 2133 8201
British High Commission: Whitehall Mansions, Xatt Ta' Xbiex, Ta' Xbiex tel: 2323 0000

Disabled Travellers

Malta is not an easy country for travellers with disabilities. The hilly streets, particularly of Valletta and Victoria, and the poor condition of the pavements, mean that getting around can be difficult. Many pavements are truly hazardous.

However, the hotels on Malta have done a great deal to accommodate people with disabilities, and exhibitions like *The Malta Experience*, for example, cater well. The natural willingness

of Maltese people can be counted upon to help if needed, but always telephone ahead to check facilities.

For further information regarding facilities for disabled travellers, contact the Health Education Unit, (tel: 2124 1484) or the National Commission for the Handicapped, (tel: 2148 7789). Tourist information centres can also advise on the accessibility of sites and museums. Malta International Airport offers help to disabled travellers both on arrival and on departure.

Security & Crime

The islands are a comparatively safe place for a holiday. There is very little violent crime and a woman needn't feel threatened when out on her own at night. Even so, common sense should always prevail. Take the usual precautions against bag snatchers or pickpockets in crowded places.

Should you be the victim of a crime you must notify the police immediately and, if necessary, seek assistance from your embassy or consulate. Contact the relevant diplomatic mission too for advice should you happen to be detained by the police.

The police are quite approachable, although rarely in evidence on the streets. There is a police station in each town.

Police General Headquarters

Malta: Calcedonius Street, Floriana, tel: 2122 4001.
Gozo: 113 Triq ir-Repubblika, Victoria, tel: 2156 2046–8.

Emergency Numbers

Malta: tel: 196.
Gozo: tel: 2156 2040.

Business Travellers

Business transactions can take time and require patience. In the Latin manner, there is a considerable amount of formality involved and some Maltese businessmen are known to be sharp operators. Also, with Malta being a small society, with much

Students

NSTS, the Student and Youth Travel organisation in Malta, is located at 220 St Paul's Street, Valletta, tel: 2124 4983/2124 6628. The Gozo office is at 45 Pjazza San Frangisk, Victoria. Both offices can provide you with an invaluable little booklet, the *Student Saver Discount Scheme*, which lists shops, exhibitions, restaurants and transport, offering reductions of between 15 and 40 percent on prices to those with an ISIC (International Student/Scholar Identity card). Entrance to museums is free to students anyway.

intermarrying, recommendations will often be for a brother, cousin or other relative, which may or may not be an advantage.

It is always advisable for any newcomer to the local business scene to do thorough research and to take advice, both legal and political. Many deals may require intricate dealings with what seems like endless bureaucracy, and this can be frustrating. On the plus side, after agreements have been reached, it is usually plain sailing. The many successful, long-established foreign companies working on the islands or with Maltese partners are proof of this.

Setting up Business

The Government has introduced many attractive incentives for companies considering manufacturing on the islands. These include considerable tax-free concessions, soft loans, training grants and a choice of ready-made factories at subsidised rental on industrial estates close to areas with a large workforce.

Contact: Malta Development Corporation, Triq P-Industrija, Qormi, tel: 2144 1888, fax: 2144 1887, www.investinmalta.com

Malta Freeport

Malta Freeport is the island's customs-free distribution and cargo-handling zone, located in Marsaxlokk Harbour. The Freeport is free of customs and excise duties, income tax, exchange control and other duties. Benefits are guaranteed by law for 15 years. Information is available from the Malta Freeport Corporation Ltd, Freeport Centre, Port of Marsaxlokk, Kalafrana BBG 05, tel: 2165 0200, fax: 2168 4814.

To promote Malta as an international financial and trading centre, the government has enacted legislation to transform the island into a financial centre. Contact the Malta Financial Service Centre, Attard; tel: 2144 1155, fax: 2144 1188, www.freeport. com.mt.

Conference Centres

Many hotels offer excellent conference facilities. These include the Crowne Plaza, Le Meridien Phoenicia, New Dolmen Hotel, Corinthia Palace, Corinthia San Gorg, Corinthia Marina, Westin Dragonara, Radisson Bay Point, Suncrest and the Hilton Malta.

The government's own centre, the Mediterranean Conference Centre in Valletta, is excellently equipped with halls that can accommodate between 70 and 1,400 delegates in theatre style. Its Great Ward is claimed to be the longest exhibition hall in Europe. Contact Mediterranean Conference Centre, Valletta; tel: 2124 3840, fax: 2124 5900, www.mcc.com.mt.

Medical Treatment

General Medical Care

Malta follows the World Health Organisation's recommendations for health safety. Pharmacists and chemists have quite wide prescribing powers and most well-known prescribed drugs are generally available here. Visitors with specific requirements must ensure they have an adequate supply of medication, or bring a prescription to present to the pharmacist or doctor.

Britons who fall ill are able to take advantage of a reciprocal free medical care agreement between the two countries. This entitles treatment for a period of up to one month. Reciprocal health agreements also exist between EU countries and provide differing degrees of exemption for different nationalities. Full details of individual agreements are available from the Department of Health, tel: 020 7210 4850. All doctors on Malta and Gozo speak English and, probably, Italian.

Pharmacies

There are numerous pharmacies and chemists throughout the islands, though they have no recognisable symbol by which to identify them. Most keep normal shop opening times, from 8.30 or 9am until 12.30pm and then 4–7pm. A roster of pharmacies open over the weekend is listed in the weekend newspapers. The qualified staff can dispense many products without a doctor's prescription.

Ambulance/Emergency Service

Malta: tel: 196.
Gozo: tel: 2156 1600.

Principal Hospitals

St Luke's Hospital:
Gwardamanga, near Valletta; tel: 2124 1251/2123 4101.
Gozo General Hospital:
Triq l'Arcisqof Pietru Pace, Victoria; tel: 2156 1600.

There are also a number of government-run health centres and district health centres (polyclinics) in the towns and villages which are able to offer first aid.

Business Hours

Malta opens early for business with the working day usually running from 8.30am–5pm. In the summer months work will start and finish even earlier.

Shops are generally open Mon–Fri 9am–7pm, with a long siesta-like lunch break between 12.30pm and 4pm, and mornings only on Saturdays. However, in tourist resorts some shops may open throughout the day and at weekends.

Most businesses close on public holidays, though museums may operate Sunday opening hours. For a list of public holidays *see Public Holidays and Festivals, page 286.*

Etiquette

Churches
Women, on entering church, must cover shoulders and avoid plunging necklines. If they are deemed to be unsuitably attired they may be handed a scarf to cover up, or refused entrance. A similar principle applies to men with shorts – though the only church that strictly applies this rule is Ta' Pinu on Gozo.

Sunbathing
Topless and nude bathing is (officially) against the law in Malta and is punishable by fines. In fact, both are customary on certain secluded (and some non-secluded) beaches, but may attract Peeping Toms with binoculars.

Tipping

If you wish to show your appreciation, here's a rough guide:
- airport baggage 50c (total)
- 10 percent for a waiter or hairdresser
- Lm1 per week for a hotel chambermaid.
- Tipping taxi drivers is not necessary.

Religious Services

Malta is a Roman Catholic country but all religions are tolerated and services are held in various languages for foreign visitors (on Sunday). For Catholics there are as many churches for Mass as there are days of the year.

In English
Rabat: St Dominic's, St Dominic's Square, 11.15am.
St Paul's Bay: Parish Church, St Paul's Street, 11am.
Sliema: St Patrick's, St John Bosco Street, 7.30, 9 and 10am, 6.30 and 7.30pm.

Valletta: St Barbara's, Republic Street, noon.

In Italian
Valletta: St Catherine of Italy, Victory Square, 11am.

In French
Valletta: St Barbara's, Republic Street, 10am.

In German
Valletta: St Barbara's, Republic Street, 11am.

Other Denominations
Anglican: St Paul's Anglican Cathedral, Valletta, tel: 2122 5714. Holy Trinity, Rudolph Street, Sliema, tel: 2133 0575.
Union Church of Scotland and **Methodist:** St Andrew's, South Street, Valletta, tel: 2122 2643.
Greek Orthodox: 83 Merchants Street, Valletta, tel: 2122 1600.
Jewish: The Synagogue, Spur Street, Valletta. Secretary of Jewish Community, tel: 2162 5717.
Ecumenical: The Seminary, Triq Enrico Mizzi, Victoria, Gozo. Services in English on first and third Wednesday of every month, 11.15am.

Islamic Centre: Corradino Hill, Corradino, tel: 2169 7203.

Getting Around

Orientation

Malta is a small island and nowhere is more than half an hour or so by bus from Valletta, which is the central terminus for nearly all services. The same rule applies to Gozo, which is even smaller, and all bus journeys radiate from the capital Victoria.

Car hire is recommended for its cheapness and the flexibility it offers over the bus service, but be warned that the quality of driving is erratic, to say the least.

By Bus

Since so many local people depend upon the buses, the system is both reliable and inexpensive. On Malta, the main bus station is just outside the city gates of Valletta and the majority of routes terminate here. Fares are calculated according to zones, (1, 2 or 3), but never cost more than a few cents. Services begin at about 5.30am and stop at about 10pm on weekdays, at 11pm weekends. Check the departure time of the last bus you require as they do vary. For bus information on Malta, call 2125 5165.

Gozo's main bus station, at Victoria, is on Triq Putirjal (tel: 2155 9344/5). Around Gozo, the buses are less frequent and finish earlier than on Malta. Use freephone 800 77 2393 for all enquiries.

Between Islands

By Boat
The Gozo Channel Company operates a car ferry (which also takes foot passengers) between Cirkewwa on Malta and Mgarr on

Gozo, offering up to 21 return crossings daily from 5.30am. Journey time is about 25 minutes. During the summer, services continue into the night and there is a non-stop shuttle service during peak holiday periods. The No. 45 bus from Valletta and the No. 48 from Bugibba connect with the ferries. Another ferry does morning and evening connections between Sa Maison/Valletta (Malta) and Mgarr (Gozo). There's also a high-speed catamaran service that leaves from The Strand in Sliema and Sa Maison on Malta.

For more detailed information on timetables contact the Gozo Channel Co:

Mgarr (Gozo)
tel: 2155 6114/2156 1622.
Cirkewwa (Malta)
tel: 2158 0435/6; 2157 1884.

If your destination is Comino, the Comino Hotel runs a ferry service throughout the year (open to all, including non-guests). It departs Comino 6.50am, 9.05am, 11.10am, 2.50pm and 4.45pm. Departs Cirkewwa 7.30am, 9.35am, 11.40am, 3.30pm and 5.25pm.

To confirm details, contact the Comino Hotel, tel: 2152 9821.

Helicopter

Helicopteros del Sureste has a helicopter service linking Malta and Gozo, with plans for other destinations. There are 18 flights a day in summer and eight in winter; the trip takes 15 minutes. Tel: 2156 1301; www.helisureste.com

By Taxi

Taxis are generally white and, more often than not, are Mercedes. As with all chauffeur-driver cars and buses, the trio of letters on their registration number will end with a "Y".

You can pick one up at the various ranks around town, at the airport, harbours and outside hotels. Street hailing is not normal, though on a Saturday night, passing cabbies may hoot to let you know they're available for hire.

It is wise to insist that either the meter be switched on, or make sure you agree a price before you start your journey. All garages run chauffeur-driven cars as taxis too.

Carriages

Karrozzin are today more of a tourist attraction than a practical means of getting from A to B. But a jaunt in a Maltese "surrey with a fringe" *gharry* is a labour-saving and picturesque way to take in the sights of Valletta, St Julian's, Sliema or Mdina. Your driver will halt every now and then to tell you a little about each view or monument. The average tour costs about Lm5 (bargain first) and usually includes a chance to be photographed at the reins.

Driving

Driving Conditions

Ask any Maltese about driving on their islands and they'll laugh and warn you to go carefully. The most important thing to remember is that though they may drive on the left (like the British), the mentality on the roads is pure Mediterranean. Do not expect direction signals. Overtaking on the inside, reversing into main roads and cutting up is the norm. There are many traffic lights, and a long series of roundabouts which seem to enlarge as the traffic grows heavier.

Saturday night in the Paceville, St Julian's and Spinola Bay areas is one long rush hour and at the weekends good weather brings out all the island's cars, with families heading for the seaside and countryside beauty spots. Coast roads are heavily congested. Whatever the provocation, drive defensively. The speed limits are 64 kph (40 mph) on highways and 40kph (25 mph) in built-up areas.

Licences

All current national and international driving licences are recognised. Visitors arriving by car should ensure that they are covered by a Green Card with insurance extension to cover Malta.

Fuel

Petrol stations are open daily 7am–6pm but only a few open on Sundays and public holidays. Some stations accept cash only, while others have an automatic pump in operation out of hours. In Gozo, stations are in Victoria or on the road to Mgarr's harbour. Fuel is comparatively inexpensive.

Parking

Parking is always difficult and fines are imposed if you leave your car blocking an exit or in a restricted zone; tow zones and traffic wardens are in operation.

Car Hire

All the familiar European firms such as Hertz and Avis have car rental services, and there are also innumerable small garages that will rent you a car at even more attractive rates. Make sure that the car is an equally attractive proposition, and check insurance cover and liability.

Rates are from about Lm8.50 per day for six days. Prices are subject to increases during the holiday season, so book well in advance if visiting in the summer. Payment by credit card is fine for large companies; smaller hire firms may prefer cash. The minimum age for hiring a vehicle is generally 25 and you will need to produce a valid driving licence or international driver's permit. Chauffeur-driven cars are quite popular with tourists and most car-hire companies also offer this service.

Malta

Alamo: through the licencee, John's Garage, at
38 Villambrosa Street, Hamrun;
tel: 2124 5038.
Avis:
50 Msida Seafront; tel: 2124 6640.
Hertz:
66 United House, Triq il-Gzira, Gzira;
tel: 2131 4636/7; 2131 9939.
Percius:
85 Triq Annibale Preca, Lija;
tel: 2144 2530.

Wembley's Rent-a-Car:
50 St George's Road, St Julians;
tel: 2138 9871;
St Andrew's Road, St Andrew's;
tel: 2133 2074.

Gozo:
Gozo Garage:
5 Triq Luigi Camilleri, Victoria;
tel: 2155 2908, fax: 2155 6866.
Mayjo Rent-a-Car:
Triq Fortunatu Mizzzi, Victoria;
tel: 2155 6678.

Cycles & Motorbikes

Cycling is not recommended in much of Malta because of the heavy volume of traffic and poor standard of driving. The situation is somewhat better on Gozo, but you should still take great care. Beware, too, of badly pot-holed roads.

Bicycles and motorbikes are available for hire throughout the islands:
Cycle Store:
135 Eucharistic Congress Street, Mosta; tel: 2143 2890.
(Bicycles only).
Victor Sultana:
New Building, Main Gate Street, Victoria, Gozo; tel: 2155 6414.

Motorbikes Only:
La Ronde:
10 Triq Belvedere, Gzira;
tel: 2132 2962.
Peter's Scooter Shop:
175A D'Argens Road, Msida;
tel: 2133 5244.
Albert's Scooter Shop:
200 St Albert's Street, Gzira (also in Bugibba); tel: 2158 3308.

Where to Stay

Hotels

All the hotels on the islands are classified from 1–5 stars, which can be differentiated as follows:

5-star: Superior standard. Fully air-conditioned. All rooms with private bath and shower, radio, television, telephone. 24-hour room service. Bar, restaurant, coffee shop, pool, sports facilities. Laundry, pressing, dry cleaning. Shops, hairdresser.
4-star: High standard. Air-conditioned. All rooms with private bath or shower, radio, telephone. Room service breakfast to midnight. Bar, restaurant, pool or beach facility. Laundry, pressing, dry cleaning. Lounge. Shops, hairdresser.
3-star: Good accommodation. All rooms with private bath or shower. Bar and restaurant. Lounge. Front office 24 hours. Laundry, pressing and dry cleaning.
2-star: Modest accommodation. At least 20 percent of rooms with private bath or shower. Breakfast facilities. Telephone or service bell in rooms. Front office during day; porter at night.
1-star: Small hotel. Shared bath or shower. All rooms with hand basin. Breakfast facilities. Office service during day; night porter.

Hotel Listings

MALTA

The following is a list of 3–5 star accommodation on Malta.

Attard
Corinthia Palace
de Paule Avenue
Tel: 2144 0301
Fax: 2146 5713

In the centre of the island, near San Anton Palace. Decorated in a grand manner, with indoor and outdoor (heated) pool. Transport provided to Valletta and to San Gorg Lido at St George's Bay. **5-star.**

Cirkewwa
Paradise Bay
Tel: 2152 1166
Fax: 2152 1153
In an isolated setting on the northern tip of Malta, near the ferry quay to Gozo and popular Paradise Bay pebble beach. Heated indoor and outdoor pools. **4-star.**

Golden Bay
Golden Sands
Golden Bay, Ghajn Tuffieha
Tel: 2157 3961
Fax: 2158 0875
In an attractive location above one of Malta's most popular sandy beaches. Good for young families. Pools, tennis. **3-star.**

Gzira
Milano Due
113 The Strand
Tel: 2134 5040/1
Fax: 2134 5045
Right on the waterfront by the excursion boats. All 108 rooms have air-conditioning and TV. **3-star.**

Marsaskala
Corinthia Jerma Palace
Tel: 2163 3222
Fax: 2163 9485
This is the only major hotel to be found on the south side of the island. Features a pool, watersport facilities, tennis, gym and a sauna. **4-star.**

Mellieha
Mellieha Bay
Ghadira
Tel: 2157 3841
Fax: 2157 6399
Facing into Mellieha Bay, a short walk from the long sand beach. Popular with groups. Features pools, watersports, tennis and nightly entertainment. **4-star.**
Mercure Selmun Palace
Selmun, near Mellieha
Tel: 2152 1040
Fax: 2152 1159

A large modern hotel attached to a former Knights' fortress in a relatively isolated location, but with beach nearby. Features a pool, watersports and tennis. **4-star.**

Qawra
New Dolmen
Tel: 2158 1510
Fax: 2158 1532
A popular, large family hotel midway between Qawra and Bugibba, facing into the bay. Features pools, watersports, tennis court, gym and Oracle Casino. **4-star.**

Price Guide

Prices are per double room including breakfast during high season:
5-star more than Lm70–140
4-star Lm40–Lm70
3-star Lm30–Lm45

Sol Suncrest
Qawra Coast Road
Tel: 2157 7101
Fax: 2157 5478
Huge hotel with 919 beds, including self-catering apartments. Well appointed. On the waterfront with its own beach, pools and restaurants. **4-star.**

St Julian's
Golden Tulip Vivaldi
Dragonara Road
Tel: 2137 8100
Fax: 2137 8101
Situated in the centre of everything that happens in Paceville and St Julian's. Comfortable and well-furnished, it is surrounded by bars and restaurants – so don't expect a quiet time here. **4-star.**
Hotel Inter-Continental
St George's Bay
Tel: 2137 7600
Fax: 2137 2222
This is a new luxurious leisure complex with superb environment and landscaped gardens. **5-star.**
The Forum
St Andrew's Road, St Andrew's
Tel: 2137 4729
Fax: 2137 0324
Set a 10-minute walk from St

Julian's resort area or the nearest rock beach. Features pool, sauna, gym and tennis court. **4-star.**
Corinthia San Gorg
St George's Bay
Tel: 2137 4114/6
Fax: 2137 4039
Opened in 1995, this is one of the Corinthia Group's flagship hotels. Good location and excellent facilities that include a wide choice of restaurants on its own beach and a well-appointed lido. Features a business centre and executive suites. **5-star.**
Hilton Malta
Portomaso
Tel: 2138 3383
Fax: 2138 6386
New waterside luxury hotel and apartment complex, including Malta's tallest building, the Portomoso Tower, which houses prestige offices. Also encompasses a yacht marina, superb conference and sports facilities and several bars and restaurants, including the Thai Blue Elephant Restaurant. **5-star.**
Radisson Bay Point
St George's Bay
Tel: 2137 4893/4
Fax: 2137 4895
Sited at the entrance to the bay in a commanding position. All rooms with views. Excellently appointed with good conference facilities. **5-star.**
Rafael Spinola
Upper Ross Street
Tel: 2137 4488
Fax: 2133 6266
In a quiet side street off the bustling main section of the resort area, this small comfortable hotel (only 32 rooms) is nicely decorated and has good service. **3-star.**
Westin Dragonara
Dragonara Road
Tel: 2138 1000
Fax: 2138 1347
This stylish and comfortable hotel has 311 sea-view rooms, set in landscaped gardens that also house the casino and the Reef Club beach lido where Malta's smart set gather. Features good conference facilities, shops, watersports and a dive school. **5-star.**

Sliema
Crowne Plaza
Tigne Street
Tel: 2134 3400
Fax: 2134 3410
In a quiet residential area but within easy walking distance of sea front and shops. Features an excellent heated family pool, tennis court, sauna, gym and four restaurants. Conference facilities are also available. **5-star.**
Howard Johnson Diplomat
Tower Road
Tel: 2134 5361
Fax: 2134 5351
Centrally placed along the Sliema Promenade with good sea views. **4-star.**
Fortina
Tigne Sea Front
Tel: 2134 3380
Fax: 2133 9388
Comfortable family hotel on the waterfront with a magnificent view across the harbour towards Valletta. Features an excellent pool, gym and tennis court. **4-star.**
Imperial
1 Rudolph Street
Tel: 2134 4093
Fax: 2133 6471
In central residential Sliema. Unpretentious, sedate clientele. Features a large pool in a garden area. **3-star.**
Plevna
2 Thornton Street, Qui-Si-Sana
Tel: 2133 1031
Fax: 2133 3558
A quiet friendly family hotel in residential section but close to shops, cafés and rock beaches. Own beach facilities with pool a short walk away. **3-star.**
Preluna Towers
124 Tower Road
Tel: 2133 4001
Fax: 2134 2292
On Sliema's main promenade, minutes from a shopping area and cafés. Has a small heated pool and good nearby beach facilities. Also features watersports, a gym, tennis court, sauna and nightclub. **4-star.**
New Tower Palace
Tower Road
Tel: 2133 7271
Fax: 2131 1235

Newly refurbished hotel with 45 pleasing rooms, most with view over seafront promenade. Smooth rock beach across the road and close to shopping centre. Features a roof restaurant and bar. **3-star.**

Tigne Court
Qui-Si-Sana
Tel: 2133 2001
Quiet family hotel facing the sea on residential waterfront. 84 rooms, some of which have a sea view. Cafés and shops nearby. Own beach facilities. **3-star.**

Victoria
Gorg Borg Olivier Street
Tel: 2133 4711
Fax: 2133 4771
Nice small hotel in residential Sliema but close to the town's amenities and beach. Good restaurant. **4-star.**

Ta' Xbiex

Best Western Les Lapins
Ta' Xbiex Sea Front
Tel: 2134 2551
Fax: 2134 3902
Set in the harbour alongside the Msida yacht marina. Features a pool and tennis court. **4-star.**

Valletta

Castille
Castille Square
Tel: 2124 3677
Fax: 2124 3679
Next to the Upper Barraca Gardens, it has 38 simple rooms. Rooftop restaurant with views, pizza café in basement. **3-star.**

Le Meridien Phoenicia
The Mall, Floriana
Tel: 2122 5241
Fax: 2123 5254
One of Malta's most prestigious hotels, set right outside the main gate of Valletta, catering mainly to business travellers. **5-star.**

Price Guide

Prices are per double room including breakfast during high season:
5-star more than Lm70–140
4-star Lm40–Lm70
3-star Lm30–Lm45

GOZO

Marsalforn

Calypso
Tel: 2156 2000
Fax: 2156 2012
On popular, busy waterfront next to beach, with 84 rooms and 12 apartments. Features floodlit tennis court, squash courts and international dive centre. **3-star.** (Currently being renovated to upgrade to a 4-star.)

Mgarr

The Grand
Triq Sant Antnin, Ghajnsielem,
Tel: 2155 6183
Fax: 2155 9744
Stylish hotel with spacious rooms and stunning views over Mgarr harbour and the Gozo Channel to Malta. Features a good-sized rooftop pool, sauna, fitness and games room, roof-garden restaurant and conference hall. **4-star.**

L'Imgarr
Triq Sant'Antnin, Ghajnsielem
Tel: 2156 0455
Fax: 2155 7589
Spectacular position overlooking the harbour. Features 74 rooms, the majority with comfortable sitting rooms, all with balconies, air-conditioning or ceiling fans, mini-bars and cable TV. Several have impressively large terraces. Also features a good restaurant, two pools, sauna, gym and conference facilities. Roof-top dining is available in summer. **5-star.**

Sannat

Ta' Cenc
Tel: 2155 6830
Fax: 2155 8199
Regularly listed as one of the Mediterranean's top hotels. Elegantly understated, single-storey complex in a tranquil location. A few independent suites and 84 rooms, all with terrace or private garden. Features two pools, one heated. Access to rock beach and sea nearby. **5-star.**

Xaghra

Cornucopia
Triq Gnien Imrek

Youth Hostels

There are very few youth hostels, but one is the Hibernia in Sliema providing 118 beds.
Tel: 2133 3859.

Tel: 2155 6486
Fax: 2155 2910
Pretty hotel on a hill outside village with 48 rooms and 5 suites. Features a swimming pool. **4-star.**

St Patrick's
Xlendi
Tel: 2156 2951
Fax: 2155 6598
Seafront hotel at the head of the bay. Air-conditioning or ceiling fans, mini-bars and cable TV in all 49 rooms. A few have Jacuzzi baths and huge balconies. Attractive restaurant and water's-edge terrace, plus roof garden with plunge pool. **4-star.**

COMINO

Comino
Tel: 2152 9821/9
Fax: 2152 9826
Peaceful, simple hotel on its own private bay with a separate block of 45 apartments. Excellent watersports facilities. Professional tennis tuition, diving school. **4-star.**

Farmhouses in Gozo

These four-square mini-fortresses, built several hundred years ago, are an integral feature of Gozo's villages and countryside. Many have been renovated and are available for holiday lets. Expect to pay from Lm60 to Lm100 per day. The main agents for arranging this kind of accommodation are:

Gozo Farmhouses
3 Triq I-Imgarr, Ghajnsielem
Tel: 2156 1280/1
Fax: 2155 8794
Offers rustic simplicity combined with mod cons. Most have pools, Jacuzzis and a hairdryer. Some have TVs, washing machines and telephones. A cook is available.

Gozo Village Holidays
11 Triq il-Kapuccini, Victoria
Tel: 2155 7255
Fax: 2155 8397
Offers attractively decorated
retreats: no television, no
telephone, but most have pools.
Meals can be delivered from the Ta'
Frenc Restaurant.

Holiday Complexes

Holiday complexes on Malta are
mainly self-catering apartments.
Prices for the following vary from
the equivalent of 3-star to 4-star
hotel rates.

Corinthia Mistra Village
Xemxija Hill, St Paul's Bay
Tel: 2158 0481
Fax: 2157 7802
Very popular hotel and self-catering
apartments comprising 255 rooms.
Excellent amenities, regular
children's entertainment. Pools,
restaurants, tennis, dive school.
4-star
Bugibba Holiday Complex
Triq it-Turisti, Bugibba
Tel: 2158 0861
Fax: 2158 0867
Set in central Bugibba. Self-catering
apartments and hotel rooms. **3-star**
Ramla Bay
Ramla Bay, Marfa
Tel: 2152 2181
Fax: 2157 5931
Perfect location facing Comino.
Good watersport facilities and
qualified instruction for sailing and
windsurfing. **4-star**
Sunny Coast
Qawra Road, Qawra
Tel: 2157 2964
Fax: 2157 6820
Large, well-maintained complex in
quiet position facing into bay. **4-star**

Where to Eat

Restaurant Listings

While Maltese cuisine may not rank
among the world's greats, there are
lots of very good things to eat
around the islands. Refer to *A Taste
of Malta, page 97*.

A government levy of 10 percent
is added to all restaurant bills; this
is not a service charge.

MALTA

Attard
Rickshaw
Corinthia Palace Hotel
Tel: 2144 0301
This Oriental restaurant serves
up the flavours of the Far East
including Chinese, Malaysian and
Vietnamese dishes. Popular at the
weekend. **$$$**

Marsaskala
Fisherman's Rest
St Thomas's Bay
Tel: 2163 2049
A very informal fish restaurant
set on the edge of the ramshackle
buildings at the water's edge.
Simple cooking, friendly casual
service. **$**
Grabiel
Marsaskala Bay
Tel: 2163 4194
A modern family-run restaurant
that has built up a serious local
following: people drive across the

Price Guide

Prices are for a three–course
meal for two with local wine:
$$$ Lm21–Lm35
$$ Lm16–Lm20
$ Lm10–Lm15

island for the sea-date and
clam starters, the octopus stew
and the prawn platter. Booking
recommended. **$$$**
La Favorita
Gardiel Street
Tel: 2163 4113
Set on a minor road to St Thomas's
Bay, this informal, noisy restaurant
is known for its fish. Crowded at
weekends, booking essential. **$$**

Marsaxlokk
Ir-Rizzu
The Waterfront
Tel: 2165 1569
Renowned for its fresh fish dishes.
Outdoor roof terrace in summer.
Booking essential. **$$**
Skuna 2
4 Duncan Street
Tel: 2165 7033
Fish dishes served right on the
waterfront. **$**

Mdina
Medina
7 Holy Cross Street
Tel: 2145 4004
A romantic setting in a pretty
courtyard with a tall oleander tree,
the Medina draws a loyal clientele.
International cooking with British
overtones. Speciality nights. **$$**

Mellieha
The Arches
113 G. Borg Olivier Street
Tel: 2152 3460
Large, brightly lit, very smart place,
with bustling service and large
portions. Roof open in summer.
Varied international menu. Booking
advisable. **$$$**
Giuseppi's
25 St Helen's Street
Tel: 2157 4882
A fine example of a truly Maltese
restaurant, both in its decor and in
its cooking. The menu changes daily
depending on what is available in
the local market. Very popular;
booking essential for dinner. **$$**
Il Mulino
45 Main Street
Tel: 2152 0404
Set in a windmill, this typically
Maltese restaurant attracts both
locals and visitors. **$$**

Café Life

Caffe Cordina
Set at the very heart of Valletta in Republic Square, Cordina is not only the city's most prestigious café, but a Maltese institution, renowned for the quality of its confectionery. All traditional seasonal cakes can be bought here. Parcelled up in the distinctive Caffe Cordina wrapping, these make good presents, particularly if you are invited into a Maltese home.

Cordina is typically Italian in its outlook, from the spelling of *caffe* to the long centre counter where regulars stand, having first paid for and collected a receipt at the cash desk for their order. It is a favourite meeting place where, mid-morning, everyone orders espresso or cappuccino with a couple of riccotta *pastizzi* (hot, savoury cheesecakes). There are small tables for waiter service inside and a number on the square outside – though catching a busy waiter's eye can be rather difficult. Light lunches are served daily and Cordina closes around 8pm. Tel: 2123 4385.

Mosta

Lord Nelson
280 Main Street
Tel: 2143 2590
An attractive restaurant featuring excellent Maltese home cooking. Even familiar international dishes take on a special flavour. Very popular, very fashionable and very casual. Booking is essential. **$**

Qawra

Gran Laguna
Triq il-Qala
Tel: 2157 1146
Ambitious Sicilian cooking of a high quality which attracts a loyal Italian clientele. Renowned for its pasta and fresh fish. Booking is advisable in summer months. **$$**

Il-Garra
Qawra Road
Tel: 2158 3297

Set in the White Dolphin Complex, this restaurant is cheap, generous and cheerful with an excellent bar service. **$**

Savini
Qawra Road
Tel: 2157 6927
Located on the outskirts of Bugibba, this is a converted farmhouse with open-air terraces especially for dining in the hot summer months. Features rich Italian cooking and silver service. Regarded as one of the island's top restaurants. **$$$**

St Julian's

Caffe Raffael
Spinola Road
Tel: 2135 2000
Pizza-pasta restaurant that has a large terrace. Excellent value given its unbeatable bayside location. **$**

La Dolce Vita
159 St George's Road
Tel: 2133 7806
Busy bayside restaurant favoured by a young, trendy, noisy crowd. In summer, the rooftop restaurant is open. Features pasta and fish specialities. Booking is recommended. **$$**

Peppino's
31 St George's Road
Tel: 2137 3200
Popular restaurant among visitors (who sit on the roof terrace in the summer). Featuring a ground-floor bar serving good, inexpensive lunches. Also a late-night meeting place, particularly at weekends. **$$**

Pizza Hut
St George's Road
Tel: 2137 7617
A pretty setting, popular with young families. **$**

Saddles
132 Main Street
Tel: 2133 9993
At the hub of St Julian's Bay, this is the meeting place of the beer and hamburger brigade. Fast sports, cars and motorbikes keep the regulars in constant motion. **$**

San Giuliano
Spinola Bay
Tel: 2133 2000
Considered to be *the* meeting place with an international clientele. Very

attractive interior with great view over St Julian's waterfront. Booking recommended. **$$$**

Sumatra
139 Spinola Road
Tel: 2131 0991
Popular with locals looking for a change of cooking. Specialises in Malaysian, Singaporean and Indonesian cooking. **$**

St Paul's Bay

Gillieru
Church Street
Tel: 2157 3480
For many decades the Gillieru has catered for Maltese who travel miles for its fresh fish, and it prides itself on the variety of fish always available. Grilled fish can be excellent, but check which is fresh, and which is frozen. Jutting out into the sea, with an open terrace in summer, it has an unstuffy and friendly atmosphere. **$$$**

Da Rosi
45 Church Street
Tel: 2157 1411
Small, friendly, family-run restaurant with a fine range of fresh fish dishes. Booking essential at weekends. **$$**

Sliema

Barracuda
194 Main Street
Tel: 2133 1817
Smartly decorated restaurant overlooking Balluta Bay. Pricey, but highly recommended by regulars, most of them business people. **$$$**

Christopher's
Ta' Xbiex Seafront, Ta' Xbiex
Tel: 2133 7101
Considered by many to be the best restaurant on the islands. Costly, except for business lunches. Casual but smart. Booking essential at weekends. **$$$**

Price Guide

Prices are for a three-course meal for two with local wine:
$$$ Lm21–Lm35
$$ Lm16–Lm20
$ Lm10–Lm15

Galeone
35 Tigne Sea Front
Tel: 2131 6420
One of Sliema's most popular casual restaurants, with Victor Bezzina cooking in the kitchen. His recommendations are always worth following. Fish, steaks and, as a starter, *spaghetti all' arabbiata* are invariably excellent. Booking is recommended as the restaurant is small. **$$**

The Blue Elephant-Hilton
Portomaso
Tel: 2138 3383
Enjoying the reputation of the international Blue Elephant chain. Excellent Thai food, but very pricey. **$$$**

Piccolo Padre
194 Main Street
Tel: 2134 4875
A fun pizzeria beneath the Barracuda restaurant. A buzzing place popular with the young, families and children. Some tables have views over harbour and sea. No bookings taken. Expect to queue at weekends. **$**

Ponte Vecchio
Tower Road
Tel: 2134 4591
A Maltese-international restaurant where fish is the speciality. Tables on pavement during summer. **$$**

Valletta

Because Valletta tends to shut down after 7pm on most evenings, many of its restaurants are open only at lunchtime or have limited opening days for dinner.

Blue Room
59 Republic Street
Tel: 2123 8014
The bistro-style Blue Room has a reputation for serving excellent Cantonese dishes. Popular with the local smart set in the evenings. Booking recommended. **$$**

Bologna
59 Republic Street
Tel: 2124 6149
Well regarded for its Maltese-Italian cooking and a popular lunchtime rendezvous for Valletta'a business community. **$$**

Fenkata

A *fenkata* – an evening at a village café where fried or stewed rabbit is served with lots of red wine – is a popular casual event for a crowd of friends. But go with a Maltese host; these meals need to be booked and a successful evening can depend on knowing the café owner. Favourite places are in **Bahrija**, and **Mgarr** (Malta) where two bars with long-standing fans are **il-Barri** (tel: 2157 3235) and **Ta' Soldi** (tel: 2157 2535), which seats 600 people and is excellent value.

British Hotel
276 St Ursula Street
Tel: 2122 4730
This basic hotel dining room occupies a prime position atop the bastion walls overlooking Grand Harbour. Be sure to book a table on the balcony, which offers an unbeatable view of Grand Harbour. Try the rabbit and finish with ricotta and almond gâteau. **$**

The Carriage
Valletta Buildings, South Street
Tel: 2124 7828
Don't be put off by the unprepossessing exterior, as inside is an elegant roof-top restaurant with pretty decor and imaginative cooking of consistently high standards. Dashing young owners cater to a smart clientele. House specials are invariably delicious, particularly the vegetarian dishes. Lunch Monday–Friday. Dinner Friday and Saturday only. Booking essential. **$$$**

De Robertis/La Cave
Castille Hotel
Castille Square
Tel: 2124 3677/8
De Robertis roof restaurant has fine city views, particularly by night. International dishes. Friday and Saturday only. Booking essential. **$$**. La Cave is an underground wine cellar serving pizzas and pasta, plus all the best local wines.

Fanelli's
293 St Ursula Street
Tel: 2125 5961

Very personal service in this basement wine-cellar. Superb food and warm hospitality. **$**

Giannini
St Michael's Bastion (off Windmill Street)
Tel: 2123 7121/2123 6575
Consistently rated among the island's top restaurants, set in a patrician house with panoramic views over Marsamxett Harbour. Pasta, fish and roasts in the Maltese manner are excellent. So is the welcome and the service. A restaurant for power-lunching as well as romantic interludes. Lunch served daily (except Sunday); dinner daily. **$$$**

Malata
Palace Square
Tel: 2123 3967
Excellent Maltese and southern Italian menu that appeals to politicians (parliament is across the road) and businessmen. *Ravjul* (Maltese ravioli) and fish are favourite dishes. Can be crowded and boisterous. **$$**

Le Meridien Phoenicia
The Mall, Floriana
Tel: 2122 5241
Attractive verandah setting in the summer. International cuisine and wines. Jackets required for men in the evenings. **$$$**

Da Pippo
136 Melita Street
Tel: 2124 8029
Good wholesome Maltese food served in a crowded casual atmosphere. Lunches only; it is very popular so booking is essential. **$**

Rubino
53 Old Bakery Street
Tel: 2122 4656
Old cake shop turned into venue for fashionable lunches Monday to Saturday or relaxed dinners on Tuesday and Thursday (closed Sunday). The changing menu includes traditional Maltese dishes as well as Italian cooking. Good atmosphere, good food, friendly crowd. Booking is advisable. **$$**

Sicilia
1 St John Street
Tel: 2124 0569
The tiny interior seats just 14 but outside is a small square with views

of Grand Harbour. Popular with locals and tourists, particularly for its pasta and fish. Open Mon–Fri lunchtime only. **$$**

Trattoria Palazz
43 Old Theatre Street
Tel: 2122 6611
Underground (steep stairs), but air conditioned, in the ancient foundations of the *Biblioteca*. A small popular *trattoria* with welcoming atmosphere, excellent pasta dishes and fresh fish. Conveniently located for the Manoel Theatre. Closed Sunday. Booking advisable. **$**

GOZO

Gharb
Jeffrey's
10 Triq il-Gharb
Tel: 2156 1006
Excellent little *trattoria* hung with local artwork. Courtyard dining in summer. Local and vegetarian specialities with ingredients fresh from the cook's own farm. The restaurant serves dinner only. Closed Sunday and winter months until about Easter. Booking advisable. **$$**

Salvina's
21 Frenc tal-Gharb
Tel: 2155 2505
Pretty little restaurant in traditional rustic stone village house. Local and international cuisine. Dinner only. Closed Thursdays. **$$**

Marsalforn
Il-Kartell
Marina Street
Tel: 2155 6918
Set on the water's edge, friendly atmosphere, good fish, local dishes and pasta and pizzas. **$**

Ta' Frenc
Marsalforn Road
Tel: 2155 3888
Stylishly converted farmhouse. Wide range of international dishes elegantly presented. Open for dinner only. **$$$**

The Republic
24 Triq ix-Xatt
Tel: 2155 6800
Trattoria with small beach-side

Price Guide

Prices are for a three-course meal for two with local wine:
$$$ Lm21–Lm35
$$ Lm16–Lm20
$ Lm10–Lm15

terrace. Closed Mon and mid-Dec–mid-Feb. **$**

Otter's
Triq Santa Marija
Tel: 2156 2473
Perched just above the sea with sunbeds at hand for a siesta; alternatively, outdoor heating is also provided for chilly evening dining. Ring-side view of waterpolo matches on summer Saturday afternoons. Good fish, pasta and salads. **$**

Mgarr
Manoel's
27 Triq Manoel de Vilhena
Tel: 2156 3588
Housed in an old fort. Varied menu and a fine view of the colourful fishing boats bobbing in the harbour. Dinner only. Closed in winter. **$**

Il-Kcina tal-Barrakka
28 Manuel de Vilhena Street
Tel: 2155 6543
Small pretty restaurant at harbour's edge, with imaginative menu. Slightly cramped. Open summer only. Booking advisable. **$$**

Victoria
Il-Panzier
Triq il-Karita
Tel: 2155 9979
Gozo's most elegant restaurant features summer dining in a soothing leafy courtyard. The limited menu is offset by superior Italian cuisine. Closed Monday. **$$$**

Central Coffee House
20 Pjazza Independenza
Tel: 2155 1039
A tiny café/bar packed with World War II memorabilia. Light, cold lunches of traditional Gozitan fare and the proprietor's own wine. Closed evenings and Sunday. **$**

Ta' Ricardo
4 Triq il-Fosos
Tel: 2155 5953
Wine barrels topped with fresh

bread and tomatoes mark the entrance to what is one of the oldest houses in the Citadel. Traditional Gozitan light, cold lunches and wine made on the premises. An excellent pit-stop after exploring the walled city. **$**

Xaghra
Gesther
Vjal it-8 ta'Settembru
Tel: 2155 6621
Authentic local food and atmosphere. Very casual. Extremely good value. Lunches only. Closed Sunday. **$**

Oleander
10 Pjazza Vittorija
Tel: 2155 7230
Excellent local dishes, fish and steaks; can be noisy inside but tables set outside in summer months provide a view of the bustling village square. Closed Monday. **$**

Xlendi
Paradise
Trejqet il-Madonna tal-Karmnu
Tel: 2155 6878
Fondly known by its aficionados as the Elvis Presley Memorial Bar; pictures of "the King" abound. Basic comforts but excellent simple cooking, including fresh fish and jumbo prawns. Tables outside in summer. Exceptionally good value. Closed Mondays. **$**

Stone Crab & Ta' Karolina
Marina Street
Tel: 2155 6400
Possibly the most popular summer restaurant in Gozo. Fish a great speciality. Booking essential. **$$**

Culture

Theatre

There is one major theatre on Malta, the **Manoel Theatre** in Valletta, and two on Gozo, the **Astra** and the **Aurora**, though these are less important than the Manoel. Tours of the Manoel Theatre are given Mon–Fri 10.30am, 11.30am and 4.30pm; Sat 11.30am and 12.30pm. On Wednesday at 12.30pm there is a free concert in the theatre's recital room; there is also a gift shop, a café and restaurant

Museum Times

Many museums and all temple sites are government-run and follow the same hours.

Malta
1 Oct–15 June Mon–Sat 8.15am–5pm, Sun 8.15am–4.15pm; 16 June–30 Sep daily 7.45am–2pm; closed on public holidays.

Gozo
1 Oct–31 Mar Mon–Sat 8.30am–4.30pm, Sun 8.30am–3pm; 1 Apr–30 Sep Mon–Sat 8.45am–4.30pm, Sun 8.30am–3pm; closed on public holidays.

These hours are subject to frequent changes, so if you've set your heart on visiting a particular museum, it's wise to ring them or check with the tourist office, tel: 9973 0000.

Opening times vary for privately run museums and attractions, though most open daily from around 9 or 10am to 5 or 6pm.

The Ministry of Tourism publishes a full events calendar listing annual and one-off events. The Manoel Theatre also publishes updated information regarding forthcoming performances, and traditional pantomime during Christmas.

Cinema

The annual Film and Video Competition, organised by the Malta Amateur Cine Circle, is held in June. In November the Golden Knight International Film and Video Festival takes place.

The island's main multiplex (with 15 cinemas in one complex) is in Paceville. There are also cinemas at Bugibba and Paola, Marsaskala, and in Victoria on Gozo.

Nightlife

Nightlife on Malta is for the most part unsophisticated and revolves arounds bars, karaoke-style establishments and nightclubs.

Most activity centres around Paceville and St Julian's. The best-known and longest-established clubs are **Matrix** on St George's Road and **Havana** in St George's Bay, both in Paceville. Both attract top international DJs.

Here are a few of the other contenders:

Paceville/St Julian's
Empire, Paceville
Barro Latino, Paceville
Places, Paceville

St Paul's Bay/Qawra/Bugibba
Il Fuego, Qawra
Reflections, Sol Suncrest Hotel, Qawra

Gozo
La Grotta, Xlendi
Wilderness.
Both of these are open air

Casinos

For an evening of black jack, roulette and other traditional casino games there is the long-established

Special Events

- **January:** Folk Festival.
- **Mid-July to mid-August:** Malta Festival; orchestral concerts, chamber music, jazz, theatre, cinema and art exhibitions; events spread over the island.
- **Last week July:** Malta Jazz Festival.
- **November:** The Malta International Choir Festival.

Casino at the Dragonara Palace (tel: 2131 2888) in Paceville, and the **Oracle Casino** at the New Dolmen Hotel, Bugibba, tel: 2158 1510. Both also have a hall of slot machines. The **Casino di Venezla**, located on the Vittoriosa waterfront, is the latest casino to open (tel: 2180 5580).

Casinos have a smart-casual dress code. No visitor under 18 is allowed entry and everyone must have a means of identification, such as a passport.

Sport

Participant Sports

The islands have a near-perfect climate for year-round sports. Although watersports are the main activity, there is also a good choice of land-based sports too. *For further information, see pages 127–129.*

Diving

A network of associations ensures that Malta has first-rate diving instructors and excursion leaders. There are numerous licensed schools and all equipment can be hired. A list of licensed diving schools is available from tourist offices.

Sporting Events

A non-stop calendar of events fills the year. Listed below are some of the annual highlights.

- **February:** Malta Marathon.
- **March:** International Snooker Tournament.
- **April:** International Archery Tournament, Marsa Sports Club.
- **May:** Sicily to Malta Windsurf Race.
- **June:** International Air Rally.
- **June/July:** International Lawn Tennis Summer Open Tournament.
- **August:** Rimini–Malta–Rimini Yacht Race.
- **September:** Football season starts.
- **October:** Autumn Series Yacht Races; Middle Sea yacht race – from Malta to Sardinia, and back.
- **November:** Four-Wheel Drive Rally of Malta and Gozo.

Diving contacts in Malta include:

FUAM (Federation of Underwater Activities in Malta), PO Box 29, Gzira, Malta.

APDS (Association of Professional Diving Schools), Msida Court, 61/2 Msida Sea Front, Msida, Malta.

If you wish to take a diving course, you will need a medical certificate confirming good health.

Some of the best areas for diving include: Ahrax Point (Cirkewwa), Anchor Bay, Qawra Point and Wied iz-Zurrieq on Malta; Ras ir-Qieqa and St Marija Caves on Comino; Reqqa Point, Dwejra Point and Mgarr Ix-Xini on Gozo.

In case of accidents there is a decompression chamber located at St Luke's Hospital at Gwardamanga. There is also a professional air and sea rescue service.

Golf, Tennis & Squash

Malta's par 68 golf course is at the Marsa Sports Club. The well-equipped complex also has 18 tennis courts, a polo field, badminton and squash courts, an archery field, plus football and cricket pitches. Many other sporting federations hold their events here. Weekly membership is available.

For further details, call 2123 2842/2123 3851. The Royal Malta Golf Club also welcomes visitors. For information call tel: 2124 2914.

Spectator Sports

Football

Soccer is a passion in Malta. League and international football matches are perfect occasions for fans to drive around town leaning on their horns, waving their team colours from the window.

The season is September to May, with top matches played at the modern National Stadium at Ta' Qali. For details of matches see the local press.

Horseracing

The racetrack at Marsa stages trotting races on Sunday with a break in July and August. There is a café and betting facilities. Tel: 2122 4800.

Water Polo

There are several water polo pitches on the islands, with the national pool at Tal-Qroqq. There is a water polo league championship, and team matches are played throughout the summer with fans getting as heated and argumentative as football fans.

Other Activities

Horse Riding

Several stables are centred around the Marsa racetrack. Some hotels may also arrange for riding trips in the countryside with Golden Bay Horse Riding.

Ten-Pin Bowling

A ten-pin bowling centre is situated at the Eden Super Bowl, St George's Bay, St Julians, tel: 2134 1196/2131 9888. Open every day from 10am to past midnight.

Walking

The wilder parts of Malta and Gozo are favourite places for ramblers to stride out, especially in spring when the landscape is carpeted with wild flowers and the trees are coming in to bud.

Rock Climbing

The island has some challenging scenery to tempt the climber. The sport is organised informally on the islands but expertly run. Groups can provide you with climbing equipment, but it's best to have the correct footwear to start with. The most popular areas for climbing are below Dingli cliffs, at Ghar Lapsi, and at Ghargur.
Contact Malta Rock Climbing, 12/4 Star Lodge, Misrah San, Alwigi, B'Kara BKR 10, www.malta-rockclimbing.com email: info@malta-rockclimbing.com

Shopping

What to Buy

Shopping in Malta is small-scale but all the leading designer brands are available. Maltese crafts are limited to blown glass, lace and metalwork. Gold and silver craft are a speciality and much sought after.

Lacemaking
Endless hours of nimble-fingered work go into the creation of intricate tablecloths, napkins, place mats, collars, shawls and delicate

Crafts & Markets

Some crafts can be found in the local markets but the typical tourist souvenir shop is not the kind of place to go unless you want Malta kitsch.
- **Malta Crafts Centre**: St John's Square, Valletta, tel: 2122 1221.
- **Ta' Qali Crafts Village:** Ta' Qali, Malta.
- **Fontanella Crafts Centre:** La Fontana, Xlendi–Victoria Road.
- **Ta' Dbiegi Crafts Village:** Limits of St Lawrence, Gozo, tel: 2155 6202.
- **Open-air markets:** a daily market takes place in Merchant's Street by St John's Cathedral until noon. On Sunday a larger market is held just outside City Gate, by the bus station, in St James' Ditch. Here you'll find cheap tapes and CDs, famous-name jeans and T-shirts, plus the usual souvenirs such as lace tablecloths. The fleamarket stalls are the most interesting part. Visit Marsaxlokk's colourful fish market on Sunday.

blouses. Lace is on sale everywhere, most famously at the open-air quayside market at Marsaxlokk.

Knitwear
When the winter sea breezes blow you will appreciate the islands' Aran-style woollens which come in heavy-duty styling and in some unusual colour combinations. This is a speciality of Gozo. Woven wool rugs in cream and white are also popular.

Glass
Glass from Malta is easily distinguished by its clear, bright colours, taking inspiration from the Mediterranean skies and sea.

You can see craftsmen at work and buy directly from **Mdina Glass** at Ta' Qali Crafts Village.

You can also watch this beautiful craft performed at **Gozo Glass** in Gharb. And Gozo Glass organises courses in glassmaking for beginners. This is a hands-on experience in the craft of "hot" glassmaking, including the use of colours and cold shop work. Studio time is available on an hourly, daily or weekly basis. All tools and equipment are supplied, and accommodation can also be arranged. For further details, contact 9 Gharb Road, Gharb, GRB102, Gozo, Malta. Tel: 00356 2156 1974, fax: 00356 2156 0354, e-mail: info@gozoglass.com

Gold and Silver
Filigree silver jewellery is a trademark of the islands and is available everywhere. Gold is also very popular. The small shops of Valletta, particularly those of St Lucia Street, are the most rewarding places to shop.

Basketware and Wickerwork
These are local crafts that serve a practical purpose. Most Maltese homes use cane blinds on doors and windows to block out the summer sun, but there are smaller items to take home.

Children

What to Do

Despite its popularity as a family holiday destination, Malta has relatively few attractions or even natural features (such as soft sandy beaches or grassy parks) which appeal specifically to children.

Perhaps the most important thing to consider is whether you require a sandy beach. If this is a major consideration, then base yourself close to Mellieha or Golden Bay.

The most child-friendly spot is White Rocks, home to **Splash & Fun Waterpark, Mediterraneo Marine World** and a dinosaur-themed playground. However, you can do all of these quite easily in a day.

The other well-advertised family attraction is **Popeye Village**. By mainland European standards, however, it is very low key and will occupy only a few hours at most.

The good news is that the locals, in true Mediterranean style, love children and there is little in the way of food and drink or sanitary conditions that is likely to cause problems. Do beware of the sun however, and keep children well covered up.

Leading hotels provide entertainers to organise activities for children – and grown ups.

Language

Malti, or Maltese, is spoken daily in Malta and Gozo but nowhere else in the world. It is a Semitic language with roots that go back to Phoenician and Carthaginian times. Given that it is both complicated and of no use outside the islands, the Maltese people *never* expect visitors to speak to them in Malti.

English is the second language and is spoken, or at least understood, by the vast majority of the population. However, it is useful to know a little Maltese if only to pronounce place names properly. And of course it is good manners, and pleasing to both parties, to be able to return the most basic greetings and phrases in Malti.

Pronunciation Tips

There are 29 letters in the Maltese alphabet: five familiar vowels (pronounced long or short, depending on the position in the word) and 24 consonants. There is no "y".

The additions to the Roman alphabet are c·, g·, x, which are dotted like an i, and gh and h·. Dotting the consonant changes the way it is pronounced:

dotted c· becomes the English ch – as in church;

dotted g· as the soft j in the French word *je* (or the second syllable in pleasure);

dotted x as in zebra. (Without a dot, z is *ts*, as in nuts.)

gh, although common is not pronounced.

h is silent unless it is crossed *h*-like a t; then it is pronounced, as in hand.

q is a glottal stop, faintly like a k, impossible to most visitors.

m when it is at the beginning of a word is pronounced *im*.

Place Names

The following is a list of Maltese towns and villages and how to pronounce them.

Birgu	*beer-goo*
Birzebbuga	*beer-tsay-boo-jah*
Bugibba	*boo-jee-bah*
Dwejra	*dway-ruh*
Ggantija	*j-gan-tee-yah*
Gharb	*ahrb*
Hagar Qim	ajar eem
Luqa	*loo-ha*
Marsaxlokk	*marsa-schlock*
Mdina	*Im-deena*
Mellieha	*mell-ee-ah*
Mgarr	im-jar
Msida	*im-seeda*
Naxxar	*na-shar*
Paceville	*par-tchay-ville*
Qawra	*ow-rah*
Tarxien	*tar-shin*
Xaghra	shah-ra
Xewkija	show-key-yah
Xlendi	sch-len-dee

Useful Words/Phrases

Good morning *bongu (bon-jew)*
Good evening *bonswa (bon-swah)*
Goodbye *sahha (sa-ha)*
(also "Cheers", when drinking)
How are you? *kif int?*
I'm very well, thank you female response: *thaba grazzi (ta-ba grat-see)*, male response: *thajeb grazzi (ta-szeb gratsee)*
Do you speak English? *Int tit kellem bl'Ingliz? (int-tit-kellem blin-gleez)*
Please *Jekk-joghbok (yeck yogbock)*
Thank You *Grazzi (grat-see)*
Yes *Iva (eeva)*
No *Le (le,* with *e* as in "get")

Further Reading

History

The Cross and the Ensign: a Naval History of Malta, 1798–1979 by Peter Elliot. HarperCollins (1980). The first detailed account of the British Navy's connection with Malta.

The Great Siege: Malta 1565 by Ernle Bradford. Penguin (1964). Compelling account of the struggle between the Knights of Malta and the Ottoman Empire for the control of the Mediterranean.

Malta Convoy by Peter Shankland and Anthony Hunter. Collins (1961). A classic account of Operation Pedestal, the convoy that braved all the enemy could throw at it in 1942 as it sailed to save Malta from starvation and surrender in the islands' second great siege.

Malta: A Panoramic History by Anthony Abela. Progress Press, Malta (1997). A lively gallop through 5,000 years.

Siege: Malta 1940–1943 by Ernle Bradford. Penguin (1987). Malta's second great test of wartime fortitude written with the immediacy of a novel.

The Story of Malta by Brian Blouet. Progress Press, Malta (1993). A rich comprehensive history, engagingly recounted.

Malta: A Thorn in Rommel's Side by Laddie Lucas. Penguin (1992). Gripping account of the 18 months when Malta was the most bombed spot on earth and Lucas was commanding the islands' top-scoring squadron.

Lord Strickland, Servant of the Crown, 2 vols, by H. Smith and A. Koster. Progress Press, Malta, (1986). The life of a remarkable man who played a dominant role in the government of both Britain and Malta.

Archaeology

Before Civilization by Colin Renfrew. Penguin (1990). One of Britain's foremost archaeologists shows how the carbon dating of Malta's prehistoric monuments changed the whole theory of human development and proved that Maltese temples are the oldest free-standing buildings known to man.
Malta: An archaeological guide by David Trump. Progress Press, Malta (1990). The essential guide to Malta's astonishing prehistoric remains.

Architecture

British Military Architecture in Malta by Stephen C. Spiteri. Spiteri (1996). A detailed study with many plans and photographs.
Malta: A Guide to the Fortifications by Quentin Hughes. Said International (1993). Reprint of a classic guide to Malta's forts and bastions.
5,000 years of Architecture in Malta by Leonard Mahoney. Valletta Publishing (1996). A Maltese architect takes a learned look at the architecture that makes the islands so distinctive. Finely illustrated.

Art

Iconography of the Maltese Islands 1400–1900 by Mario Buhagiar. Progress Press, Malta (1987). A critical survey of 500 years of painting in Malta by a leading art historian.
International Dictionary of Artists who Painted Malta by Nicholas de Piro. Said International, Malta (1988). Illustrated biographies of 600 artists from many nations spanning several centuries.

Miscellaneous

Saints and Fireworks by Jeremy Boissevain. Progress Press, Malta (1996). An instructive and entertaining survey of religion and politics in rural Malta.

Images of Malta and photographs by Daniel Cilia with text by Geoffrey Aquilina Ross. Miranda Publications, Malta (1990). Personal views, both written and in photographed.
Malta 360° with photographs by Attilio Boccazzi-Varotto with text by Geoffrey Aquilina Ross. Priuli & Verlucca, Italy (1985). Coffee-table book with sweeping photographs that capture scenes usually overlooked.

Fiction

For Rozina ... a husband, and other Maltese Stories by Francis Ebejer, Progress Press, Malta (1990). A charming insight into the minds and manners of the rural Maltese by one of the country's finest writers.
The Kappilan of Malta by Nicholas Monsarrat. Pan (1994). A wartime love story interwoven with a whole sweep of Maltese history.

Other Insight Guides

Insight Pocket Guide: Malta is a perfect companion on the ground, offering a series of tailor-made itineraries designed to help readers get the most out of Malta during a short stay.
Insight Compact Guide: Malta offers the reader an on-the-spot reference guide full of interesting facts and figures.
Insight Guide: Sicily explores Malta's nearest neighbour and closest historical companion.
Insight Guide: Italy gives a fascinating insight into Italy's history, culture, cities and countryside. Informative text combines with captivating photography.

Feedback

We do our best to ensure the information in our books is as accurate and up-to-date as possible. The books are updated on a regular basis, using local contacts, who painstakingly add, amend and correct as required. However, some mistakes and omissions are inevitable and we are ultimately reliant on our readers to put us in the picture.

We would welcome your feedback on any details related to your experiences using the book "on the road". Maybe we recommended a hotel that you liked (or another that you didn't), as well as interesting new attractions, or facts and figures you have found out about the country itself. The more details you can give us (particularly with regard to addresses, e-mails and telephone numbers), the better.

We will acknowledge all contributions, and we'll offer an Insight Guide to the best letters received.

Please write to us at:
Insight Guides
PO Box 7910
London SE1 1WE
United Kingdom
Or send e-mail to:
insight@apaguide.co.uk

ART & PHOTO CREDITS

Eddie Aquilina 98, 191, 208, 276

Jonathan Beacom back cover right, 124/125

Bodo Bondzio 4/5T, 260R

Camera Press 62/63, 66, 68, 69, 70, 71, 72

Daniel Cilia 92, 99, 240/241, 252/253, 257

Philip Enticknap/The Travel Library 128

Glyn Genin front flap top & bottom, spine bottom, back cover left & centre, back flap top & bottom, 1, 2T, 2B, 4BL, 4BR, 5B, 8/9, 25, 81, 82, 101, 116/7, 126, 134/5, 138, 145, 149T, 149, 151T, 153T, 160, 163T, 165T, 169, 171T, 173T, 173, 179T, 181T, 187T, 187, 191T, 200, 201, 204, 207T, 209T, 212/3, 215, 216, 217T, 217, 218, 219T, 219, 220, 229T, 231T, 231, 233T, 235T, 248, 249, 251T, 251, 257T, 258, 260L, 261T, 264/5, 272/3, 278, 279, 280

Chris Hellier/Corbis 181

Illustrated London News 19, 64, 65, 67

Bob Krist 10/11, 14, 20, 31, 76, 83, 86/87, 90, 100, 108/109, 168, 214, 233, 254, 266/267, 268, 274

Lyle Lawson 6/7, 12/13, 16/17, 18, 21, 22, 23, 28/29, 30, 33, 38, 39, 42/43, 45, 54/55, 56, 58, 73, 74/75, 79, 80, 84/85, 88, 89, 91, 93, 94/95, 96, 97, 104, 105, 106/107, 110, 111, 112, 113, 114, 115, 118, 120, 121, 127, 129, 130/131, 132/133, 136/137, 142/143, 144, 147, 148, 150, 152, 153, 154, 155, 158/159, 161, 162, 163, 164, 166/167, 170L&R, 171, 172, 174/175, 176, 177, 179, 180, 182/183, 184, 185, 189, 190, 192, 193, 194/195, 196/197, 198, 199T, 202/203, 207, 209, 221, 224/225, 226, 227, 228, 230, 234, 235, 238/239, 242, 244/245, 246, 247, 250, 259, 261, 262/263, 269, 275, 277

Erich Lessing/AKG London spine top, back cover bottom,

Neil A Lukas 151

Paul W Murphy 24, 26/27, 32, 119, 188, 199, 205, 229, 232, 270, 271

Adam Woolfitt/Robert Harding Picture Library 104

Sovereign Order of St John 36, 37, 40, 41

Topham Picturepoint 77, 78

Cartographic Editor **Zoë Goodwin**
Design Consultants
Carlotta Junger, Graham Mitchener
Picture Research **Hilary Genin**

Picture Spreads

Pages 52/53
Top row, left to right: Paul W Murphy, Lyle Lawson, Paul W Murphy, Courtesy of St John's Ambulance; *Centre row, left to right*: Paul W Murphy, Topham Picturepoint; *Bottom row, left to right*: Paul W Murphy, Paul W Murphy, Bob Krist.

Pages 122/123
Top row, left to right: Daniel Cilia, Bob Krist, Lyle Lawson, Glyn Genin; *Bottom row, left to right*: Bob Krist, Glyn Genin, Lyle Lawson.

Pages 156/157
Top row, left to right: Paul W Murphy, Glyn Genin, Paul W Murphy, Glyn Genin; *Centre Row*: Glyn Genin; *Bottom row, left to right*: Glyn Genin, Verdala Press Services, Glyn Genin, Paul W Murphy.

Pages 236/237
Top row, left to right: Glyn Genin, Lyle Lawson, Glyn Genin, Glyn Genin; *Centre row*: Glyn Genin; *Bottom row, left to right*: W H Bartlett/Mary Evans Picture Library, Glyn Genin, Lyle Lawson, Glyn Genin, Erich Lessing/AKG London.

Maps Colin Earl

© 2005 Apa Publications GmbH & Co. Verlag KG (Singapore branch)

Index

Numbers in italics refer to photographs

a

accommodation 292–5
agape tables 25, 191
air rally 300
aljotta 98
Anchor Bay 219
Arab influence 18, 23–4, 25–6, 185, 189
Archaeological Museum (Gozo) 251
Archaeological Museum (Valletta) 148, 154, 221, 227
archaeology 18, 21–6, 111, 189–90, 227–8, 230, 231–3, 236–7
Archbishop's Curia 114
architecture 111–14
Armier 218
Attard 199, 200
  Corinthia Palace Hotel 200
  San Anton Palace and Gardens 199, 200
  Santa Marija church 113, 199, 200
auberges 46, 112, 154
  see also Valletta; Vittoriosa
audio-visual/multimedia shows 150, 152, 153, 188, 249, 255
Azure Window 261, *262*

b

Bahar-ic-Caghaq (White Rocks) 215
Ball, Sir Alexander 51, 57, *58*, 152
Balluta Bay 208–9
Balzan 199
Baptism of Christ 173
Barbarossa brothers 37
baroque architecture 113–14
Barry, Edward Middleton 114
beer 101, 156
The Beheading of St John the Baptist 77, *173*
Belisarius 25
Belli, Andrea 114, 154
Bertie, Fra Andrew (Grand Master) 53
betting 127, 128
Bighi 153
bird reserve 218
Birgu *see* Vittoriosa

Birkikara 201
  Church of St Helena 201
  Church of Santa Maria 113, 199
birth customs 120
Birzebbuga *14*
Black Pearl (floating restaurant) 208, *277*
Blitz of Malta 69–73
Blondel, Mederico 112, 114
Blue Grotto 231, *232*, 277
Blue Lagoon *126*, 128, 255, *267*, 269, 271, 275–6
boat trips 275–7
boats 120, *174–5*
  see also luzzu
bocci 129
Boffa, Sir Paul (Prime Minister) 77
Borg in-Nadur 231
Borg Olivier, George (Prime Minister) 80, *150*
Il Borgo 33, 38, 177
Bormla *see* Cospicua
bowling 129
Bradford, Ernle, *Siege: Malta 1940–1943*, 65
hragoli 97, 99
brass bands *122–3*
bread *88*, 100
British influence 19, 51, 57–60, 77–9, *156–7*
  see also World War II
Bronze Age 228, 231
  see also cart tracks
Bronze Cross 71
Bugibba 216, *217*
Buonamici, Francesco 112, 113–14
Burmarra 216
buses 105, 119, 147
Buskett Gardens 234–5
Buzi (bailiff) 57
Byron, Lord 58–9

c

Cachia, Domenicho 201
Caffe Cordina 148–9
Cagliostro 49
cakes 100–101
Calypso's Cave 258–9
Cammileri, Charles *147*
Carafa, Gregorio (Grand Master) 172
Carapeccia, Romano 114
Caravaggio 173
  St Jerome 77, *173*
carnival 101
cars 92, 105–6, *156*
cart tracks *22*, 234, 262
Carthaginians 22–4

Cassar, Gerolamo 112, 113, 114, 145, 147, 150, 154, 161, 169–70, 235
catacombs 25, *26*, 190–91
Catania (Sicily) 278
Cave of Darkness 230
cave dwellers 21, 230, *231*
caves and grottoes *24*, 190, 258–9
Chambray, Jacques de 255
Chapels of the *langues* 171–2
Charles V of Spain (emperor) 26, 194
Charlotte Louise 276
Chattes Gessan, Annet de Clermont de (Grand Master) 172
Chevers, Sarah 49
Christianity 18, 24–5, 26
Christmas customs 120
church architecture 113, 199
church clocks 119
Churchill, Sir Winston 60, 65, 73, *157*
cippi 23
Cirkewwa 218, 255
Clapham Junction 234
Co-Cathedral of St John, *see* St John's Co-Cathedral
Cold War Summit Monument 231
Coleridge, Samuel Taylor 58
Comino 255, 269–71, *274*
  Hotel Comino *269*, 271
Conventual Church *see* St John's Co-Cathedral
Corsairs 37
Cospicua (Bormla) 177
  Church of the Immaculate Conception 177
Cotoner, Nicolas (Grand Master) 171, 172
Cotoner, Rafael (Grand Master) 170, 171
crafts 201, 261
Cros, Louis du 154
cruises 275–7
cycling 129

d

Dark Ages 18, 23, 25–6, 111
death customs 120
devil 119
dghajas 120, 157, *174–5*
Dingli, Tommaso 198, 199, 228
dinosaur-themed playground 215
disco, open-air (La Grotta) 262
Disraeli, Benjamin 45, 60
diving *126*, 127, 233

Dobbie, Sir William (governor) 66
dockyards *79*, 177, *180*
dolphins 215
Dragut 37–40
drinks 101
Dungeon (Mdina) 187–8
Dürer, Albrecht 194
Dwejra Point 261–2

e

Eden Superbowl 129
education 82
emigration 89
Erardi, Stefano 190
Etna (Sicily) 278–9
European Community 15, 19,
    80–81
Evans, Katherine 49

f

Faith (biplane) 65
Fat Ladies 22, 148
Favray, Antoine de 112
Fenech Adami, Eddie (Prime
    Minister) 81
fenek 96, 97, 99
fenkata 99, 221
festivals *(festi)* 89, 90, 92, 101,
    122–3, 125, *156–7*, 200,
    234–5, *241*, 247
figolli 101
Filfla 233
film studios 181
fireworks *122–36*
fish *95–6*, 99–100, 127
fishing *89, 230*
Floriana 113
    Archbishop's Curia 114
folklore 119–20, 251, 261
Fontana 262
food 97–101
Fort Chambray 255
Fort Manoel 207–8
Fort Ricasoli 153, 181
Fort St Angelo 25, 33, 38, 39, 45,
    52, 153, 179–80
Fort St Elmo 38, 39–41, *52–3*,
    145, 150–51, *152*
Fort St Michael 39, 40, 45
Fort St Rocco 181
Fort Tigne 205
fossils 230
Freedom Monument 178
freeports *81*, 82, 231
French influence *50–51*
friezes 164, 165
Fungus Rock *259*, 261–2

g

Gafa', Lorenzo 114, 193, 250
gambling 92, 127, 128
game 269
gardens 199–200, 234–5, 247,
    279
George Cross 70, *73*, 151
Ggantija temples *12*, 21, 111,
    257–8, *258*
Ghadira *see* Mellieha Bay
Ghadira Bird Reserve 217
Ghajn Hadid Bay *215*, 217
Ghajn Tuffieha Bay 220
Ghajnsielem 249, 255
ghaqaq ta'l-ghasel 97, 101
Ghar Dalam 21
Ghar Lapsi 233
Gharb *260*, 261
    Church of the Visitation 261
    Folklore Museum 261
Gharghur 199
Ghawdex, *see* Gozo
Ghaxaq *86*
Giardini, Giovanni 173
glass 201, 208
Gnejna Bay 221
Gobelin tapestries *161*, *162*,
    163–4, *165*
Golden Bay 128, *214*, *219*, 220
golf *127*, 129
Goya 194
Gozo 38, 243–62, *132*
    see also Victoria
    Gozo 360 Degrees (audiovisual
        show) 249
    Gozo Heritage (audiovisual show)
        249, 255
    hotels 294
    restaurants 298
Grand Harbour *57*, *62–3*, *67*, *133*,
    142–3, 153, *157*, 180
    cruises 275
Grand Masters **33**, 46–8, 49, 163,
    170
    see also individual names
Grand Master's Palace *30, 33,
    38–9*, *59*, *61*, 112, 145, 149,
    158–9, 161–5, 192
    Ambassadors' Room (State
        Room) 165
    Hall of St Michael and St John,
        see Supreme Council Hall
    Neptune Courtyard *160*, 161–2
    Pages' Waiting Room (Yellow
        Room) 164
    State Dining Hall 165
    Supreme Council Hall 163,
        164–5

Tapestry Room (Council
    Chamber)*161 162*, 163–4,
    165
Grand Master's Summer Residence
    200
Great Siege (1565) *34–5, 38, 39*,
    37–41, 164
    Frieze 164
    Monument *148*
grigal 128, 277
Grognet de Vasse, Giorgio 114,
    198
Gudja 199

h

Hagar Qim *16–17*, 21, 231–2, *233*
Hal Saflieni, Hypogeum 21, 221
Hamrun *123*, *156–7*
Hompesch, Ferdinand von (Grand
    Master) 50, 228
Hompesch Arch 228
horse-racing 127, 128–9, 234–5,
    247
horse-riding 129, 220
hospitality 90
Hotel Comino *270*, 271
hotels 292–4
humour 92
hunting 218, *257*, 269
Hypogeum of Hal Saflieni 21, 227

i–J

Illustrious (carrier) 66, 67, 68
independence 19, 77–9
industry 82
Inland Sea 261, 277
Inquisitor 47, 48
Inquisitor's Palace 114, 178–9
Inquisitor's Summer Palace 234
International Boat Show 277
International Fair (Naxxar) 199
Islamic influence 18, 23–4, 25–6
Isola *see* Senglea
Ittar, Stefano 114
jewellery-making 201

k

Kalafrana Freeport container
    terminal *81*, 231
Kalkara 181
kawlata 97, 98
Kinnie 101
Knights' hospital, 207–8
    see also Valletta, Sacra
        Infermeria
Knights Hospitallers exhibition 152

Knights of St John, 18–19, 26, 31–33, *52–3*, 111–14
  see also **Grand Masters**
knitwear 261
Kuncizzjoni 157

l

La Cassiere, Jean Evesque de (Grand Master) 161
La Grotta (disco) 262
La Valette, Jean Parisot de (Grand Master) 37, 39–41, *44*, 45, 145, 170, 178
Labour Party 81
lace 201, *242*, 261
lampuki 99
langues 46, 171–2
Laparelli de Cortona, Francesco 113, 145–7, 249
Lascaris Castellar, Jean Paul de (Grand Master) 47
Lascaris War Rooms 73, 153–4
Last Supper 173
Lazzareto Creek 208
Lear, Edward 258
leather-work 261
Lija 199, 200
L'Isla *see* **Senglea**
L'Isle Adam, Philippe Villiers de (Grand Master) 32, 180
Little Armier 218
lore 119–20
Luke, Sir Harry (governor) 58, 61
  luzzu *116–17*, 120, *226*, 229, *231*, *269*, *276*

m

Madliena 157
Madonna Tal-Providenza 232
majjistral 128, 277
Malta Experience (audio-visual show) 152
Malta Freeport 82
Malta George Cross – the Wartime Experience (audio-visual show) 150
Maltese cuisine 97–101
Maltese customs 90, 119–20
Maltese Light Infantry 51
Maltese people 89–92
Maltese Venus 231
Malti language 18, 23–4, 61
Manno brothers 194
Manoel Island *11*, *202–3*, 207–8, 277
Manuele, Antonio 251
marathon 129

Marfa Ridge 218–9
marinas 208, 277
Maritime Museum 179
markets 154, 229
Marsa Race Track 127, 128
Marsa Sports Club *127*, 129
Marsalforn 260
Marsamxett Harbour *11*, *202–3*
Marsaskala 129, 228, *229*
Marsaxlokk *224–7*, 229–30
  Malta Freeport 82
Mazzuoli, Giuseppe 173
Mdina 111, *182–4*, 185–9
  Banca Giuratale 180
  Bastion Square 189
  Bishop's Seminary 114
  Carmelite church 114, *185*, 188
  Casa Iguanez *187*, 188
  Cathedral 111, 114, 188, 192–4
  Museum 114, 194
  Greek Gate 186
  Hole in the Wall 176
  Main Gate *182–3*, 186, 187
  Mdina Dungeon 187–8
  Mdina Experience (multimedia show) 188
  National Museum of Natural History 187
  Palazzo Falzon *188*, 189
  Palazzo Gatto–Murina 188
  Palazzo Santa Sofia 180
  Palazzo Vilhena 187
  Tower of the Old Standard 187
  Triq Villegaignon 188
Mdina Glass 201
meat 98–9,
  see also **rabbit dishes**
medieval architecture 111
Mediterranean Film Studios 181
Mediterraneo Marine World 215
megalithic temples 21–2, 111, 148
Mellieha 217, *218*
  Bay (Ghadira) 128, *129*, 217, *218*
Meryon, Dr Charles (diarist) 59
Mgarr 221, 255
military parades *74–5*, 151
minestra 97, 98
Mintoff, Dominic (Dom) (Prime Minister) 77, 78, 79, 80
Mnajdra temples 21, *23*, 231, 232–3
Mnarja festival 125, 234–5
Modica (Sicily) 278
Mondion, Charles François de 112, 114
money 286

Mosta (Dome) 114, *196–7*, 198, *199*
Mount Etna (Sicily) 278–9
Mount Scebberas 38, 40, 45, 112, 145
Mountbatten, Lord Louis 154
mqaret *99*, 101
mqarrun fil-form 97
Msida 208, 277
Marina 208, 277
multi-media shows, *see* **audiovisual/multi-media shows**
museum opening times 148
music *122–3*
Muslim influence 18, 23–4, 25–6
Mussolini, Benito 61, 65, 79
Mustafa Pasha 39–41
Mystic Marriage of St Catherine 172

n

Napoleon 19, 50–51, 152, 154
Nasoni, Nicolo 162
National Library (Biblioteca) 114, 149
National Museum of Fine Arts 114, 152, 154
National War Museum 151
Nationalist Party 81, 91
Natural History Museum (Gozo) 251
Natural History Museum (Mdina) 187
Naxxar 41, 198–9
  Our Lady of Victory church 198, 199
  Palazzo Parisio 198–9, *199*
Neolithic period 21, 111, 216, 230, 231–2, 257–8, 262
neutrality 81, 82
nightlife 209

o

Ohio (tanker) *69*, 72
Order of St John of Jerusalem *see* **Knights of St John**
Ottoman Turks 31–2, 37–41

p

Paceville 209
Palmieri, Cocco (bishop) 193
Paola 227
Paradise Bay 218
passegiata 89, 208
pasta 97, 98

pastizzi 100, 122
Paule, Antoine de (Grand Master) 172, 200
Perellos, Ramon (Grand Master) 162, 164, 172, 193, 250
Perellos Battery (Comino) 270
Perez d'Aleccio, Matteo 164, 192
Peter's Pool 229
Pevsner, Nikolaus 169
Phoenicians 22–4, 25, 230
Pinto de Fonseca, Emanuel (Grand Master) 49, 154, 161, 171, 190, 205
pirates 49, 243, 255, 270
pizzas 100, *101*
pleasure cruises 275–7
Pleistocene fossils 230
Pomskizillious Toy Museum 258
Popeye 208
Popeye Village 219–20
population 89
post 154
pottery 201, 261
Pozzallo (Sicily) 278
prehistory 18, 21–2, 148, 262, *see also* cart tracks; temples
President's official residence 200
Preti, Mattia 112, 113, 169, 170, 171, 194, 249
Pretty Bay *81*, 231
Prime Minister's summer residence 234
Publius 25, 192
Punic Wars period 24, 148, 247
Pwales (Paul's) Beach 216

q

Qawra 215, 216
Qbajjar *253–4*, 260
Qormi 199
qrun 120
Quaker incident 49
quarries *82*
qubbajt 101

r

Rabat *25*, 185, 186, 189–91
    Augustinian Priory 114
    Mnarja Festival 129, 234–5
    Museum of Roman Antiquities 189–90
    St Agatha's Catacombs 25, 191
    St Paul's Catacombs 25, *26*, 191
    St Paul's Church 113, 190
    St Paul's Grotto *24*, 190
    St Publius' Church 113, 190
    Wignacourt's College 114

rabbit dishes *96*, 97, 99, 221, 235
Ragusa (Sicily) 278
Ramla Bay (Gozo) 259, *260*
Ramla Bay (Malta) 218
religion 91–2
restaurants 295–9
Rhodes 31
Rohan, Emmanuel de (Grand Master) 172
Roman period 18, 24, *25*, 111, 148, 189–90, 260
ross fil-forn 98
Rothmans Grand Prix snooker 129
Round Gozo cruise 275
Round the Islands cruise 275
Round Malta cruise 275
Royal Malta Yacht Club 208

s

Sacred Island (audio-visual show) 153
sailing *125–6*, 127, *272–3*, 276–7
    see also yachting
St Agatha 191
St Agatha's Catacombs 25, 191
St Anthony 119
St Charles Borromeo 172
St George's Bay 129
St Jerome 77, 173
St John Ambulance Association 53
St John the Baptist, The Beheading of 77, *173*
St John's Co-Cathedral *49*, 112, 113, 148, *166–8*, 169–73
    Cathedral Museum 172, 173
    Chancel and Choir 173
    Chapels of the *langues* 171–2
St Jude 119
St Julian's *134*, 205, *207*, 209
    Paceville 209
    Spinola Bay *204*, *205*, 209
St Luke 192
St Mary (Virgin Mary) 119
St Mary's Battery 270
St Mary's Bay 270, 271
St Mary's Tower 270
St Michael 172
St Paul 152–3, 190, 192, *193*, 194, 216
St Paul's Bay 216, 276
St Paul's Catacombs 25, *26*, 191
St Paul's Grotto *24*, 190
St Paul's Island *212–3*, 216
St Publius 25, 192
St Rita 119
St Thomas Bay 229
saints 25, 119, *122*, 153, 190, 191

Salina Bay 215
salt pans 215, *253*, 260
San Blas 259
Sannat 262
Saqqajja Hill (Rabat) 129, 234–5
Schermerhorn, E.W. *Malta of the Knights* 31, 50
Sciberras, Antonio 148
Scott, Sir Walter 59, 148, 169
scuba diving *see* diving
sea trips 275–7
Seabelow (MV) 276
seafood 99–100
Seated Woman 231
Selmun Palace 216
Sengle, Claude de la (Grand Master) 180
Senglea (Isola, L'Isla) 38, 41, 45, *176*, *177*, *179*, 180–81
September 8th (anniversaries) 41, 73
shooting migrating birds 218
shopping 205, 208
shrines 119, 260–61
Sicily 278–9
    invasion of 73
Siege Bell (World War II) 152
Siege of Malta (1565), *see* Great Siege
Siege of Malta (1940–42) *see* World War II
Siggiewi 234
silver-working 201, 301
Skorba temples 221
Sliema *11*, *81*, 153, 205–9
    Bisazza Street 208
    The Front 208
    Manoel Island *203*, 207–8
    pleasure cruises 275–6
    Strand 207
    Tigne 207
Slug Bay 218
snooker 129
soups 98
Spanish influence 26, 32
Spinola Bay *204*, *205*, 209
Spinola Palace 209
Spirit of Malta 276
Splash and Fun Water Park 215
sport 127–30
Stone Age 18, 21–2, 111
Strickland, Sir Gerald (Lord) (Prime Minister) 60–61
superstition 119–20
sweets 100–101, *122–3*
swordfish 100
Sylvester Craters (Etna) 278–9

t

Ta' Cenc *261*, 262
Ta' Dbiegi Craft Village 261
Ta' Hagrat temple 221
Tal-Providenza 232
Taormina (Sicily) 278, 279
  Corso Umberto 279
  Giardini Naxos 279
  Giardino Pubblico 279
  Palazzo Corvaja 279
  Teatro Greco *279*
tapestries *161, 162*, 163–4, *165*, 173
Ta' Pinu *12*, 260–61
Ta' Qali Crafts Village 201
Tarxien temples 21–2, 227–8
Ta' Xbiex 208
taxis 291
temples 18, 21–2, *23*, 111, 148, 221, 227–8, 231–2
tennis 271
Les Tenures des Indes *161, 162*, 163–4
Thackeray, William Makepeace 59, 169
theatres *147*, 150, 247–8
Three Cities *41*, 68, *142–3*, 177–81
Tiepolo, Gianbattista 164
timpana 97
torta tal-lampuki 97, 99
Tote 127, 128
tourist influence 92
toy museum 258
trucks *102–3*, 106
Turks 31–2, *34–6*, 37–41, 45

u

underground churches 191
  see also catacombs
underwater sports *126*, 127, 233
underwater viewing 276

v

Valletta *41*, 45, 112–14, *115*, 145–61
  in 1840 *60, 112, 113*
  Archaeological Museum 148, 154, 221, 227
  Auberge d'Allemagne 114, 154
  Auberge d'Aragon 154
  Auberge d'Auvergne 154
  Auberge de Baviere 154
  Auberge de Castile *45, 110*, 114, *133*, 154, 201
  Auberge de France 154
  Auberge de Provence *47*, 148, 154
  Auberge d'Italie 154
  Basilica of Our Lady of Mount Carmel (Carmelite Church) *145*, 150
  Biblioteca (National Library) 114, 149
  Caffe Cordina 148–9
  Casa Rocca Piccola 150
  Cathedral, *see* St John's Co-Cathedral
  City Gate (Republic Gate) *46*, 147
  Customs House 114
  Ferreria (arsenal) 112
  Fort St Elmo 38, 39–41, *52–3*, 145, 150–51, *152*
  Grand Master's Palace, *see* Grand Master's Palace
  Hospital of the Order, *see* Sacra Infermeria
  Hostel de Verdelin 113
  Jesuit College 113
  Knights Hospitallers exhibition 152
  Lascaris War Rooms 73, 153–4
  Law Courts 148, 154
  Lower Barracca Gardens 152
  Main Guard 149
  Malta Experience 152
  Malta George Cross – the Wartime Experience 150
  Manoel Theatre *147*, 150
  Mediterranean Conference Centre 151–2
  National Library (Biblioteca) 114, 149
  National Museum of Fine Arts 114, 152, 154
  National War Museum 65, 151
  Palazzo Parisio 154
  Palazzo Verdelin 150, *153*
  Post Office 154
  Republic Square (Queen's Square) 148, *149*
  Royal Opera House *71*, 114, 147
  La Sacra Infermeria *40, 42–3*, 46, 50, 112, 152
  Sacred Island (audio-visual show) 153
  St Francis' church 114
  St Mary of Jesus church 114
  St Nicolas' church 113
  St Paul Shipwreck church 153
  St Paul's Anglican cathedral 114, 154
  St Rocco's church 114
  Siege Bell 152
  slaves' prison *48*, 112
  Strait Street (The Gut) 150, 156
  Upper Barracca Garden 153, *157*
  Valletta Experience (audio-visual show) 150
"La Vallette", *see* La Valette, Jean Parisot de
Vaubois, Claude 50, 51
vegetables 98
vehicles 92, 105–6, *156*
Verdala Palace 235
Verdale, Fra Hugues de (Grand Master) 235
Verres (Roman governor) 24
Victoria 247–51
  Armoury 251
  Cathedral 114, 250–51
  Citadel *52–3*, 111, 249–50
  museums 251
  Old Town 248–9
  Palace of the Governors of Gozo 250
  Pjazza Independenza (It-Tokk) 248
  prisons 251
  Rundle Gardens 247
  St George's Basilica 248–9
  theatres 247–8, 249
  Triq ir-Repubblika 247
Victoria Lines *157*
Vilhena, Antonio Manuel de (Grand Master) *31*, 171, 187, 188
Visconti, Horatus (Inquisitor) 234
Vittoriosa (Birgu) 39, 41, 45, *108–9*, 111, 112, *174–5*, 177–80
  Auberge d'Angleterre *52*, 154, 179
  Church Museum 178
  Church of St Lawrence 114, 177–8
  Freedom Monument 178
  Inquisitor's Palace 114, 178–9
  Maritime Museum 179

w

water-taxis, *see* dghajsas
waterpolo 129, 209
watersports 127–8, 129, 217, 271
weaving 201
weddings *91*
Westin Dragonara Hotel 209
White Rocks (Bahar-ic-Caghaq) 215
Wied-iz-Zurrieq 231

Wignacourt, Adrien de (Grand Master) 172
Wignacourt, Alof de (Grand Master) 278
windmill 258
winds 128, 277
windsurfing 128, *129*
wine 101
World War II 19, 65–73, 151, 153–4
Blitz (Siege) of Malta 69–73
wrecks 127

x

Xaghra 257, 258
Ninu's Cave 258
Pomskizillious Toy Museum 258
Ta' Kola Windmill 258

Xerri's Grotto 258
Xemxija 216
Xewkija Rotunda (Xewkija Dome) 198, 255–7
Xlendi 262
xlokk 277

y

yachting 208, 217, *271*
see also sailing

z

Zabbar
Hompesch Arch 228
Our Lady of Graces church *114*, 199, 228
Zebbiegh 221

Zebbug 113, 199
Zondadari, Marc'Antonio (Grand Master) 172
Zurrieq 231

A
B
C
D
E
G
H
I
J
a
b
c
d
f
g
h
i
j
k
l

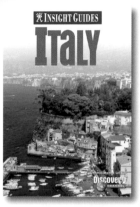

INSIGHT GUIDES

The classic series that puts you in the picture

Alaska
Amazon Wildlife
American Southwest
Amsterdam
Argentina
Arizona & Grand Canyon
Asia's Best Hotels & Resorts
Asia, East
Asia, Southeast
Australia
Austria
Bahamas
Bali
Baltic States
Bangkok
Barbados
Barcelona
Beijing
Belgium
Belize
Berlin
Bermuda
Boston
Brazil
Brittany
Brussels
Buenos Aires
Burgundy
Burma (Myanmar)
Cairo
California
California, Southern
Canada
Caribbean
Caribbean Cruises
Channel Islands
Chicago
Chile
China
Colorado
Continental Europe
Corsica
Costa Rica
Crete
Croatia
Cuba
Cyprus
Czech & Slovak Republic
Delhi, Jaipur & Agra
Denmark

Dominican Rep. & Haiti
Dublin
East African Wildlife
Eastern Europe
Ecuador
Edinburgh
Egypt
England
Finland
Florence
Florida
France
France, Southwest
French Riviera
Gambia & Senegal
Germany
Glasgow
Gran Canaria
Great Britain
Great Gardens of Britain
  & Ireland
Great Railway Journeys
  of Europe
Greece
Greek Islands
Guatemala, Belize
  & Yucatán
Hawaii
Hong Kong
Hungary
Iceland
India
India, South
Indonesia
Ireland
Israel
Istanbul
Italy
Italy, Northern
Italy, Southern
Jamaica
Japan
Jerusalem
Jordan
Kenya
Korea
Laos & Cambodia
Las Vegas
Lisbon
London

Los Angeles
Madeira
Madrid
Malaysia
Mallorca & Ibiza
Malta
Mauritius Réunion
  & Seychelles
Mediterranean Cruises
Melbourne
Mexico
Miami
Montreal
Morocco
Moscow
Namibia
Nepal
Netherlands
New England
New Mexico
New Orleans
New York City
New York State
New Zealand
Nile
Normandy
North American &
  Alaskan Cruises
Norway
Oman & The UAE
Oxford
Pacific Northwest
Pakistan
Paris
Peru
Philadelphia
Philippines
Poland
Portugal
Prague
Provence
Puerto Rico
Rajasthan

Rio de Janeiro
Rome
Russia
St Petersburg
San Francisco
Sardinia
Scandinavia
Scotland
Seattle
Shanghai
Sicily
Singapore
South Africa
South America
Spain
Spain, Northern
Spain, Southern
Sri Lanka
Sweden
Switzerland
Sydney
Syria & Lebanon
Taiwan
Tanzania & Zanzibar
Tenerife
Texas
Thailand
Tokyo
Trinidad & Tobago
Tunisia
Turkey
Tuscany
Umbria
USA: The New South
USA: On The Road
USA: Western States
US National Parks: West
Venezuela
Venice
Vienna
Vietnam
Wales
Walt Disney World/Orlando

INSIGHT GUIDES

The world's largest collection of visual travel guides & maps